Softly,
As I Leave
You

Also by Priscilla Beaulieu Presley

Elvis and Me: The True Story of the Love Between Priscilla Presley and the King of Rock N' Roll

Softly, As I Leave You

LIFE AFTER ELVIS

PRISCILLA BEAULIEU PRESLEY

with Mary Jane Ross

GRAND CENTRAL

New York   Boston

Copyright © 2025 by GLDE, Inc.
Cover design by Milan Bozic
Cover photo of Priscilla Presley by Ron Galella/Getty Images
Cover photo of Graceland by Raymond Boyd/Getty Images
Cover copyright © 2025 by Hachette Book Group, Inc.

Hachette Book Group supports the right to free expression and the value of copyright. The purpose of copyright is to encourage writers and artists to produce the creative works that enrich our culture.

The scanning, uploading, and distribution of this book without permission is a theft of the author's intellectual property. If you would like permission to use material from the book (other than for review purposes), please contact Permissions@hbgusa.com. Thank you for your support of the author's rights.

Grand Central Publishing
Hachette Book Group
1290 Avenue of the Americas
New York, NY 10104
grandcentralpublishing.com
@grandcentralpub

First Edition: September 2025

Grand Central Publishing is a division of Hachette Book Group, Inc. The Grand Central Publishing name and logo are registered trademarks of Hachette Book Group, Inc.

The publisher is not responsible for websites (or their content) that are not owned by the publisher.

The Hachette Speakers Bureau provides a wide range of authors for speaking events. To find out more, visit hachettespeakersbureau.com or email HachetteSpeakers@hbgusa.com.

Grand Central Publishing books may be purchased in bulk for business, educational, or promotional use. For information, please contact your local bookseller or email the Hachette Book Group Special Markets Department at Special.Markets@hbgusa.com.

Print book interior design by Amy Quinn

Library of Congress Cataloging-in-Publication Data

Names: Presley, Priscilla, 1945– author. | Ross, Mary Jane, author.
Title: Softly, as I leave you: life after Elvis-a memoir / Priscilla Beaulieu Presley;
    with Mary Jane Ross.
Description: New York: Grand Central Publishing, 2025.
Identifiers: LCCN 2025007396 | ISBN 9780306836480 (hardcover) | ISBN 9780306836497
    (trade paperback) | ISBN 9780306836503 (ebook)
Subjects: LCSH: Presley, Priscilla, 1945– | Television actors and actresses—United
    States—Biography. | Motion picture actors and actresses—United States—Biography. |
    Businesswomen—United States—Biography. | Rock musicians' spouses—United
    States—Biography. | Presley, Elvis, 1935–1977.
Classification: LCC PN1992.4.P74 A3 2025 | DDC 791.4502/8092
    [B]—dc23/eng/20250526
LC record available at https://lccn.loc.gov/2025007396

ISBNs: 978-0-306-83648-0 (hardcover); 978-0-306-83792-0 (large print);
978-1-538-77871-5 (signed edition); 978-1-538-77872-2 (B&N Black Friday signed Edition);
978-0-306-83650-3 (ebook)

Printed in the United States of America

LSC-H

Printing 1, 2025

To those who have left us:

My precious daughter, Lisa Marie;

My beautiful mother, Ann;

My sweet grandson, Benjamin;

Elvis, who is with me still.

And to my beloved son, Navarone, who comforts me in their absence.

I love you all tenderly, deeply, and eternally. I carry you in my heart every day.

*Softly, I will leave you softly,
Long before your arms can beg me stay
For one more hour, for one more day.
After all the years,
I can't bear the tears to fall
So softly, as I leave you there.*

—Music by Tony De Vita
—Lyrics by Hal Shaper
—As performed by Elvis Presley

Contents

Prologue: Unchained Melody   ix

CHAPTER 1	**Letting Go**	1
CHAPTER 2	**Holding On**	17
CHAPTER 3	**Separate Ways**	31
CHAPTER 4	**Saying Goodbye**	47
CHAPTER 5	**Keeping the Faith**	61
CHAPTER 6	**Suspicious Minds**	77
CHAPTER 7	**Acting Out**	93
CHAPTER 8	**Love Me Tender**	109
CHAPTER 9	**Coming of Age**	123
CHAPTER 10	**Memories**	139
CHAPTER 11	**Leaving Las Vegas**	155
CHAPTER 12	**Guest Star**	171
CHAPTER 13	**Second Thoughts**	187
CHAPTER 14	**Raise Your Voice**	201
CHAPTER 15	**Poison Apples**	219
CHAPTER 16	**Storm and Grace**	237
CHAPTER 17	**Peace in the Valley**	253
CHAPTER 18	**Don't Be Cruel**	267
CHAPTER 19	**Lights Out**	285
CHAPTER 20	**Midnight**	299

Epilogue: Raven   313
Acknowledgments   319
About the Authors   321

Prologue

UNCHAINED MELODY

"Wait for me, wait for me."
I'll be coming home, wait for me.

I AM WALKING DOWN A ROAD. ALL AROUND ARE TREES, LUSH and green. I don't know where I am, but the place feels familiar. Behind me and to my left walks a handsome young man in a navy pilot's uniform. He keeps an eye on me from a few feet away, making sure I am safe.

My mother walks with him, young again, the lines smoothed from her beautiful face. I hear her voice. "Did you eat dinner? You need a good night's sleep for tomorrow. Remember to hold your head up high when you walk out on stage."

"Yes," I reply, "I will."

Grandma is to the right of me, holding my arm, stroking it gently when I get tired or distressed. "I'm here, young'un. I'm still listening. You can always talk to me."

My rescue dogs skitter about, exploring the path, then returning to me for a pat on the head. Their tails wag excitedly.

Lisa Marie and Benjamin walk slightly ahead of me, their arms around each other. Lisa turns around and looks me in the eye. "I'm sorry, Mom."

"I'm sorry too, sweetheart."

As she turns back around, I ask her, "Did you take your bath?" It is an old joke, and Lisa laughs.

"Yes, Mom, I took my bath."

Benjamin turns toward me. "I'm all right, Nona. I really am."

I look into his eyes and say, "I know."

To my left walks Elvis. His body is lean and strong again, his deep blue eyes clear. When he looks down at me, his face fills with tenderness.

"Yittle all right?"

"Her's all right."

"Does her miss him?"

"Every day, Sattnin', every day." Taking my hand, he threads his fingers through mine, resting lightly where the ring used to be. I feel the warmth.

But I keep walking, my eyes firmly on the road ahead, for I know that it is taking me home.

Softly, As I Leave You

CHAPTER 1

Letting Go

I'm caught in a trap, and I can't get out
Because I love you too much, baby.

WHEN I LEFT ELVIS PRESLEY, I WAS TWENTY-seven years old. I had spent half of my life as his wife or girlfriend, going straight from my parents' home to his. I knew almost nothing about the world outside his orbit. My choice to leave was terrifying for me and unfathomable to his millions of fans. What they didn't understand was that I did not leave Elvis because I no longer loved him. I loved him as much on the day I left as on the day we married. I left Elvis because I needed a life of my own. I was living his life. Just as Elvis was searching for the meaning of his life, I was searching for mine.

The split with Elvis was complicated and long in coming. We had been together thirteen years when I left, almost half of my life. The world outside was changing, but behind the gates of Graceland, his mansion in Memphis, Tennessee, things remained the same. When Elvis and I became serious in 1963, I was eighteen years old and very much a product of my generation. Like my mother before me, I grew up learning how to please a man. The expectation for girls in the 1960s was to find and secure a good husband. I worked hard to meet those expectations. I went to charm school to learn how to dress and do my makeup. My attitude suited Elvis, who was also a product of his generation. He loved to buy me pretty things, including beautiful clothes. I happily took his advice on clothing and makeup as he shaped me into his perfect woman. I didn't resent it; I embraced it. I wanted to please my man.

Pleasing my man, though, involved a great deal more than the way I looked. Like all girls, I studied home economics, learned how to create a happy home, and read magazine articles on how to behave with a man. I was taught never to be forward—pushy. Elvis couldn't stand pushy girls. There were rules for almost everything girls did back then. I should never phone a boy, for that would be forward. It was up to him to call me. A woman's purpose was to meet her man's needs before considering her own, if she thought about hers at all. I was to make sure my husband had his favorite food prepared to his liking, whenever he wanted it. I was to listen to my husband without expecting him to listen to me. It was not my place to offer my own opinions unless he asked. I should never question his instructions or behavior. If he came home late or stayed out all night, he didn't owe me an explanation. These things were his prerogative as head of the household. Most important, I felt it was my job to keep him happy, not the other way around.

Social traditions also prepared me for marriage. When I was in the ninth grade, the year I met Elvis, my school had a contest where the boys could bid on the girls. If a boy had the winning bid on a particular girl, he "owned her" for the day. She had to follow him around, serve him his lunch, and carry his books. The boys competed for the girls, but the girls also competed with one another. The girl who got the highest bid was the winner, the most popular girl. That year, I won. The whole contest is unthinkable by current standards, but at the time, it was fun. It also foreshadowed the endless competition for Elvis's attention that would characterize my marriage.

I embraced these social norms without question. For many years, they guided my marriage. I loved caring for Elvis. I cherished the role of the devoted homemaker. Whenever we stayed at the ranch, where we didn't have staff, I eagerly and lovingly took over Elvis's care. Every night, I laid out his pajamas, and I took on the roles of the servants by day. I am nurturing by nature, so caring for him wasn't difficult for me.

In addition to the conservative mores of the time, marrying a Southern man created additional expectations for both Elvis and me. Much has been made of the ten-year age gap between us, but it wasn't unusual in the South. It certainly wasn't considered pedophilia. After all, thirty-three-year-old Rhett Butler had first attracted Scarlett O'Hara when she was sixteen. Of course, they were fictional characters, but they were symbolic of a cultural reality. Jerry Lee Lewis had famously married his wife when she was thirteen. So had Edgar Allan Poe, another Southern icon. I, fortunately, wasn't a child bride. Though Elvis and I had started a relationship when I was fourteen, it didn't become a romantic relationship until I was seventeen. We waited to have sex until he married me at twenty-one. The fact remains, however, that there were ten years between us.

There was some logic to an age gap between spouses. Older men could be good husband prospects because they were more mature and well established socially and economically. From the Southern men's point of view, choosing a younger woman made it easier to function as the head of the household, guiding their young wife's behavior and opinions. This extra code of etiquette was layered onto Elvis's expectations of me as a wife. Elvis was a Southern man who expected his woman to be pretty, submissive, and charming. Twenty-four hours a day. I would even wrap my hair in toilet paper after Elvis fell asleep to keep my hairdo intact. Then I'd get up early to fix my hair and eye makeup before he woke up. The problem, of course, was that as I grew into adulthood, the power imbalance created by the age gap with Elvis remained. It was difficult for us to have a marriage of equals when Elvis was used to being in charge.

I did my best to meet all of his expectations. I had never learned to cook, but with a full staff at Graceland, I didn't need to. I made attempts to cook a meal in the beginning, but the results were barely edible. Although I was clearly not destined to be a chef, I was careful to ensure that Elvis got his favorite foods on time. I consulted with the cook daily, sometimes several times a day, to make sure Elvis's preferences were met. Each time he returned home, I greeted him in a lovely outfit, with styled hair and full eye makeup, and made a fuss over him. I also listened to Elvis talk endlessly, sometimes all night, even when he read me passages from philosophy books at three in the morning. I tried never to question his behavior. He resented anything that sounded like criticism. He felt no need to explain his relationships with other women. I was to trust him and ignore whatever I might hear.

Elvis never forced me to do any of these things. Both of us knew what the expectations were when I married him, and for a long time, I accepted them. Elvis's behavior fit the standards of the time. In many ways, he was a good husband. He never abused me, physically or emotionally. Though his temper could be explosive, he rarely exploded at me. With me, he was usually gentle and often tender. He was also extremely generous. He bought me beautiful things, expensive gifts, amazing jewelry. I still wear the diamond cross he gave me. I had much to be grateful for in my marriage. The difference between him and other husbands, though, was that he was Elvis Presley. He had money, a loyal entourage constantly serving his needs, and millions of fans. But I loved him, and because I did, I strove to be the perfect Southern wife of the era. Eventually, though, the struggle wore me down, and I began to feel like the proverbial bird in a gilded cage.

Elvis lived in a world of his own making. He really was the king of all he surveyed. We—the guys and I—slept when he slept, ate when he ate, watched what he liked on TV. It was normal to me, and for a long time, I didn't question it. The hard part for me was the people who made up Elvis's little kingdom. They were all male. Elvis and I weren't the typical married couple; we were two people plus an all-male entourage. I was seldom alone with my husband. When I set the table for our breakfast in the late afternoon, when Elvis usually woke up, I never put out just two place settings. At least six of the guys usually ate with us. When I'd cuddle up against Elvis to watch television, there were men scattered around the room watching with us. They'd laugh and comment and cheer when Elvis shot up the TV set. They came on trips with us and stayed in the hotel where we stayed. Except for a few precious days on our honeymoon at our house in Palm Springs, California, I shared him with the guys. About the only time I had him to myself was when we went to bed in the early hours of the morning. I never complained, for I didn't want to be seen as whining or nagging. I was trying to be the perfect wife, so sharing Elvis with the guys all the time was something I had to accept.

Elvis was surrounded by men who took care of his every need and were generously rewarded in return. When he and I got horses, the guys got horses so we could all ride. They were both his friends and his staff, and the inner circle was his family. He trusted them. In a world where it wasn't always safe to be Elvis Presley, they formed a wall of protection around him. Individually, I liked most of them. In some cases, like Joe Esposito, they became my friends, too. But the fact remained that the Memphis Mafia—a nickname they loved—was made up entirely of men. I was the only woman living in a man's world, whether we were at Graceland, in LA, or at our weekend home in Palm

Springs. Living in that world seemed wonderful to outsiders. In reality, it was a very lonely place.

Every night when we ate our dinner, I was the only woman sitting at the dining room table. I got to hear what most women don't: guy talk. I heard all the jokes and the salty language. The guys would start laughing, and I would laugh and look like I was having fun, but I didn't get a lot of the jokes. I also got to hear their uncensored assessment of the line of waiting girls. There was always a long line outside our home. Very, very pretty girls queued up at the gate, hoping to see Elvis but often willing to settle for one of the guys. The girls were the embodiment of my worst nightmare, all of them eager to replace me.

I'd hear one of the guys say, "Wow! Did you see that one? Did you see the blonde?" A graphic description would follow. And so they'd go, down the line of willing females.

Sometimes they'd choose a few of the prettiest girls and bring them in to meet Elvis. I squirmed with the memory of how I'd met Elvis the same way. I still wasn't sure why Elvis had chosen me, and I feared being replaced. Elvis had been single back then, but even married, he was accustomed to having pretty girls escorted to his presence. He'd talk to them and read to them from the Bible and from books on Eastern philosophy. And he could never resist flirting with them. He enjoyed charming them. He sometimes held the girls over my head as a threat.

He'd say, "If you don't want to listen to me, there's plenty of girls who will." And there were. I could see them from our front window or, worse yet, sitting in our living room.

I would sit there thinking, "Oh my gosh, I just hope and pray Elvis doesn't go for this girl." I was afraid to leave him on his own. I didn't want to visit my parents, because that meant there could be someone else stepping in while I was gone.

It was even more uncomfortable because most of the guys were also married. Sometimes the guys would date the girls they brought to meet Elvis, and I saw what was going on. Their wives were my best friends, but I had to keep silent. There was an unspoken code that I would never tell what I saw going on with the guys.

And then there were all the girls I didn't see. I usually stayed at Graceland when he was shooting a film on location, but I would hear the rumors about him and his costars. The celebrity magazines and papers were full of gossip about Elvis and glamorous girls I'd never met. I felt inadequate next to them, out of place on the sets. The actresses could have conversations with Elvis that I couldn't have; they were all in the movie business. They had so much in common with him, and they were so much more experienced than I was. I was just the girl at home, waiting for her man to come back.

The stories had been circulating since Elvis and I first dated. He had famously dated Ann-Margret and Shelley Fabares for a while before we were married, while I was living at Graceland as his girlfriend. I started seeing stories about Elvis and Ann-Margret in Las Vegas, where they were filming. And I'd seen a picture of them going to a show together. I began to panic. When I finally asked Elvis about Ann, he dismissed the rumors. He didn't like me asking him about other girls. It was against the unspoken female behavior code. I had no right to ask.

He just said what he always said when I got worried: "Don't you ever worry. No one's going to take your place."

But those were just words. The pictures told a different story.

The problem didn't stop when we got married. The knowledge that he always seemed to have actresses that he was very close to ate away at me.

Once Elvis started touring full-time, my anxiety deepened. I rarely saw him, and I couldn't help obsessing about the girls throwing their room keys on the stage for him nightly. I couldn't get over the gnawing anxiety. The isolation, the days and weeks without my husband, magnified my fears and began to crush me.

Making everything worse was the fact that Elvis lost interest in me sexually once Lisa was born. He had never been able to make love to a woman who'd had a child. He had put his mother on a pedestal, and after Lisa was born, he put me on one, too. It is impossible to make love on a pedestal. I wore sexy negligees, applied my eye makeup carefully, and tried to initiate lovemaking. Nothing worked. Elvis remained flirtatious and very affectionate with me, but that was all. He was hesitant to have another child. After all, I had gotten pregnant the first time we made love. His hesitation intensified my fears. The loneliness and sense of helplessness weighed heavier with every passing month. It was exhausting. I felt like I was, as the song goes, caught in a trap with no way out. I never want to experience that fear, that insecurity, again.

Small wonder that I became involved in an affair with my karate instructor, Mike Stone. I had started taking karate to get out of the house and develop my own interests. Ironically, I was also doing it to please Elvis. When we met Mike in Hawaii at a karate tournament, Elvis was very impressed. Mike was a great karate master, better even than Chuck Norris. At the time, women rarely learned karate, a sport and an art form Elvis deeply admired and practiced himself. I would show Elvis the moves I'd learned, and he would proudly have me show off to the guys.

What neither of us foresaw was the way karate empowered me. I was good at it, and after years of feeling helpless, it was wonderful to have mastery of my body and my environment, at least for short periods. While Elvis was away from home, performing and spending time with other people, I spent hours training with Mike. My self-confidence grew, and I experienced more of the outside world as I went to tournaments with Mike and met other people. The other couples I met exchanged opinions freely with their mates, a contrast with my marriage I couldn't help noticing. For the first time, I began to see a different way of living. Then one day, a mailbox full of letters at our Palm Springs house ripped apart the ties that bound me.

Once the Las Vegas concerts started, Elvis had rented a home in Palm Springs, a place where he could relax when he wasn't performing. One weekend when he was out of town, Joanie Esposito (Joe's wife) and I drove out to Palm Springs to collect the mail and check on the house. When I turned the key in the mailbox, however, what poured out wasn't bills or junk mail. The mailbox was stuffed full of letters from girls.

Many were for Elvis. Others were for the boys, including Joanie's husband. All the guys were cheating on their wives. The letter writers gushed about spending time at the house having romantic interludes with the men. One letter to Elvis was signed Lizard Tongue. The graphic image was jarring. I finally held written proof of what I'd always feared. I was deeply hurt, but I was also furious.

I called Elvis and demanded an explanation. He immediately tried to shift the blame to me. *Why had I gone to the house? Why was I going through the mail? Was I snooping on him? It was none of my business what was in that f-ing mailbox.* When that tactic failed, he resorted to saying the girls were all lying.

This time, though, turning the tables didn't work. If Elvis was having affairs that were none of my business, then it was none of his business what I was doing. The close friendship that Mike and I had developed turned into an affair.

The affair itself was wrong, of course. Both Mike and I were married, however I rationalized it, and both of us had children. But as a young woman experiencing the exhilaration of being desired again, I fell headlong into the relationship.

Contrary to rumor, though, my involvement with Mike was not the reason I left Elvis. The marriage had been crumbling for years, and when it finally imploded, Mike Stone was just one catalyst. The other was Lisa Marie.

When I'd first learned I was pregnant with Lisa, I'd been stunned. Elvis and I had only been married a few weeks. Until we married, I had stayed home at Graceland for four years as his girlfriend while Elvis led a glamorous life in Hollywood. Our wedding had meant I could finally come out in the open. I could now travel with Elvis, attend public events, and claim him as my own in the eyes of the world. I was so excited. But when I got pregnant on my wedding night, those dreams fell apart. Neither Elvis nor I was ready for a child. He worried about what fatherhood would do to his career. His fans were still adjusting to him being a married man. But his anxiety went beyond his career. He had never been around children and felt unprepared to raise a child.

I, on the other hand, knew exactly what we were getting into. As the oldest of six children, I knew about the diapers, the baby's constant need for attention, the lack of sleep. There would be no traveling, no romantic interludes for us to focus on each other. For weeks, Elvis and I worried in silence about what was to come. At my lowest point, I even wondered how I'd feel if I had an accident and miscarried. I felt so guilty that I was even having these thoughts.

It was Elvis who finally brought things to a head. He looked at me one day and asked if I wanted to have an abortion. He told me he'd support whatever I wanted. His words were a wake-up call.

The enormity of it hit me head-on, and I began to cry.

I told him, "No! We can't do that. This is our *baby*!"

Things changed after that. We were bringing a new life into the world. A new generation. The first time I felt the baby move, it was magical. Fear and dread were replaced by growing excitement and tenderness for our unborn child. When we actually held Lisa Marie in our arms for the first time, we fell hopelessly in love with her. We could not imagine our lives without her.

Loving her, though, didn't automatically make things easy. Elvis was a typical man of his time, expecting me to do all the physical care of our daughter. Changing a diaper was unthinkable to him, and he was repulsed when she smeared her food or spit up. Keeping her fed and groomed was my job, and I wanted to do it. He loved to hold her, but only when she was scrubbed and clean and clothed in cute little dresses. Complicating things for me was the fact that I now had to accommodate two schedules: Lisa's and Elvis's. Lisa's day started in the early morning and ended in the late evening. In between, she needed constant attention. Elvis still lived like a night owl, going to bed a few hours before Lisa woke up and waking four hours before she went down for the night. Just as Lisa needed me to be there for her during the day, Elvis expected me to be there for him all night. It was exhausting and ultimately impossible.

At first, Lisa and I went with Elvis to Palm Springs on the weekends, in part because of my well-founded fear of giving somebody else a chance to take my place in my absence. The desert house wasn't a good environment for a child. It was too hot to be outside, and there were no other kids around. At that time, none of the guys had children. It was the same all-male world I was accustomed to. Elvis would stay up until the television stations closed down for the night, and he wanted me to stay up with him, as I always had. I would put Lisa to bed and then watch TV with him. But when our daughter would wake up and start crying, Elvis didn't want me to go to her. He wanted me to stay with him and watch television. And the problem wasn't just when we were in Palm Springs. I began to feel like I was living two lives, one tending to my daughter and the other keeping my husband happy. I was serving two masters, torn between being a good mom and being a good wife. Though Elvis loved Lisa deeply, he was accustomed to coming first, to having his needs attended to. He was a generous man, but he was unprepared to share me.

Finally, I got a nanny. I had to because of Elvis's lifestyle; otherwise, I would never have been able to sleep. But I became jealous of a nanny taking care of my daughter when I should be taking care of her. I felt guilty about having a nanny there when Lisa woke up in the middle of the night and started crying.

Elvis always said, "She'll take care of it," meaning the nanny.

And the nanny would take care of it, but for me, it was very painful. Lisa should have had her mother there to comfort her. I felt guilty that I was not being the mother to my child that I should be. I struggled to find a way to make the situation work, but it was painful trying to keep our family together. I felt like a failure as both a mother and a wife.

Eventually, I had to choose. I was caught in a perfect storm of loneliness, isolation, jealousy, and guilt. By the time Lisa was four years old, I knew I had to make a decision.

So I realized it was time for me to go. Elvis was stunned. So were the guys. His fans were incredulous. How could I leave the man everyone wanted? But I realized that the situation would never change. I could never have a life of my own in the velvet cocoon I lived in.

I wanted our family to change as little as possible once I left. I knew my departure would be hard on Grandma Minnie Mae, Elvis's paternal grandmother, who loved me like her own. She was everybody's grandma, and we all cherished her. Grandma had lived with Elvis for years, even coming to Germany after his mother's death. Elvis nicknamed her Dodger, and I sometimes called her that, too.

I had always kept Grandma company when Elvis was gone, spending long hours sitting next to her in her arm chair as she talked. She would pick at the side of her hair and stare at the floor as she gradually slipped into a reverie. Grandma would tell me about Elvis's parents, Gladys and Vernon, when they were young and when Elvis was growing up. She would also talk about her ex-husband and what a philanderer he was, constantly cheating on her. He had treated her badly and rarely come home. She had no idea that Elvis cheated on me, too, for Elvis kept that from her, and I loved her too much to put my worries on her. She was deeply grateful to Elvis for making sure she was well taken care of at Graceland. I could sense her feelings as she would talk about the past and about how Elvis never left her. She would listen to my stories, too. Grandma was one of the few women I got to talk to. When we weren't talking, we'd watch old movies and soap operas together. She loved her soaps. Her favorite was *As the World Turns*. She would have been so proud to see me on *Dallas*.

Telling Grandma I was leaving Elvis was one of the hardest things I've ever done.

I sat down next to her and said, "Grandma, I have something to tell you. I'm leaving. I'm leaving Elvis."

"What?! What did you say? But you two young'uns love each other so much," she protested. She twisted her hair in anguish.

"I will always love Elvis, Grandma, always love him, but I have to leave. It's time for me to go."

She absorbed this information in silence.

Then she took my hand and began to rub it. "When are you leaving? And why are you leaving?"

"It's time to go, Grandma. I can't take what I see anymore. It's time."

"I understand, young'un." And I believe she did. "Am I going to see you?"

"Yes, I'll be back. I'll see you. I promise."

"Oh, this is..." and her voice trailed off. Still clinging to my hand, she said, "When will you be back?"

"I'll always let you know. I'm going to call you, too."

Finally, she said, "Okay. You call me."

And I did. When Elvis went on the road, and I knew she was on her own, I would call her and talk like in the old days. I would ask her how she was doing and how she was passing the time. In the years that followed, whenever I could, I would go to Graceland and visit with her. Four or five times a year, we'd talk and watch old movies together. I did that until she passed. You don't just marry a person; you marry a family. I remained married to Elvis's family. Lisa Marie and I were Presleys. That never changed.

As difficult as it was, I never regretted my decision to leave Elvis. But I never ceased to mourn it.

CHAPTER 2
Holding On

And I guess I never told you...
You were always on my mind.

The first few months were rough. Angry and humiliated, Elvis fixated on Mike Stone. Elvis thought I was leaving because of Mike. It was easier to blame another man than to face the truth. I didn't leave because of Mike Stone. And I didn't leave because Elvis had forced himself on me when he found out about Mike. He had not. Elvis had felt emasculated. He'd needed to prove to himself and to me that he could make love "like a real man," the way he imagined a karate master doing it. Elvis made love to me *forcefully*, not *forcibly*. His usual tenderness and consideration for me were missing. It was emotionally hurtful, and it left me with an unhappy memory of my last experience of sexual intimacy with Elvis. But it was not the reason I left.

Elvis found the thought of me with another man unbearable. In the weeks after my departure, he told the guys that Mike had to die. He even asked Joe to find a hit man. Joe warned me to be careful. When I offered to bring Lisa to Vegas for one of Elvis's shows, Joe advised against it. Seeing me might set Elvis off. Over time, and with a lot of persuasion from his father and the guys, Elvis gradually calmed down and gave up the idea of killing Mike, thank God. Once, in anguish, he even asked me if it had been his fault, if he had been "too blind" to see what he had. Though he said little, I think Elvis pondered the loss of our marriage long and deeply. I still have one of his favorite books of philosophy in which he printed in the margin, "Through loss of love, you sometimes only realize the gift you were given." Elvis had never had someone leave him before. It must have been gut-wrenching for such a proud man to look his own failures in the eye.

Elvis was the one who told his father when I left. Vernon understood because he was with Elvis all the time. He was there when Elvis was with other girls in Vegas. Vernon never blamed me or made it hard for me. I had a close relationship with him. That never changed.

I stayed in touch with Colonel Tom Parker, too. When he got a home in Palm Springs, I'd go to visit him. And he would call and check on me to see how I was doing.

I'd say, "I'm doing well. Thank you, Colonel."

"Well, you need anything, you know who to call."

I also stayed in touch with some of the guys, especially Joe, and several of the wives. Joanie and I remained close, and Elvis's double first cousin Patsy Presley and I remained best friends. I had known her since I was a teenager.

We all knew Elvis needed another woman, and it was the guys' job to find her. Five months after I left, the boys invited Miss Tennessee to one of Elvis's movie nights at the Memphian Theater. Her name was Linda Thompson, and she was beautiful. Elvis was at his most charming, and Linda reportedly fell for him instantly. Things got easier for everyone, including me, once Elvis and Linda began a relationship. Surprisingly, I wasn't jealous. When I left the marriage, I had left the crushing burden of fear and jealousy behind. I could finally breathe, and with my newfound freedom, I gained perspective. I knew Elvis needed a good woman to take care of him, and I liked Linda. The wives told me she was a good person who seemed to really care about Elvis. Having a beautiful woman of his own on his arm soothed Elvis's ego and helped heal his heart. It also lessened my burden of worry about him.

When I first left, I didn't really know where I was going. My only homes, or at least houses, were shared with Elvis. Mike Stone suggested I look in Marina del Rey, a small waterfront community west of LA. I had never been there, so I drove over to take a look and loved it immediately. It was charming. There was a small harbor with boats docked there, and I could smell the ocean just yards away. I rented a pretty little apartment tucked into an alcove of the harbor. I wasn't looking for a permanent home yet; I was still figuring out what I was going to do. My sister, Michelle, moved in with Lisa and me to help us get settled. I felt safe there, and it would do as my temporary refuge.

Mike did not move in with me. In the beginning, especially, we were both cautious about him having contact with Lisa. We didn't know where the relationship was going, and I didn't want Lisa hurt. Mike usually came when Lisa was gone, occasionally making short visits with both of us to get to know her. We kept things platonic when she was around. I was very concerned about her well-being and tried to protect her emotionally as much as possible. I didn't want to add to the physical and emotional upheaval she was already going through. Lisa was almost five years old by then, old enough to be observant but too young to understand the complicated relationships I was negotiating. She knew Mike only as Mommy's friend. She called him Mikey.

Elvis and I gradually began talking again. We had always made Lisa's birthdays a big event, so as her fifth birthday approached, we agreed I would bring her to Vegas at the end of January to celebrate with both of us. Since he was doing a concert series there, the party was in Elvis's suite at the Las Vegas Hilton. I dressed Lisa and myself in matching mother-daughter outfits that my friend Olivia Bis had made for us. The dirndl-style dresses laced up the front and were made of a blue and red paisley print. They were pretty and unique, appropriate for both a woman and a young child. As always at Lisa's parties, the room was filled with balloons and food and over-the-top gifts from Elvis. We made our best effort to be festive and show Lisa Marie that nothing had changed in the family. After the party, we went to Elvis's eight o'clock performance.

That show was Lisa's first experience of seeing the frenzy surrounding her daddy. She had heard her father play and sing sometimes at home, but she had only the vaguest idea of what he did and no idea of the hysteria he inspired. The show was sold out as usual, the hotel lobby filled with the Elvis souvenirs the Colonel always provided in abundance. The venue was packed with excited fans, and there was a murmur as the guys escorted us to our seats. A few people noticed us, looking at us and whispering, but everyone was polite. No one approached us. The guys sat around us, constantly monitoring our safety. We were about eight rows back. The first rows were filled with pretty girls, strategically placed next to the stage to scream and swoon when Elvis started to sing. Elvis knew how to work a crowd, to bend down and murmur sultrily or plant a kiss on a girl in the front row.

Lisa was sitting on my lap, being quiet as I had asked her to, when the lights came up onstage, and the theme from *2001: A Space Odyssey* blasted out. Her eyes grew big as she saw her daddy, resplendent in his bejeweled costume, commanding the stage. She was rapt as he began to sing, and she looked at me occasionally with wonder. She became very excited when Elvis greeted her in the audience and everyone applauded. When the crowd screamed and cheered, she cheered with them. When they stood up, she stood up. Sometimes she looked around at the crowd, taking it all in. I could see the realization dawning that Elvis wasn't just Daddy; he was someone very special.

A couple of numbers before the show ended, Joe ushered Lisa and me out the back way, through the kitchen, and backstage to the dressing rooms. We heard the loudspeaker announcement that became iconic over the years: "Elvis has left the building." There was a long wait while Elvis showered and changed; then he came out and hugged me, picking up the sleepy little girl in my arms. That was the night Lisa Marie discovered that her father was the King. It was also the night she began to realize she was the little princess. Before, she had just been Lisa. Now she was Elvis Presley's daughter. It was an identity that both enabled and haunted her for the rest of her life.

Over the next eight months, as our attorneys argued about the terms of the divorce, Elvis and I reached an agreement ourselves. We worked out a financial settlement and, most importantly, a plan to share custody of Lisa. We were prepared to move forward.

On October 9, 1973, eighteen months after I'd left Elvis, we met at the Santa Monica Courthouse for the divorce proceedings. Michelle came with me, and Elvis was accompanied by Joe and Vernon. I was stunned when I saw Elvis. His weight had ballooned, and he was bloated and sweating. He hardly looked like himself anymore. As we sat in the judge's chambers, listening to him read the decree, Elvis and I held hands. I ran my fingers over his. They were so swollen that they felt like a stranger's hand.

I whispered to him, "Sattnin', is him all right? Is her [meaning Linda] taking good care of him? Making sure him eats and staying with him until him falls asleep?"

The judge was puzzled. He paused at one point and asked us if we were sure we wanted a divorce. We assured him we did. A wave of pain and nostalgia washed over me. I listened to the judge pronounce us divorced and then walked out into the sunshine, still holding hands with the man I loved. Who, I had no doubt, still loved me. We embraced and kissed each other on the cheek. I gave him a little wave as he got into the car, and he winked at me. Our life together had ended legally, but it had ended gently.

I remained in the apartment in Marina del Rey until the divorce was final. Once that was settled, I began to look for a place near the home Elvis and I had once shared in Holmby Hills, a neighborhood in LA. I found a beautiful house on a one-acre estate in Beverly Hills. It was built in 1951 and had a secluded feel to it. There was a pool and tennis court and beautiful foliage, with plenty of walkways and hiding places for Lisa to play in, and a patio area where Lisa and I could entertain. There was a fence around the property and a high gate for safety. The house itself was lined with large windows that brought the outside in, and it had high, beamed ceilings. It was beautiful, and I set about decorating it with enthusiasm. It was the first place that felt like home after I left Elvis. I ended up living there for forty-seven years. I raised my children there, and eventually, it became Nona's house, the place where my grandchildren came.

Most important at the time, my new home was close to Elvis's house. I wanted to be nearby in case Elvis ever needed me, and I wanted to keep the family together as much as I could. That was important for all of us. I didn't want the family to be physically separated any more than necessary. Elvis and I were still connected, very concerned about each other. It had been an unusual marriage. It was an unusual divorce. As I'd told Grandma when I left, the love was still there. If anything, the relationship was better because we were now free. The barriers that once stood between us were gone.

I took responsibility for ensuring that Elvis saw our daughter. I was the one who said, "Lisa can come. Okay? When I'm making arrangements, I'll make sure that Lisa sees you." He greatly appreciated that.

I wanted Lisa to be there when Elvis came back from his tours or from Graceland. I wanted him to have the security of knowing she was there whenever he wanted to see her. If Lisa wanted to visit her dad after school, I'd drop her off. If I couldn't take her, my housekeeper would. One way or another, I made sure she saw her daddy.

Elvis would tell me if it was a good time for her to visit, for he was moving around a lot on tour. If he was only going to be someplace for two or three days, we would postpone the visit. It all depended on his schedule. If he was in Vegas or at Graceland for two weeks, we'd work something out. We took turns having her for Christmas, and if there was an Easter or summer break, she'd be with him for extended periods. He spent most of his long breaks at Graceland. One of the guys would fly to LA and get Lisa and then bring her back. They were all friends that she was comfortable with and Elvis trusted. It was a great arrangement.

It worked well in almost every respect. But there was one glaring problem. Even when in physical proximity, Mommy and Daddy lived in different worlds. At Mommy's house, things were calm and structured. In Daddy's world, the King reigned. Elvis still spent his days with the guys, still ate breakfast late in the afternoon, still went to bed at two or three in the morning or later. It would never occur to him to change his habits just because his daughter was there. It never did. At Daddy's house, she could play all day with her friends and with all the toys at Graceland. Elvis got Lisa her own golf cart so that she could roar around the grounds. She raced over the lawns and plants. Lisa was never one to stay within the lines. She would wander into the kitchen if she got hungry and insist that the cook provide her with her favorite foods. One time, she demanded an entire chocolate cake. When the cook resisted her nutritional choices, Lisa would say, "I'll tell my daddy, and he'll fire you!"

If the nanny tried to impose a schedule, Lisa would threaten to have the nanny fired, too. She was a little terror. Elvis didn't follow up on her threats to fire the staff; he apparently thought it was cute.

Lisa went to bed when she wanted to, often when Elvis did. If he and the guys were busy, she'd stay up. There was an endless succession of expensive gifts. Elvis even bought her a tiny mink coat and a diamond ring. I would call every night while Lisa was there, just to make sure everything was all right. If Elvis came on the phone, I'd ask if Lisa had eaten dinner or taken her bath or been put to bed. He would assure me she had. Often, Grandma's daughter Delta would call me back well after midnight to tell me Lisa hadn't eaten dinner, was refusing to take a bath, and hadn't been put to bed. It was funny but exasperating.

When I confronted Elvis about the situation, emphasizing the importance of giving our daughter guidelines and values, he replied, "The hell with values. Let the kid have fun."

It was an exaggerated version of the permissive divorced-dad syndrome, supersized because he was Elvis Presley. From a child's point of view, his indulgence was unconditional love. I saw it differently. I thought it was a recipe for disaster. Years later, describing her childhood self, Lisa said, "I was a pint-sized tyrant. Then I went home, and my mom had to deal with me." The good-cop/bad-cop contrast in the way Elvis and I parented Lisa affected my relationship with my daughter. As much as my daughter loved me, I could never compete with her daddy. She adored him. And in Elvis's defense, he adored her, too. He saw nothing wrong with the freedom he gave her.

Elvis always needed a support system, and fortunately, he still had that in his entourage. He had grown very concerned about his personal safety by then, particularly in Vegas. If there was a rumor about a possible threat or any odd behavior in the crowd at a concert, Joe and the guys took care of it. And they remained his social circle, there to horse around with, to joke with, to keep him company.

I was his go-to when there were problems with the guys. If he got upset with one of them, he'd tell me. He called to tell me he'd fired Marty Lacker, saying, "That damn m*****f****r! You know what he did?" Blah, blah, blah. A lot of curse words. He would let it all out, raging. Sometimes he'd go on for over an hour.

I'd say hardly anything, just mumbling, "Oh! Uh-huh. Hmmm."

If I started talking, he'd say, "Listen to me!"

Other times, he would make a call from his car phone, just checking in.

I'd say, "How are you doing?"

"Just driving around. How's it going? What are you doing?"

"Is everything okay?"

"Yeah."

He'd let me know what was going on or talk about some argument he'd had with his dad or one of the guys. Sometimes, he would be upset with Dee, Vernon's wife. Their marriage was on the rocks. Family things.

I never really knew when he was going to call. It happened at all hours. He'd usually take the moment when his girlfriend was out. If she was there, he'd use the phone in his bathroom or dressing room while she was in the other room. After Mike and I broke up, I would take the call in another room if I was with someone when the phone rang. I never acknowledged that the caller was Elvis if I was with another man. Talk about ruining the mood! Elvis never asked if I had a boyfriend, and I never discussed my boyfriends with him. Conversely, I never discussed Elvis with anyone I was dating. I didn't date a lot of men, and I didn't listen to Elvis's music when I did. It would have been unwise and unkind. And contrary to some tell-all interviews, he *never* called when I was making love to someone!

Elvis sometimes came over when he was in LA. He'd be out driving around with one of the guys, usually Joe, and decide to stop by unannounced. He never had a plan. It was always pretty much at the moment. A bell outside by my gate let me know he was coming. He usually came in the evenings or late in the day because he never got up early. When he'd come through the door, he would give me a kiss or a hug. Then he'd sit and talk for a while. He always sat with his legs crossed, jiggling his foot constantly. Elvis could never sit still. I thought it was cute. One time, my mother was there, and they talked for a while.

If Lisa was there, I'd sit near him so that she could sit on our laps together. He usually had one of the guys with him. Every now and then, he came alone, but usually, there was someone with him.

It was good. I liked our relationship. It was actually a better relationship because there was no pressure. Everything was out in the open. He didn't have to hide things anymore.

I would ask, "Are you still dating Linda?"

"Yeah, I'm still dating her."

"Is she treating you well?"

"Yeah."

I understood that Elvis had to have a woman. Starting with his mother, he'd had a woman by his side since birth. He did not want to be alone. Once he became famous, it was important to his image to be seen with a beautiful woman. When Linda Thompson left him four years after I had, he was desperate. She had been his first serious relationship after me, and now she had left, too.

As always, the guys were on the lookout for a replacement woman for Elvis. One of them told him, "There's this girl that just won queen of something in Memphis. You want me to bring her over?"

Her name was Ginger Alden. They picked her out, introduced her to Elvis, and that was it. It was a done deal. She was a very pretty young woman. Was she in love with him? Nobody close to Elvis thought so. She was only twenty years old, too young to cope with Elvis's complex needs, and she already had a boyfriend. However, her mother, I was told, was intent on Ginger's being with Elvis. He was a big prize. Ginger didn't want to see

Elvis on the weekends, because she wanted to be with her boyfriend, so she was constantly making up excuses to stay home. She didn't want to be on tour with him, either. I didn't know Ginger well, so I can't speak from experience, but I heard about her constantly from the guys and their wives. They did not think it was a good relationship. And I worried about that. I worried because Elvis wasn't being taken care of. I became even more concerned when it was rumored they were engaged. The marriage, if it were ever to happen, would have disaster written all over it.

Elvis continued to be affectionate with me. He still called me Sattnin', his nickname for his mother. It came from the word *fattening*, referring to the fact that Gladys was plump. It was a term of affection, and it clearly didn't apply to me literally. I was thin. But it was Elvis's way of telling me how much he loved me, as he'd loved his mother.

It was endearing. And he continued to talk baby talk with me. It was his love language. He called me "him's girl."

He'd tell me, "Him misses him's girl."

I would reply that her missed him, too.

Other times, he'd call me Yittle, meaning "little," "little her." "Where's Yittle? Yittle, come here."

Or Nungin'. Nungin' was "young'un." He still used my pet names.

Then one Christmas, as he was leaving my house, he kissed me on the forehead and looked at me. There was a moment, and then he said, "Someday. Maybe someday."

Him and her. Maybe someday.

CHAPTER 3

Separate Ways

I see a change is coming to our lives.
It's not the same as it used to be.

Though I kept the Presley name when Elvis and I divorced, I did not remain the same Priscilla Presley. I had been either Elvis's girlfriend or Elvis's wife since I was a teenager. That was, and is, how the world identifies me. When I left, I was suddenly confronted with the reality of figuring out who I was without Elvis. It was the second-biggest identity crisis of my life. The first occurred when I was eleven years old.

I grew up in a military family, the oldest of six children. The only name I had ever known for myself was Priscilla Ann

Beaulieu, my middle name honoring my mother. My father, I believed, was an air force officer named Paul Beaulieu. He was a devoted family man, a little gruff and distant as military men tended to be, but he was good to me, and I loved him. Then one afternoon when I was eleven, my parents were next door having dinner with the neighbors when I got bored and started looking through a closet. I saw a small suitcase-shaped box, and when I opened it, I found a folded American flag, a locket on a chain, and photographs of my mother. She was with a young man, and they were holding a baby. I knew the baby was me. I had no idea who the man was.

I called my mother on the phone, crying, and said, "Mom, Mom, Mom, I found these pictures, and it's not Dad, and I don't know who he is."

My mother replied, "I'll be right there," and came home immediately.

She gently explained that when she was eighteen, she fell in love with a navy pilot. He was her first love. His name was James Wagner. My name when I was born was Priscilla Ann Wagner. I listened with my eyes wide open as she told me that James was my biological father. He was a military man like my other father, Paul. Jim was killed in a plane crash when he was flying home to see me. He was in a small plane, with a friend piloting. The weather was bad that day, and they had crashed into a mountain that was hidden by the fog. Both men died. I was only six months old at the time. He and my mom had been married for a little over a year.

Mother was focused on me, on telling the story gently, but even at that age, I could tell how difficult it was for her to tell me this. Losing her first love in a plane crash had devastated her. She told me what a wonderful man he was. He was smart, and he had a friendly, outgoing personality. He whistled whenever he walked down the street, saying hello to everyone. His parents were very loving, and they had embraced her.

Then, when I was three years old, she had met and married my father—my stepfather. Dad was very jealous of Jim and made my mother promise never to tell anyone, including me, about him. Dad legally adopted me, changing my name to Beaulieu, and Jim Wagner was never mentioned again. When I was still very small, before she and Dad married, my mother had taken me regularly to visit my Wagner grandparents. Those visits stopped when she married Dad. He wouldn't allow it. She told me that my real father had loved me very much and that I would have loved him, but I couldn't talk about him. Out of respect for my stepdad, she asked me to promise never to tell anyone, not even my siblings, about my first father. I kept that promise for over twenty years. I often wondered about my real father and whether my siblings would feel the same about me if they knew I wasn't a real Beaulieu.

It wasn't until years after Elvis and I divorced that I finally told my brothers and sister who my real father was. I was told that a journalist had discovered the identity of my true father and was publishing an article about it. They were surprised, but that was all. I was still their big sister. And I finally had the freedom to reach out to my Wagner family. I was able to meet my grandmother and uncle. They had followed my life for years in the news but had resigned themselves to never seeing me again. Becoming part of their family, too, was an important step in making me whole.

Discovering I was a Wagner had been painful and confusing. Discovering who I was without Elvis was sometimes confusing, but it was also an adventure. Most people struggle with their identity as teenagers. When I was a teenager, I adopted Elvis's identity. Now, in my late twenties, I was going through a belated process of self-discovery. Discovering my identity the second time was liberating.

I was also discovering a new personal style. The black eye makeup of the 1960s was replaced by the more natural look of the 1970s. I even lightened my eyebrows like the model Twiggy, whose blonde elfin looks and huge eyes had made her world famous. I experimented with hairstyles and hair colors, from brunette to blonde to strawberry. Now I could part my hair in the middle if I wanted to. Elvis had always hated hair parted in the middle, but now it was up to me. In addition to the sheer fun of experimenting with different styles, I discovered that the new looks had the added advantage of making me relatively anonymous. People were used to identifying me by my black hair and black-lined eyes. With my new, evolving appearance, I could go out with friends and not be recognized.

Wearing anything I wanted also gave me a heady sense of freedom. Fashion was like my playground. I hadn't resented dressing to please Elvis when I was with him. I liked his taste, and I'd enjoyed the way his face lit up when I wore something he loved. He thought high heels were sexy, and I liked looking sexy for him. But now I had choices. I still wore heels when I wanted to dress up, but I loved going out wearing flats. I could wear denim, too, jeans or denim jackets. Elvis never wore jeans and didn't want me to wear them. He associated them with the poverty of his childhood, when he couldn't afford anything else to wear. Now I wore classic styles, long flowy dresses, vivid colors, and feminine prints. It was the 1970s, and long dresses were in style. I didn't like the hippie look, complete with fringe, but I did like the embroidery and embellishments of the decade. I could wear anything I wanted; the only limitations were my own taste and the comfort of the clothing. I was nearly thirty years old, and it was the first time I was able to experiment with clothing. I'd gone from wearing clothes my parents liked to wearing clothes Elvis liked. Now the only one I had to please was me.

I had always had a sense of style, which I got from my mother. Mother was always impeccably dressed, and I used to look at her and think how pretty she was. She had modeled to make some money before she met my stepfather. I had briefly modeled, too, after I attended the Patricia Stevens finishing school. I was a table model in a fancy restaurant; it was the only job I had ever had. Even when I was quite young, I liked to add personal details to what I wore. I would embellish my sweaters with collars and my skirts with linked metal belts. I loved ties and would wear bow ties with some of my outfits. I was chosen Best Dressed in the ninth grade. I was always interested in fashion.

Going into the fashion business was a natural fit for me. I had become friends with Olivia Bis when she had a designer boutique in Beverly Hills. I used to buy clothes from her whenever Elvis had a Vegas opening. I shopped there for almost everything because I loved her style. She sold one-of-a-kind, beautiful clothing. Because of my interest in design, she would work with me to create what I wanted. I'd bring something in and say,

"I really like this," and we'd work together to create a garment I loved. She was so open, so good to work with. Olivia and I became good friends. Before Elvis and I divorced, I talked to her about buying part of her business and joining her. Elvis liked Olivia and her designs, so he'd agreed. After he and I separated, I became actively involved in the business. Olivia and I opened a shop on Robertson in Beverly Hills and called it Bis and Beau. I was involved in the design process, and I loved every aspect of co-owning the shop.

Not long after we opened, I received another exciting opportunity. I was contacted by the *Ladies' Home Journal*, one of the leading women's magazines of the time, and asked to do an interview for a cover article. Never having done an interview before, I was wary. But Sandra Shevey, the journalist who had reached out, assured me that it was a legitimate request, telling me not to worry about tabloid-style coverage. She even gave me editorial approval. Everyone connected with the article was wonderful, and Sandra was sweet. I was a nervous wreck when the time came for the interview, but apparently it didn't show. I was described as very "poised." The article came out in August 1973 and focused on how it felt to be an independent woman, on my own and living with my daughter. It was exciting to have an article written about my new life, and it was great PR for Bis and Beau as well.

Olivia mentored me in the early months of the boutique opening, teaching me a great deal about the clothing business. For example, I would bring in something I liked in silk and suggest that we use a similar fabric.

Olivia would tell me, "Well, you know, sometimes silk can be difficult to work with. And people can't throw it in their washing machine; they have to take it to the cleaners. Customers don't like that."

I gradually learned about fabrics and what's best to use commercially. Texture was as important to me as the look of an outfit. I don't like to wear clothing that is scratchy or otherwise uncomfortable on the skin. You buy something beautiful, but if you haven't considered the texture, you might regret the purchase. You take it home and put it on and realize you've made a big mistake. We had great fabrics at Bis and Beau. A woman whose specialty was fabrics worked with us and brought us a wonderful selection. A talented team of tailors, seamstresses, and craftspeople made much of our clothing. Customers could have outfits made for them or choose from a select variety of ready-made clothing. Our clothing was often very hip, ahead of the curve. We also had some timeless looks. We gave people choices, and they liked that.

One of our most popular creations was embellished jeans and denim jackets. We were one of the first stores to sell them. We also carried a range of styles, from gowns to miniskirts. I designed a line of watches with Swiss-embroidered bands that I called Mikibeau. We quickly developed an A-list clientele. Some of them were open to our suggestions; others already knew what they did or didn't want. I too am like that. I have very distinct taste. We got to know the clients' preferences over time.

Cher always wanted something sexy and different that you couldn't find anywhere else. When she told me, "Priscilla, I love this," it was huge. Cher loved our clothing!

Liza Minnelli came in; so did Natalie Wood. She was tiny and cute as a button. Victoria Principal came in often. I had no inkling that within a few years, I'd be costarring with her on a hit series.

Sometimes if I wasn't there, Olivia would call me and say, "Oh my God, you're not going to believe who's here. Oh my God."

I'd go, "Who?"

One time it was Barbra Streisand. Another time it was Lana Turner.

I said, "Lana Turner? Are you kidding me? She's an icon." Hearing she had visited our boutique gave me chills. Miss Turner was very old-school sophisticated, with classic lines and turned-up collars. So elegant. We were thrilled to death that we had such top people coming into our store.

I was involved not only in the designs but also in the day-to-day running of the store. I worked there when Lisa was at school or with Elvis. I loved showing the customers our designs. For the first time, I was working and getting paid, comanaging my own business. I was hardworking, organized, and detail oriented. I discovered I had an instinctive sense of what customers wanted. I learned that I was a natural as a businesswoman, and my self-esteem soared. It was an exciting discovery, and the sense of freedom and independence I experienced was amazing. I felt useful, like I was contributing.

And I was meeting people, friends of my own, some of whom remain friends to this day. I still had a few of my old friends: Elvis's cousin Patsy, Joanie Esposito, and a couple of the other wives from my days with Elvis. But now I was meeting people through other avenues, through my own interests and activities. Before, everyone I knew was someone I'd met through Elvis.

Now I was going out more on my own, with people of my own choosing. When I was with Elvis, I had to be with him whenever he was home. I didn't want to go out, because I was always afraid that when I went out the front door, the guys would bring another girl through the back door. Now I chose where I wanted to go and who I wanted to be with.

Though I was happy at Bis and Beau, after three years, I decided to sell my share back to Olivia. Much as I loved the work, I had begun to feel that I was becoming a liability to the business. Word had gotten around that I co-owned and worked at the store. People began referring to the business as "Priscilla's shop," which wasn't fair to Olivia. Elvis fans would gather there in hopes of seeing me. They would peer through the front window, looking for me. Some of the bolder ones came inside and surrounded me, asking for my autograph. The situation made our clients uncomfortable and made me even more so. The focus was shifting from the shop to me personally. I came in less and less, because I had become a distraction. I felt responsible, though in reality, there was nothing I could do about other people's behavior. Olivia and I talked and agreed that I would sell my share back to her. It was a difficult decision, but it was the right one.

Admittedly, my life became simpler when I was no longer working at the store. Even when I was working, I was a hands-on mom. My priority had always been Lisa Marie. I was there to wake her up in the morning, feed her breakfast, and get her ready for school. I would braid her hair or put it in ponytails and make sure she was presentable. She looked so cute in her little uniform. I dropped her off at school myself and made a point to be home while she did her homework. I wanted to be the one to make sure she had a good dinner and a bath and went to bed early on school nights. I wanted to tuck her in and kiss her good night.

My sister lived with us part of the time, and she was wonderful with Lisa. I also had staff members to help me. They would provide backup if needed, but Lisa didn't like being left alone with the staff. Besides, I wanted to be there. She was my life.

I worked hard to keep Lisa out of the public eye. She was very recognizable because she looked so much like Elvis, with the same sleepy, deep blue eyes. She was still spending time with her dad, still visiting Graceland on breaks, still shuttling back and forth between two very different worlds. That was a challenge for both Lisa and me. Keeping her out of trouble sometimes felt like a full-time job. Strong-willed and stubborn, she tended to barge ahead without thinking things through. She was also mischievous.

Lisa once told Linda Thompson, "My mommy doesn't like you." My daughter went on to explain that this was because Elvis took Linda on tour more often than he had taken me. Linda thought her comment was funny; so did I when I heard about it. Actually, I did like Linda because she took good care of Elvis, but Lisa liked to stir things up. It made life more interesting. When she grew up and looked back at that time in our lives, she said she sometimes felt like she was the bull, and I was the china shop. I spent a lot of time picking up the pieces.

After leaving Bis and Beau, I soon realized that I would have other business opportunities that required less time away from home. I was being approached by people interested in working with me on a variety of projects. Sometimes the offers appealed to me. Sometimes they didn't. I accepted the position of chief spokesperson for Wella Balsam, a popular line of hair products. I did commercials for the products and occasionally traveled to events where I represented the company. I liked the products and enjoyed the work. Another offer was one I couldn't turn down fast enough. It came from *Playboy*. The magazine wanted me to pose for the cover and centerfold. It sent me several samples to show what the publication wanted. Of course, I had seen *Playboy* magazines before. I'd found a cache hidden under my brother's bed when he was a teen, and all of Elvis's guys had copies. In fact, one of my stipulations was that all copies be removed when Lisa visited Elvis in Vegas. I knew, of course, that the magazine contained "girlie pictures." But it was one thing to know this and another to go through the magazine page by page, picturing myself in it. The whole idea made me very uncomfortable. That was one avenue I definitely didn't want to pursue.

By 1975, my relationship with Mike Stone had come to an end. We had spent three good years together, but his world was karate. It had brought us together when we first met, but over time, our interests diverged. Mike was his own man. I learned a lot from him.

Shortly after our breakup, I began dating Robert Kardashian. I was introduced to him by Joanie Esposito, who was now divorced and seeing Robert's brother, Tom. (She later married Tom.) We double-dated for a while. Robert was a sweet man, and I liked him. But after a few months, I realized it wasn't going to work out. Robert had a demanding job as an attorney, working long hours five days a week. By the time the weekend rolled around, all he wanted was a quiet night at home with popcorn and a good movie. It was fine at first, but I gradually grew restless. I am more active by nature. I wanted to be out and about, doing something. Robert wanted to get married, but I knew it wouldn't work. I wasn't ready to marry again. We remained friends, though, and twenty years later, I saw the agony he went through during the O. J. Simpson trial. Robert was fiercely loyal, and he loved O. J. like a brother. In Robert's role as Simpson's defense attorney, his personal loyalty to O. J. created a conflict. The realization that his friend had committed the murders nearly destroyed him. Ten years later, Robert's daughter Kim called me from the hospital shortly before he passed away. Robert and I had one last conversation before he died. He was the kindest of men, and I remember him with great affection.

My next romantic relationship was in sharp contrast to Robert. Elie Ezerzer was the top hairdresser at the Vidal Sassoon Salon in Beverly Hills. Vidal was then the face of the haircutting world, the Elvis of hair. Hearing that I wanted one of the new cuts that were coming into style, a friend recommended Elie. As I waited to see him for my appointment, I watched him with other clients. Just to see him work was amazing. His hands were beautiful, and every touch of the hair was done with absolute precision. He would make a tiny cut, move to the side to look at it, then look at it in the mirror before he proceeded. It was like watching an artist, except instead of sculpting clay or marble, he was sculpting hair.

And he was handsome, a tall French Moroccan man who dressed impeccably in a suit and tie. He walked with confidence, like he was somebody. He had such an air about him, even in the way he smoked a cigarette. He was just cool. The women loved him. When it was my turn, he sculpted my hair into a beautiful chin-length bob. Before long, we were dating.

I soon learned that he had an artistic temperament as well. Elie was passionate, volatile, and exciting to be with. But he was also jealous. If I waved to someone, he'd ask, "Who's that guy? How do you know him?" It was a little intense, though it took a while for me to realize how intense. After a few months of dating, things came to a head. I had gone with Michelle to visit friends in Hawaii. My sister and I got one room with a big bed to share. One of my friends was a well-known singer there, and we went to his show. Afterward, we went out with him and his friend and another girl. We drank a little wine and talked. It was a nice evening. Then, at about one in the morning, Michelle and I went back to our room at the hotel. Almost immediately, the phone rang. It was Elie. He was at the hotel. He had flown to Hawaii unannounced to check up on me, to see if I was with somebody else.

"You're not in bed!" he shouted. "You said you were in bed, but you're not!"

He was furious. All I could think was that he would be able to smell the wine on my breath when he came to the room. And even though we'd been out with a group of friends, I knew he'd freak out if he discovered there was another guy among them.

That pretty much ended the relationship. It scared me when he showed up like that. I was afraid it would become a pattern. I couldn't live with that kind of jealousy.

Separate Ways | 43

Not long afterward, a mutual friend introduced me to Kirk Kerkorian. The only thing I knew about Kirk was that he was very wealthy and owned half of Las Vegas. I'd heard his name mentioned when I was there with Elvis. Kirk was a lovely man, almost thirty years older than me, well-mannered and thoughtful. Very much the gentleman. We became friends, and one day, he told me he was going to Cannes on his private plane with friends. Would I like to join them? I was excited. I had never been to Cannes, and now I would get to see it.

I was so naive. I thought it was just a trip with this lovely older man who wanted to show me the beautiful city he loved. I assumed I would have my own room. After all, there was nothing romantic between Kirk and me. Then we got there. Kirk and I had adjoining rooms on his yacht. Connected rooms. For the first time, I wondered what was going to be expected of me, and I started to panic. While Kirk was resting that afternoon, I went for a walk. I realized I'd gotten myself into a situation I wasn't ready for. I felt like a prostitute, as if I were trading my body for a trip to France. I knew I couldn't do it. So I went back to the yacht and made reservations for a flight home that night. Then I had to tell Kirk there had been a misunderstanding. I was very embarrassed.

But he was a true gentleman. He told me he understood. I left for the airport and flew home to LA. Kirk and I remained friends, and he never made me feel uncomfortable about what had happened. It was a wake-up call for me, though. I realized how inexperienced I was in the dating world. I had missed the adolescent dating experience, when you figure out how things work and what's expected of you. I knew everything about being with Elvis but very little about being with other men.

And there was still Elvis to deal with, complicating things. He always complicated things. He had an unfortunate habit of phoning late at night when I was with another man. It happened with Robert Kardashian. One night, Robert was sound asleep in bed with me when the phone rang at 2:00 a.m. Fortunately, he was a sound sleeper, so I leaped out of bed and grabbed the phone before it woke him. I tiptoed down the hall to the guest bedroom and shut the door to listen to the familiar voice. Elvis was calling from the hotel after a performance.

"It went great tonight, Cilla! I sang the shit out of everything, and the crowd went crazy. You should have seen them. It was a full house. Damn, I was knocking 'em out!"

The excited voice went on and on. As usual, there was no "Hi, Sattnin', how are you?" Not even a hello, as far as that went. The only reason he knew I was there was my murmured "Uh-huh, wow, great," as he drew breath in between words. It hadn't crossed his mind that I might have been asleep. It had certainly never occurred to him that I might be with another man. Despite our divorce, he still couldn't wrap his head around my being with someone else. He'd have gone ballistic, maybe literally, if he'd known Robert was in my bedroom. Elvis always carried a loaded gun, sometimes more than one. I put my hand over my mouth to stifle the sound of my yawn while Elvis continued to talk. He was as excited as a kid. It was endearing, but I was just so sleepy.

Finally, he started to wind down. His tone changed, and he switched over to his love language.

"Sattnin', is her okay?"

"Her's okay. Is him okay?"

"Yeah."

I whispered goodbye and gently set down the receiver. Then I padded soundlessly back down the hall and slipped under the covers with Robert. He stirred slightly, but he didn't wake up. He never knew Elvis had called. And Elvis never knew about Robert.

CHAPTER 4
Saying Goodbye

Take your troubles to the chapel
Get down on your knees and pray.

I HAD BEEN WORRIED ABOUT ELVIS FOR A LONG TIME. HE would sometimes talk about dying young like his mother. Gladys had died at forty-six. Elvis had never recovered from her death, and he didn't want to live long enough to lose Vernon, too. It was disturbing to hear. Was he having a premonition? Or was it just one of his moods?

Once he passed his fortieth birthday, it became obvious to everyone that his health was deteriorating. He put on startling amounts of weight, looking bloated and heavy. When I took Lisa to Vegas to see him, I was shocked by what I saw.

He no longer looked like the man I knew. Getting through his concerts was increasingly challenging for him. Exhausted and distracted, he would sometimes struggle with the lyrics to his songs. It reached the point that he couldn't finish some of his performances. His audiences noticed, but most of them would forgive anything he did. The reviewers were more direct about what they saw. On June 28, 1977, a few days after Elvis's last concert, Ken Williams of the *Cincinnati Journal News* wrote a review that was prescient: "There comes a time when a performer should step down, retire or rest.... We prefer remembering you at your peak, rather than at your funeral."

Elvis began going into the hospital regularly. I knew he was trying to rest and get away from the pressure. His medication intake had skyrocketed, and both Joe and Vernon were very worried. Joe went on the road with Elvis and saw the worst of it, but he was helpless to intervene. How did you tell Elvis Presley that he needed help? You didn't. Anything that related to his looks, his weight, or his pills was off-limits. Mentioning any of those topics only made him angry. To him, it was criticism.

If anybody mentioned pills, he'd say, "Mind your own business." It was an extremely sensitive subject.

I tried to talk to him about it myself, in the gentlest possible way. "Is everything okay, Nunjin? Is him okay?"

He'd brush me off, saying, "Yeah, yeah, yeah, him's okay."

Joe Esposito, Jerry Schilling, and some of the other guys would phone to tell me what was going on. They were very careful, for they knew it was a suicide mission if they got caught. If Elvis had known the guys were calling me about the situation, he'd have fired them. He did fire some of them, including Joe, for that very reason. When he calmed down, he hired Joe back, but he'd made his point. There were lines nobody was allowed to cross. Even me.

He kept telling me, "Don't worry, I'm fine."

But he wasn't, and we all knew it.

Part of the problem was that he did not believe he was taking drugs. Elvis defined drugs as illegal substances sold on the streets, and he was violently opposed to those. What he was taking was medication, prescribed by a doctor. That, in his mind, was a completely different thing. He'd been taking medication since he was a teenager. Most people think his drug problem started with the stimulants the army gave him, to keep him awake on patrol. But in reality, the problem had started much earlier. His mother took pills for a variety of illnesses, including depression, insomnia, and obesity. She was hospitalized for depression on several occasions. Elvis took some of Gladys's pills himself, for his own depression or insomnia, or when he was tired. In those days, doctors did not yet understand the dangers or addictive properties of these drugs. They were "mother's little pink pills." When I first met Elvis, I thought they were harmless. I was still cautious, for my mother had always told me to be careful with medication. Elvis coaxed me into trying some, but I didn't like the way they made me feel. I resisted taking them. By the time Elvis was in his thirties, the dangers of the drugs were well understood, but that didn't keep doctors from prescribing them. His doctors gave him anything he wanted. He was Elvis Presley. For unscrupulous doctors, enabling patients was a lucrative part of their practice.

Keeping Elvis healthy required continual care and monitoring. For years, I took responsibility for it. I kept a close eye on him, making sure he ate regularly and sitting with him until he fell asleep. Linda Thompson did the same thing after I left. That was one of the reasons the family and the guys—and their wives—liked her. Elvis's needs had only increased after I left. Linda had to deal with more than I had. I think I'd had the best of him. But when she also left, Elvis began spiraling rapidly downhill.

Elvis's deterioration wasn't just physical. He was declining mentally as well. By then he was taking a staggering amount of prescription opioids and barbiturates, including very high doses of Dilaudid, Percodan, Demerol, codeine, and quaaludes. These medications were designed for those with severe pain problems in the last stages of illness, not for regular use. Quaaludes were so dangerous that they were made illegal in 1984. The drugs had many physical side effects, including weakness, loss of motor skills, and a swollen larynx, all of which affected Elvis's performances. But they also carried serious cognitive and psychological risks: mood changes, serious mental impairment, a false sense of well-being, nightmares, depression, and confusion. Elvis was still on amphetamines as well, which he needed to wake up, not to mention perform. When taken in high amounts, amphetamines—uppers—can induce paranoia and outbursts of rage, both of which Elvis experienced. Each medication carried its own risks, but the cocktail of drugs given to Elvis increased the risks exponentially. He didn't recognize the symptoms that were obvious to everyone around him. Because the pills were affecting the way he felt and reasoned, any effort to talk to him about his drug intake was futile.

What was despicable about the situation was that all these medications were legally prescribed by Elvis's physicians, one of whom traveled with him on tour. With a doctor to back him up, it is no wonder Elvis wouldn't listen to his friends or family. The miracle, of course, was that he was still functioning at all. Few people could have survived the drug doses Elvis was given. Small wonder he began to feel like he was immune to the risks. The pills, and the doctors, had convinced him he was.

In April, Lisa and I went to Graceland to keep Grandma company for a few days while Elvis was on tour. But he cut the tour short because he wasn't feeling well and came back to Memphis. That evening, he called me up to his room. He was sitting on the bed in his pajamas, surrounded by his books. He looked ill, and when he talked, he slurred his words slightly. It was painful to see him like that. For a while, we talked about Lisa. Then he began talking to me about what he was reading.

He was holding one of his favorite books, Cheiro's *Book of Numbers*. Cheiro was a mystic and astrologer who used numerology to predict the future. Through a series of mathematical calculations, you could chart your ideal life path or even get advice about specific decisions. Elvis had long ago determined both of our astrological numbers and done the math to get guidance for us, separately and together. He had literally worn out three copies of Cheiro's book, replacing each copy as it frayed and began to fall apart. He was so earnest about it, underlining passages and reading them to me, still searching for answers for his life. One passage he marked said, "Work is love made visible.... And when you work with love, you bind yourself to yourself and to one another and to God."

It was like the old days, Elvis reading to me in the middle of the night.

I looked at him and thought, *You are so ahead of the game. Yet so lost.*

Finally, I gave him a hug and a kiss and said good night. I had no premonition that it was the last embrace. I would never see him alive again.

The June 1977 tour would be his last. For the most part, the concerts were a struggle for him. It was clear he wasn't well. The notable exception was the June 21 concert in Rapid City, South Dakota, a performance that became legendary. He looked exhausted during the first few songs, breathing hard and having some difficulty walking. Then partway through the performance, he told the audience he wanted to introduce "Unchained Melody," a new song he had just recorded. He was out of breath and difficult to understand, and I doubt the audience caught much of what he said. But they certainly understood what followed. As he took his seat at the piano and handed the microphone to Charlie Hodge, he seemed to be gathering his forces. When he began to sing, it was apparent that something magical was happening. His rich baritone rang out sweet, powerful, and clear, and when he asked, "Are you still mine?" it was sung from deep wells of emotion. The song built and built, and Elvis's eyes filled with tears. As he sang, he turned several times to Charlie, still holding the mic on his left, and smiled at him. It was written all over Charlie's face that he understood the importance of the moment. As Elvis finished the last, lingering note, he looked up, joyous, exhilarated. In that moment, he was the King again, and he knew it.

The last time I talked with Elvis was that August. Lisa was at Graceland, and Elvis and I agreed it was time for her to come home. She wanted to stay longer, but he was going on tour soon, and we both knew she couldn't tour with him. So we talked about his tour's end and when and where he could see her again. Would he come back to LA or go directly to Memphis? We worked out the details of who would bring her back and then chatted a little. He talked about the upcoming tour. He seemed enthusiastic about it, optimistic about turning in some good performances. His voice was clear and strong, like his old self. We laughed, and I remembered how much I loved his laughter. That was August 14.

On August 16, 1977, I was meeting my sister for lunch on Melrose Avenue. It was a strangely cold and damp day for summer in Los Angeles. As I neared the restaurant, Michelle was flagging me down from the corner across the street. When I came to a stop, she rushed over to the car. She told me that she'd just had a call from Dad. Joe Esposito was phoning all over, trying to get a hold of me. It was something about Elvis being in the hospital. My heart stopped. I knew Joe wouldn't be doing that if it was just another of Elvis's hospital stays. Something must be terribly wrong.

I did a U-turn and raced home, running traffic lights and going far too fast. Cars skidded to a halt to miss me. It's a miracle I didn't get hit. All the way home, I prayed over and over, "Dear God, please let it be all right." Lisa was at Graceland, due to come home later that day, so she was part of whatever was happening.

When I reached home, I could hear the phone ringing as I got out of the car. I prayed it would keep ringing until I reached it. I let myself into the house with shaking hands and grabbed the receiver.

It was Joe. I said, "What's happened?"

He replied, "It's Elvis."

"Oh my God."

"Cilla, he's dead. We've lost him." His voice broke.

I began screaming, "No! No, no, no, no, no!" I started to sob, and I could hear Joe crying on the other end of the line.

"Joe, where's Lisa?"

"She's okay. She's with Grandma." I asked Joe to send a plane for me, as quickly as he could, and hung up. The questions I needed answered would have to wait.

A few minutes later, the phone rang again, and when I picked it up, I heard Lisa's voice saying, "Mommy! Mommy! Something's happened to Daddy! Everybody's crying."

I could hear Vernon's voice in the background, sobbing and saying, "My son! My son!"

I told Lisa, "I know, baby," and reassured her that Daddy's plane was coming for me soon. I told her to wait with Grandma until I got there. She said she was going outside to play with her friend.

I hung up in a kind of daze. I couldn't absorb what Joe had told me. How could Elvis be dead? I had just talked to him two days before. He'd sounded good.

Joe sent Elvis's private plane, the Lisa Marie, to pick up Michelle and me, my parents, Jerry Schilling, and a handful of other close friends to fly us to Memphis. When we got to

Graceland, I found Lisa playing golf carts in the yard with one of her friends. At first, I thought it was an odd reaction, and I worried about what the paparazzi would make of Lisa playing in the wake of her father's death. But then I realized it was a child's way of escaping the reality of the silent house. I hugged her close, then went inside.

I still didn't know what had happened, so Joe told me. Ginger had found Elvis unconscious, face down on the floor of the bathroom, that afternoon. She called downstairs for help, and Joe had raced upstairs. He knew immediately that Elvis had passed, but he didn't want to believe it. My heart plummeted as Joe confirmed that Lisa had seen Elvis's body. Elvis was still face down on the floor when she saw him, his face buried in the shag carpet. Lisa had been afraid he was suffocating. Joe wasn't sure if she'd understood what she was seeing. He'd sent her to see Grandma while the ambulance came. He did chest compressions while they waited for the ambulance. A doctor continued efforts to resuscitate Elvis as they raced to the hospital, but all the efforts were futile. Shortly after arrival, Elvis was pronounced dead. Apparently, it was a heart attack.

Inside Graceland, the atmosphere was eerie. The house seemed hollow and dead. It was as if the energy had been sucked out of it—Elvis's life force. We all walked around like zombies. Vernon was distraught. He felt Elvis's passing very, very deeply. It broke my heart to see such a strong man repeatedly call out his son's name, tears streaming down his face. He was losing his only child. A part of Vernon was lost that day as well. I never again saw the energy he once had. Whenever he'd come into a room and said, "Hey, son," his face would light up with a smile. I never saw that smile again. Grandma struggled to believe that Elvis was gone. After he left us, she always carried a little handkerchief. I'd see her tearing up, and she'd wipe her eyes and whisper, "My boy."

There was no privacy for those of us closest to Elvis, including the family. People and cameras surrounded the property. Mourners waited to be admitted to the house for a public viewing of Elvis's open casket. The funeral was a nationally televised event. The streets near Graceland were thronged with tens of thousands of people. The crowds were so large by the second day that President Jimmy Carter called up the Air National Guard to help local police. It was hot and muggy, and some in the crowd fainted from the heat and from emotion. In the afternoon, thousands of people filed past the open casket that had been set up in the front hall. Lisa stayed with Elvis's body as much as she could. She didn't want to leave him. We sat on the stairs and watched as people walked by. Crowds of strangers in Elvis's home, crying and paying their respects. Some mourners had walked away from their jobs to drive sixteen hours or more to Memphis and line up along Elvis Presley Boulevard, hoping to be admitted to the house. The trip was a financial sacrifice for many of them, for much of the crowd was made up of the everyday people who identified with Elvis as one of their own. He, too, had come from poverty. He had remained loyal to his hometown and his family, and he never got above his upbringing. They felt compelled to pay their respects as they would to a family member. It was overwhelming. There wasn't room yet for our own grief.

His memorial was an international event. While mourners gathered in Memphis, Christ's Church in London held a service in Elvis's honor. Over five hundred people crowded the sanctuary and the lawn outside. At the close of the service, they all sang "Amazing Grace" in his honor. Elvis's passing was felt not just in Memphis, but around the world.

The private funeral service was held in the living room and adjoining music room, with the peacock glass framing an archway between the two. Elvis's coffin was moved into the room for the service. Vernon had hired a local preacher who didn't know Elvis and who talked primarily about Elvis's legendary generosity. The Blackwood Brothers, longtime friends and backup singers for Elvis, sang gospel songs. I sat on the couch with Lisa and Vernon, numb with grief. It was all a blur at the time, and it still is.

Lisa and I waited until we could be alone with Elvis to say goodbye. I had bought a silver bracelet engraved with the words, "I love you, Daddy," for Lisa to give him. I helped her put it around his wrist. Then we each kissed him one last time. I'm not sure it hit me until then that he was really gone. The body I had held and caressed so many times was now stiff and empty. It was an eerie, aching feeling.

A line of white Cadillacs formed the funeral procession to the Forest Hill Cemetery. Lisa and I rode with Vernon in the car immediately following the hearse. Elvis was entombed in the Presley family crypt with his mother. Two days later, after two thieves tried to steal the coffin, he was moved to the Meditation Garden at Graceland and kept under security. Gladys was moved to Graceland shortly afterward, to lie beside him. Elvis and I used to sit in that garden in the small hours of the morning, in the peace and the moonlight. I was glad they had brought him home.

Vernon had a bronze plaque made to cover the coffin, with an inscription ending, "We miss you, Son and Daddy."

I returned home to LA with Lisa, feeling that a large part of me had died with Elvis. I couldn't accept that he had passed. I'd felt Elvis would always be there. He was such a force of nature. Despite all my fears for him, I never thought he would die at the age he did. He was still so young. He'd talked so much about what he still wanted to do. He had plans for his music and for his life. Elvis wasn't ready to leave. I wasn't ready.

It was a constant battle to accept that he was gone. Every morning, I would wake up and remember, "Oh God, Elvis isn't here anymore. How can I live knowing that?" I was frightened to be in a world without Elvis in it.

There would be no more calls. I would never again pick up the phone and hear his voice. There would be no more visits, no more dropping by unexpectedly. I wouldn't be going to Graceland anymore, except to visit Grandma and Vernon. There was no more Memphis Mafia. Everybody scattered. Everything changed. I changed. I had been happy-go-lucky, always excited about where we were going or what we were doing next. I had finally adjusted to the separation, feeling free and adventurous. Optimistic. My memories of Elvis had been happy ones. When I went somewhere we'd been, I would think, "Oh my gosh, we went here." I remembered the times fans would cling to him and want pictures. They loved him and didn't want to let him go, and when he tried to escape, a trail of girls would follow him. It had been fun. He had so much charm and was so generous to loved ones and strangers alike. It filled him with joy when he was able to do something special for other people.

Now my mind was filled with images of loss. I couldn't get away from reminders of him. The media was filled with articles and broadcasts about Elvis, and his songs flooded the radio stations. If I went out, people would come over and say, "I'm so sorry." I knew they meant well, but it was painful. For a long time after Elvis passed, I rarely went anywhere. I waited a while to continue with my life.

Worst of all, I no longer had a father for my daughter. I was raising my child by myself, a brokenhearted child who had lost her daddy. When we got back home from the funeral, we were surrounded by reminders of his passing. I had to protect her from all the news reports, the unwanted attention, the nonstop condolence calls. It seemed like every newspaper and magazine had a headline about his passing. If Lisa and I went to the grocery store, I'd pull the ones with headlines out of the rack and turn them around in the checkout line so Lisa wouldn't see them. To get her away from the constant reminders, I decided to send her to summer camp. I hoped it would not only insulate her from the publicity but also take her mind off her thoughts. Joanie's kids and some of her other friends were there. I checked on her regularly at camp, and she seemed to be doing pretty well. She later said that camp had helped. When it ended for the summer, my sister and I took her out of the country to give her some privacy until the incessant publicity died down. We went to England and later to Europe. We were seldom recognized there, and we could explore the sights in peace.

There was one odd incident while we were in France. At a museum with Marie Antoinette exhibits, Lisa calmly said, "That's who I was in my past lifetime."

I went blank. *Past lifetime?* "What do you mean?"

"That's her, Marie Antoinette. I was her in my past life."

I thought, *God, where did she get that from? Did that just come out of her mouth? How does she know that? She doesn't even know who Marie Antoinette is.* It was very strange. When I finally took her back to Graceland to see Vernon and Grandma, she did better than I expected. She had friends in Memphis, and I'd have them over to play. It seemed to help her.

When Elvis Presley died, it was as though he created a vacuum. He had a charisma, a powerful life force that extended far beyond his talent or his fame. Gladys was convinced that when Elvis's twin brother, Jesse, was stillborn, Jesse's soul had merged with Elvis's. It was how she accounted for the power he had over people. He had twin souls. Maybe she was right. Elvis was a flawed human being, like all of us, but he had love, compassion, and generosity to a truly remarkable degree. He became a superstar not out of ambition but out of love for his parents and a determination to lift them out of the grinding poverty they had endured. He was the most beautiful, talented, loving human being I have ever known. He searched all his life to find the path God wanted for him. Despite the stumbles and the setbacks, I believe he found it. And I had the extraordinary honor, for a while, of walking it with him.

CHAPTER 5

Keeping the Faith

When you walk through a storm,
Hold your head up high.

E LVIS WAS ALWAYS THE SEARCHER IN THE FAMILY. When he began his spiritual quest in earnest, I was still a teenager. The piles of books, the esoteric discussions, the long hours of being read to, all left me unmoved. I was young, and I hadn't yet experienced the kind of loss and trauma Elvis had. But when Elvis passed, a yawning chasm opened in my heart, and I desperately needed answers. For the first time, I began to search for my own spiritual path. My Catholic upbringing hadn't prepared me for what I was now facing.

I'd gone with Elvis sometimes to the Self-Realization Fellowship's Mother Center (headquarters) in the Hollywood Hills. The fellowship is based on the teachings of Paramahansa Yogananda. I think Elvis liked it because it was a union of Eastern and Western religions—the teachings of Jesus and of Krishna. Elvis had read about so many religions, and this one brought them together in a simple way that made sense to him. He also liked that it focused on experiencing the loving presence of God. That was comforting to him.

Most of all, he loved talking to the fellowship's president, Daya Mata, referred to as the "Mother of the Society." Elvis kept a copy of her book, *Only Love*, by his bed. He really liked her, in part because she reminded him of his mother. Daya Mata was born eighteen months after Gladys Presley, so she was almost the same age as Gladys would have been had she lived. Daya Mata looked a bit like her, too. She had wideset eyes, dark hair going gray, and a round face. Her clothing was lovely, orange robes made of rich fabrics. When I met her, I thought she was sweet, very kind. She and Elvis had a special relationship. He always talked with her alone, though he'd share some of it with me later. He would ask her questions: *Why are we here? What are we supposed to do in life? Is there an afterlife? Do we come back? What should I be doing with my life?* He was always searching for answers.

I liked the fellowship. It is one of the most peaceful places I've ever been to, a large old white building with beautiful gardens and meditation centers. Few people were there when we visited, occasionally a monk in a simple orange robe. I don't know if it was quiet because Elvis was there and they were giving him privacy, or if it was always that peaceful. I do know that there was an amazing serenity about the place. Being there comforted me. I felt safe.

I didn't go back, though, after Elvis passed. Somehow, it wasn't the right place for me. I needed something less ethereal that would tell me how to cope with the changes I was going through, something concrete that would ease my pain. And I needed to know how to help my grief-stricken child. Through all the years with Elvis, I hadn't been ready to ask the questions he was asking about life. Now I too went searching, and what I found was Scientology. I guess timing is everything.

It was John Travolta who became my gateway to the Church of Scientology. I admired John, who was a fervent Scientologist himself. I knew that he had experienced losing a loved one, so he understood grief and loss. He took me to the Scientology Celebrity Centre on Franklin and introduced me to the people there. As he showed me around, I saw the classes the center was offering. Scientology wasn't about going to church, he told me. It was about learning, helping yourself, and growing into life. Scientology believed it was up to you to change your own life, and the church showed you how. I also learned that even when loved ones die, they're okay, and they will come back in another body. I found this belief comforting. It also piqued my curiosity. I was very eager for guidance through this painful time in my life.

I was given a copy of the bible of Scientology, a book written by its founder, L. Ron Hubbard, and titled *Dianetics*. It was a hugely popular book that had been a bestseller when it came out, and it still formed the basis of Scientology belief, referred to as "technology" by Hubbard. It laid out the principles that guided the church. Hubbard divided the mind into two sections: the analytic (conscious) and the reactive (unconscious). The analytic mind was logical; the reactive mind was emotional, the space where painful or traumatic experiences were stored. The road to healing lay in ridding the body of those stored emotions—releasing all the pain and dysfunction—so that the analytic mind was in complete control. The process required progressing through a series of stages, which Hubbard called the "bridge to total freedom." Each step up the bridge brought you closer to healing. If you reached the highest levels, you were freed of all trauma. This was called "going clear." Your mind and body were now clear of all harmful elements, and your analytic mind guided your life.

This philosophy appealed to me greatly. The thought of freeing myself from all the pain and confusion of losing Elvis gave me hope. I wanted to take control of my life. I would not only be leaving the past behind but also be guided as I moved forward in life. Scientology would show me the way, step by step.

The method Hubbard invented for going clear was called "auditing." It embodies some of the elements of therapy and of confession. Auditing relies heavily on a machine called an "e-meter" (Hubbard electrometer), which works somewhat like a lie detector. It measured and recorded my bodily stress levels. If something painful or conflicting came up, if I lied about something, or even if my mind wandered, the meter reflected that. It had a moving needle that told the auditor what I was experiencing. The auditor's job was to ask me questions, note when the needle moved, and ask me to confront what the meter was reacting to. The auditor didn't give me advice so much as direct my attention to the problem. Confrontation is big in Scientology.

Auditors didn't let you evade problems; I was guided to confront them. It was up to me to take responsibility and figure out my next steps.

I remember one of the first times auditing made me take responsibility. In Scientology belief, breaking a moral code causes harm to oneself as well as others. These personal failures are addressed in auditing. I was dating Robert Kardashian at the time and had begun to get a little bored with the relationship. When another man asked me out, I went, but I kept the date secret. The auditor immediately picked up on my deception and guilt and confronted me, essentially saying, "What are you going to do about that?"

I realized how uncomfortable I was with what I'd done, and I took responsibility. I broke it off with the other man, and then I talked to Robert. I apologized for what I'd done and told him it wouldn't happen again. It was painful and awkward, but afterward, I felt so much better about myself. I had done the right thing and freed myself of a burden.

From the first day I went, I loved the auditing. Talking about the things that I was holding inside was a wonderful relief. As the weeks of intense auditing went by, I began to get rid of my pain a little at a time. I could almost feel it coming out of me and dissipating in the air. My loss, my failures, my mistakes—all seemed to disappear. My auditing sessions lasted for up to two hours, sometimes every day. By the time I finished a session, I felt euphoric. It was almost magical. I wanted to find out more and began going to classes.

The church changed the way I lived. When I found myself in a bad situation, I stopped blaming other people. I asked myself,

"What did I do to help create this situation? What can I do differently that might change it?" I felt far less helpless, because I was in control of my life.

Eventually, I began to hear sometimes-disturbing rumors about Scientology. Other people apparently had a very different experience from mine. But for me, it was a good experience. That may be in part because I worked with the Celebrity Centre. Celebrities have a special status in Scientology. The church believes that because of their potential influence and outreach, celebrity members are especially valuable to the church. It is likely that I was nurtured with great care because I was considered an asset; I could bring in new members. And I did. Looking back, I realize I was naive about some of what went on. But at the time, the church was a welcome and valuable part of my life. It gave me something to hold on to. The doubts eventually came, but they came much later.

Fairly soon after I joined Scientology, I brought Lisa in, too. She was so broken after Elvis died. I wanted her to have a support system to help and guide her, to let her talk and get things out. She took little courses on how to handle life better, and after a while, she began auditing. I enrolled her in the Scientology-sponsored Apple School so that she would be in a healthier environment. Though Lisa was resistant at first, she grew to be both a believer and an advocate for Scientology.

It is difficult to explain how challenging it was to raise Elvis Presley's only child, particularly after he passed. As Elvis's daughter, Lisa lived with the constant threat of harm or kidnapping. She didn't realize that this was a possibility, but I did. While Elvis was alive and when she was with her father, Lisa lived in a protective shell. At Graceland, she was surrounded by walls and guards and other men who were frequently armed. She could run around and play freely and be perfectly safe. In Las Vegas, a couple of the guys were always there to ensure her safety. Elvis's home and entourage insulated her from danger. When she was with me, however, that wall of protection vanished. There were no guards at my home, no Memphis Mafia to watch over her. There was just me and my staff, consisting mostly of women. I was always afraid that something would happen to Lisa.

Raising my daughter was a challenge for both of us. She was strong-willed from the beginning. Like her dad, she just came that way. Lisa had a mind of her own, and being Elvis's daughter only reinforced it. When we went to Vegas, she had seen the fans mob her father and she had taken it all in. Her daddy was very, very special. Afterward, when we walked through the hotel, people would exclaim, "It's Lisa Marie! Oh my God. And Miss Priscilla!" People would give her things and exclaim over her. She learned she was special, too. Under the circumstances, any child would have realized that. At Graceland, while her father was alive, she was used to bossing everyone around, from the staff to her playmates. After Elvis was gone and she lived at my house full-time, the habit lingered.

She had no sense of a regular kid's boundaries. Lisa would boss her friends around: "You're going to do this, or I'm not going to be your friend!" For nine years, she had lived at least part-time in Elvis's world. Most of her friends at Graceland were the children of Elvis's employees, so they understood that Lisa was the boss. The habits she learned there followed her and were a liability in her new environment. I wanted her to grow up with a normal little girl's life. On her first day at a new school, I would ask the teacher to introduce her just as Lisa, without mentioning her last name. I didn't want her to get a big head. I never, ever told her that she would have her father's money when she grew up. I didn't want her to know until she was older.

It was difficult for her to fit into the everyday world. She often felt different, isolated. She had trouble making and keeping friends.

Her go-to line was, "I'm Lisa Presley. My father's Elvis Presley!" Sometimes she would add, "So watch it!"

I would talk to her about it and tell her she should never say that. People would find out Elvis was her father on their own, anyway. I would tell her that bragging about who her father was would make her unpopular.

She would say, "Why, Mommy?" She truly didn't understand.

I didn't want people to focus on who her dad was. I wanted them to know her as Lisa. It was hard for her to comprehend. Her sense of identity was wrapped up in her dad, maybe more so after he was gone. Being Elvis's daughter was a way of holding on to him.

I also did my best to keep magazines away from her. I would scout the gossip columns to make sure there was nothing about Elvis in them. This was especially important in the year following his death. I also scanned for inappropriate photos or articles. I made sure that at home, all the magazines and newspapers were okay for Lisa to read. I'm sure she saw some of this stuff at school, but she wouldn't find it at home. Home was a safe zone.

Keeping her on a routine was a never-ending struggle. She'd gotten used to doing only the things she wanted to do, when she wanted to do them. Now here I was, imposing order and discipline, and she hated it. When I brought her home after school, she had to do her homework before I'd let her play. Her "But all the other kids…" got her nowhere with me. This rule was particularly hard for her because she struggled with academics. I hired tutors to help her, especially with the more challenging subjects. I wanted her to learn French so that she could travel to Europe. As it turned out, learning a language was the last thing she wanted to do. But like most parents, I had dreams for my child.

And of course, there was the nightly bath ritual. Bathing had been optional at Graceland. I would draw the water, add bubble bath, and set everything up for her, but she still had to get in the bathtub herself. Did she want to? No. Did she know she had to? Yes. So she would roll her eyes and sigh and say, "Oh, Mommy," but she would get in. She never sassed me. She knew better than that. I knew a routine would be better for her in the long run, but she didn't understand that. Being the disciplinarian was exhausting. There were days when, like Elvis, I just wanted the kid to have fun.

And we did have fun. We went to Disneyland and Knott's Berry Farm and the local parks. It would have ruined the outings if we'd been recognized, but I became expert at going out incognito. I had a variety of disguises. I'd wear wigs, or I'd pull my hair back and wear a hat. I found that dark glasses seemed to draw attention, but regular glasses with clear lenses were effective. I dressed casually, like everyone else, and fit in with the crowd. I quickly discovered that bringing friends with us helped, too. Lisa alone might have attracted attention, but running around with other kids, she blended right in. Lisa and I, dressed up and on our own in Beverly Hills, might be recognized. But at Disneyland, we were just part of the crowds. I don't think we were ever recognized.

By the time she was ten, it became increasingly clear that Lisa had musical talent, but I didn't want to make a big deal about her singing, for I knew that everyone would compare her to her father. I wanted her to be whoever she wanted to be. Lisa Marie, not Elvis's daughter. If that included music someday, so be it. If not, that was fine, too.

On June 26, 1979, Vernon passed away from a heart attack. He was sixty-three years old. Lisa and I flew to Graceland for his private funeral service. It was small, with only family and a handful of friends. My heart ached for Grandma that day. Vernon's passing saddened me deeply, but it wasn't a complete surprise. He had told me that when his son went, he was ready to go. Elvis took Vernon with him when he passed, not physically but emotionally. The life went out of Vernon. He was a private man with few friends. His life had revolved around Elvis. When Elvis rose to fame, Vernon took on the role of Elvis's protector. The father carefully managed his son's money, always vigilant for fear that someone would take advantage of his son. Elvis trusted him completely. Vernon was fiercely proud of Elvis, but he wore his pride quietly and with dignity. His commemorative plaque describes him as gentle, quiet, responsible, and fair. He died quietly, as he had lived. We buried him in the Memorial Garden at Graceland with Gladys and his son. The epitaph was a quote from Tennyson: "God's finger touched him, and he slept."

Grandma was now the last surviving member of the family that had once lived at Graceland. She was the only one left except for the household staff, several of whom cared for her. The year after Vernon died, on May 8, 1980, her strong heart finally failed her. Grandma Minnie Mae Presley, "Dodger," was eighty-nine years old. Once again, Lisa and I joined the remaining relatives and friends for a small private service in the Memorial Garden. Her epitaph describes her as "The flower that never faded... The queen of our home." She guided the family through hardship and heartache, always there for the ones she loved so fiercely and who loved her back. I know. I was one of them. I grieved her passing deeply. Biologically, we weren't related. But she was my grandma, too. I worried about Lisa. In a period of three years, she had lost her father, her grandfather, and her great-grandmother. At twelve years old, she already carried a heavy burden of grief.

Elvis had left Graceland to Vernon, who became responsible for its running after Elvis passed. Before Vernon died, he told me that he had named me as the next Graceland trustee. He had put me in charge.

He said, "I trust you. Elvis loved you and left it to me. I'm leaving it to you."

I was deeply touched that he'd entrusted me with Graceland. Vernon was not a demonstrative man, so his words were all the more important to me.

I quickly learned that Graceland was in serious trouble. It was bleeding money. The care of the grounds, the staff salaries, the animals requiring care—all were ongoing expenses. With no funds coming in, the upkeep was unsustainable. By the time Vernon passed, only $500,000 of Lisa's inheritance remained. The ongoing expenses and tax debt quickly depleted those funds. I went through the possibilities with the attorney and accountant, asking how we could make this work. What could we back off on? The accountant told me that the only way to save what was left of Elvis's fortune was to sell Graceland. He had not known Elvis personally and had no concept of what Graceland meant to him. To the accountant, the property was simply a financial asset.

I said, "That will never happen," and I meant it. Graceland was Elvis's pride and joy, his refuge and sanctuary, the symbol of his life and his success. He and Gladys were buried there. So were Vernon and Grandma. To Lisa, it was her childhood home, the place that held her memories of her daddy. It had been my home, too, and I still felt Elvis's presence there. Selling it was unthinkable. I owed it to Elvis to save it. The problem was that my only experience with business was running the boutique. Saving Graceland was far beyond my skill set. I had no idea how I was going to do it, but I was determined to find out.

I rolled my sleeves up and dug in. I went to a couple of businesspeople I knew and asked them where I should start. One of the friends, Bob Wall, knew Peter Ueberroth, who had staged the 1984 Olympics so brilliantly.

I said, "I have to meet with him."

Bob arranged it, and I had a meeting with Ueberroth. I told him my situation and asked him how he was able to pull off the Olympics.

He replied, "It's the people that you surround yourself with who know people that can make an introduction."

I thought, "Oh, God. Who do I know?"

It was good advice. I asked around, and a friend suggested I connect with Morgan Maxfield. Maxfield had pioneered the idea of building gas stations at freeway exits and made a fortune doing it.

When we met, I told him, "I can't sell Graceland. I don't have the heart to do it. But I need help to keep it going."

Morgan, God bless him, said okay. We visited several historical sites together, and Morgan came up with some steps we could take to open Graceland to the public. Doing so would generate income and allow us to pay the upkeep and the back taxes. But just as I began to heave a sigh of relief, Morgan was killed when the plane he owned and was piloting crashed. I was stunned. The tragedy literally brought me to my knees. What on earth was I going to do now?

The only person I could think of who could help was Jack Soden. As Morgan's right-hand man, Jack had been with us for the site visits and the discussions about Graceland. He was familiar with the plan Morgan had developed. Jack was a good businessman and a good man. When I asked him for his help, he resisted at first. Converting a private property to a public one was not what he usually did, and he was hesitant to take the project on.

He even felt compelled to tell me, "Priscilla, I'm not an Elvis fan." I didn't need a fan, I told him; I needed a businessman. He had the business knowledge I needed to save Graceland. I was persistent, and, eventually, he agreed to help me.

The plan was to spruce Graceland up and open it to the public. It was already in good shape and would need very little work before we could open. I told him that it was important to keep family members on as staff. Patsy was the secretary; her dad and uncle were both gate guards. Billy Smith, Elvis's cousin, had worked with Elvis for years. It had been important to Elvis to employ members of his family. They needed job security and pride in their work. I intended to continue the tradition. The second story of the mansion would be roped off. I knew Elvis would have hated having strangers wander through his private space. That was one of the best decisions I made. Many fans turned out to be protective of Elvis's desire for privacy. If they overheard a guest planning to sneak upstairs, they reported it immediately. Being off-limits gave the second floor an air of mystery. Rumors that Elvis still lives there persist to this day.

The opening was a huge success. Within a month, we were able to pay back our expenses and make a profit. During my time as trustee, the value of Graceland rose to over $100 million. Graceland has become the second-most visited historic mansion in the nation. (The White House is the first.) I'm proud of what Jack and I accomplished. We did it with the help of many friends. To this day, it feels like a miracle.

By saving Elvis's home, I had saved my home as well. Lisa and I could visit whenever we wanted, and when she was twenty-five, the responsibility would pass to her. The day Graceland opened to the public was an emotional one for me. I'd believed that I would never again see Elvis's fans excitedly lined up to see him. Yet there they were. Some of them even brought their children in little Elvis costumes, with capes. They were the first of the thousands of fans I have greeted over the years—people who help me keep Elvis's legacy alive, who help keep *him* alive.

For Elvis lives on at Graceland. The fans know it. The staff and neighbors know it. I know it. We feel his spirit there. I have never been one to believe fantastic stories about spirits. But every time I walk in that door, I think, *Oh my God. He's here.* I can feel him, feel his presence. It's both haunting and comforting.

I tell people before they go in, "You'll feel his spirit there." Most of them do.

I know that whenever I miss him, I can still go home to Graceland, and he'll be waiting for me.

CHAPTER 6
Suspicious Minds

We can't go on together
With suspicious minds.

M Y DAUGHTER WAS A CONUNDRUM, COMPLICATED and challenging. Lisa was a free spirit, a determined and restless soul. She thought deeply and felt strongly but had trouble articulating what was on her mind. It wasn't until she pursued music as an adult that she could put her feelings into words. The self-image she had developed from her dad's stardom and parenting style had given her a sense of entitlement that she had trouble letting go of as she grew up. It complicated her social relationships. It also gave her a burden that she struggled to carry all her life. Under the cool teen facade lay a shy, insecure girl. She was sweet, tenderhearted, and loyal. And she was funny, a trait that became obvious in her interviews as an adult. Lisa loved and depended on me, but I'm not sure she understood until later in life how much I loved her. Elvis's love had been obvious in lavish ways. Mine showed in my commitment to careful parenting, to always putting Lisa first. She was my life after Elvis died. Getting her through her teen years was worrisome.

In many ways, Lisa was a typical teen. She never wanted to go to school, sighing pathetically and telling me she was too tired when it was time to get dressed.

I would tell her, "That's not going to work, Lisa. You're going to school." She would drag herself unwillingly into her uniform. We had that same conversation nearly every morning. We were both sick of it.

It wasn't only that Lisa didn't want to go to school; she didn't understand why she had to. School remained a foreign land to her. She had never fit in socially, and academics had always been a struggle. From her point of view, school was pointless. Lisa was easily bored, always craving new experiences. And to her, school was the most boring place there was. I tried school after school, including ones in Ventura County and Beverly Hills. I even considered a boarding school in Europe. My plan was to lease a home in Switzerland and put Lisa in school there. That way, she could come home on the weekends and I would be nearby. But she failed the entrance exam, just as she failed her classes at school. It wasn't a lack of intelligence. Lisa was smart; she mastered challenging Scientology courses with ease. The problem was that she just didn't care. School was boring, and Lisa hated to be bored.

From the time her world ended at nine years old, I think the only thing Lisa really wanted to do was go back to Graceland and be with her dad and her friends. Most teenagers are embarrassed by their parents. Maybe if Elvis had lived, Lisa would have eventually been embarrassed by him, too. But because she lost him so young, her romanticized childhood view of him lived on.

Although my daughter was sweet, she was also impulsive and didn't always use good judgment. Because she was recognizable and vulnerable, I went to great lengths to keep her out of the public eye. I was careful about who she spent time with, too. I didn't want her to be hurt or taken advantage of.

I monitored her constantly. If she said she was going somewhere, I would sometimes follow her to make sure she was there. Usually, she was. Afterward, I would sneak back home so she wouldn't find out. I would sometimes call the parents of her friends if she was supposed to be spending time at their houses.

She would tell me, "Oh, all my friends are going, and I want to go, too."

I'd say, "Well, that sounds fine, but who are these friends? Let me know so I'll know what parent to call if there's a problem." She understood that. Fortunately, I liked most of her girlfriends. But boys were another issue altogether.

Lisa was preoccupied with boys. I had the sex talk with her when she reached puberty. My mother had never had that talk with me, because such things weren't talked about in her generation. But this was a different era, and the percentage of teens having sex had risen dramatically. I was terrified she'd get pregnant. It didn't help that Lisa was drawn to bad-boy types. She was attracted to guys with motorcycles and leather. She found nice guys boring. Lisa liked things to be happening. One boy came to pick her up in a limo. He was dressed in a black leather jacket and had long hair. I knew his parents were wealthy, and I had a bad feeling about him. Lisa thought my disapproval was because of the way he looked, but the real problem was that he came across as entitled and rude. I put my foot down on that one. He was bad news.

When she was fourteen, she started to wear sexier clothes. I was really upset about the way she began dressing. I would have to send her back to her room to change, and it always sparked a disagreement. She didn't see what was wrong with the way she wanted to dress. Apparently, all the other girls were doing it, an argument that got nowhere with me.

One day, she put on a very revealing outfit. Tired of arguing, I decided it was time to teach her a lesson. So instead of putting my foot down again, I went back to my room and changed my clothes. I put on a sexy outfit with a bare midriff. Then I came back out and said, "Let's go."

Lisa was horrified. "Mommy, you're not going to wear that, are you?"

I replied, "Why? What's wrong with it?"

"Oh my gosh, Mommy, I don't want you to wear that."

"Why not?"

"Well, because you can see your tummy."

I said, "Well, you can see yours too. I don't like your outfit, either."

We got into it. I refused to back down. I finally walked out the door and headed for the street, with Lisa following me, protesting all the way. When we got to the street, I stepped off the curb and put my thumb out to hitchhike.

"Mommy!!!"

Let's just say that she got the point!

It was during this period that I began the second-longest romantic relationship of my life after Elvis. His name was Michael Edwards, and he moved in with Lisa and me when Lisa was ten. We were together for almost six years. I met him at a party through mutual friends. Michael was a highly successful model—next to Elvis, one of the handsomest men I'd ever seen. He was also charming, solicitous, kind, and fun. Like me, he enjoyed being active—swimming, horseback riding, traveling. He was usually the life of any party. He would cook, bring the food and drinks out, and entertain.

He was always attentive. If I was tired or not feeling my best, he would notice and say, "Are you okay? Can I get you anything?"

It's no wonder I fell for him. He seemed like the perfect man. A couple of my friends urged me to be cautious, however. They said he had the looks, and he had the charm, but was he a good man? A reliable one? They reminded me that it's hard to be objective when a man is so charming. My mother and dad didn't like him, either. They couldn't come up with a reason. They just didn't trust him. Your family often sees what you can't see, because you're too caught up in your feelings. But at the time, Michael seemed like the perfect man.

One incident with my mother didn't help with my parents' view of him. Now my mom was wonderful, but she was sometimes a bit Victorian. She wasn't given to public displays of affection; she hadn't been raised that way. So Michael decided my mother needed to be hugged more often.

My parents were walking out to the car one afternoon when Michael said to Mother, "You need a hug. You need to know how much you're cared for."

And he engulfed her in his arms, pulled her close, and wouldn't let go. Mother looked like a trapped animal. She tried to pull away, but Michael wouldn't let her. I'm thinking, *God, Michael, enough. Let her go!*

When I started to protest on my mother's behalf, he said, "No, she needs this. She needs to be hugged. Your dad doesn't hug her enough."

My mother said, "Let me go! Let me go!"

I felt bad for my mom, but honestly, it was hilarious. The hug seemed to go on forever. When he finally released her, she practically ran for the car. After that, she kept her distance around him in case of another surprise attack.

Though his displays of affection toward my mother were misguided rather than romantic, I did worry about him being flirtatious with other women. He was often surrounded by beautiful girls, models he worked with on his shoots. These shoots sometimes took place out of state, where he would travel to do them. I couldn't always go. I had Lisa, and I was still working for Wella Balsam. I was always a bit suspicious about what he was doing out of town, because he was so flirty. Like Elvis had been. I knew from experience that flirtation could quickly turn into something more. One time, I was visiting him on a shoot and found two partly filled wineglasses on the shelf under the bar. When I asked him about them, he brushed my question aside. But still I wondered, why would one man use two wineglasses? I later found out that he had been with another woman on that trip.

And then he began to take little trips without telling me. I have no idea where he went.

I wouldn't hear from him for two or three days, and I'd start thinking, *Well, where is he? He hasn't called me. I don't know where he is.*

I checked to see if his suitcases were there, and if he'd left his clothes in the closet. I didn't know where to call, because this was in the days before cell phones, and you needed a location to call someone. He'd eventually show up with an explanation, being solicitous and apologetic. Common sense told me something was going on behind my back, but it was hard to believe because he was so sweet with me. More accurately, I didn't want to believe it. I didn't want to accept that he was having flings with other women. You'd think I would know better after my experience with Elvis. But I remained naive because I needed to be. I wanted to believe that Michael was faithful to me.

By then, I had begun to think of the three of us—Lisa, Michael, and me—as a family. When his daughter, Caroline, who was a year older than Lisa, came to visit, we were a family of four. She and Lisa were close.

Four years into our relationship, Michael had his own test of faith—in me. Through my agency, I was invited to go to Chile and do an interview with Julio Iglesias. Along with other celebrities, I would be there for the Festival de Viña del Mar. Having never been to Chile, I was excited about the opportunity and I accepted the invitation. My sister lived with us by then, and she and Michael could take care of Lisa while I was gone. Lisa was wonderful about it.

When I called home after we arrived in Chile, my daughter said, "I'm fine! The dogs are fine! Have fun, Mommy."

The trip was exciting, and I loved the Chilean people. I didn't speak the language, but Julio was very attentive when he realized I only spoke English. He translated for me and kept an eye on me so I didn't feel uncomfortable or get lost. We got to know each other, and Julio interviewed me for a television broadcast. It's pretty funny watching it on YouTube now. Julio asked me questions primarily in Spanish, and I struggled to answer him without knowing what he'd asked. I said general, complimentary things about the country and hoped it related somehow to the question.

Julio had tremendous star power. He was handsome, suave, sexy, and very, very charming. The quintessential Latin lover. One evening, we went to a club, just the two of us, and he invited me to his room for a drink afterward. Because I'm a slow learner, I again didn't think through the expectations until I got there. Julio had clearly planned a romantic evening for us. And I will admit, I was tempted. Very tempted.

My mind was spinning. Could I do this? Have a holiday fling and then go home? Was that fair to Michael? And then my mind changed direction, to Elvis. Julio reminded me so much of him in some ways. I'd come to think of him as the Elvis of the Spanish-speaking world. Julio had the same charisma, the same sort of magnetic charm, the same flirtatiousness. He had fame and money. Women were drawn to him. Yes, he was a lot like Elvis, and that was the problem. If I became involved with

Julio, I would be back in the limelight and back in the insecurity of knowing there would always be a lineup of girls hoping for a fling with Julio. By the time he made his move that night, I knew I couldn't do it. It would be a big step backward in my life.

Julio was surprised. I don't think he was used to being turned down, and besides, he assumed I had understood his invitation when I accepted it. I said I was sorry, but I had to go. I was leaving the next day. I arrived back in LA with my heart and my conscience intact. A year or so later, I heard from him. He paid me a very nice compliment, and when my mother asked to see his show in Vegas, he greeted us warmly afterward. A class act. Michael didn't believe I had turned Julio down, but that was his problem.

I had an encounter of a different kind with another famous man not long afterward: O. J. Simpson. At a party Michael and I attended, O. J. was there with his wife, Nicole. She was standing by meekly, not saying much to anyone. She didn't seem to know a lot of people.

After a few minutes, O. J. came over to chat with Michael and me.

I said, "How's Nicole?" I had expected her to come over with him.

He looked intensely in my eyes and said, "Let me worry about Nicole. Nicole is doing fine."

I said, "Oh, okay," and looked over at Michael. The intensity in O. J.'s face frightened me. I was relieved when he walked away.

Nicole was standing alone, so a little later, I went over and said hello, then moved on. Michael stayed to talk to her. They knew each other somehow, possibly from Michael's modeling, and they began chatting.

When I looked over a couple of minutes later, O. J. was approaching them. He picked Michael up by his neck so that Michael was on his toes, beginning to choke.

O. J. said, "You fuckin' stay away from her!" Then he set Michael down.

My mouth was open in disbelief. When Michael came back to me, he was shaking like a leaf. I was not surprised when O. J. was put on trial for killing Nicole years later. I'd gotten a glimpse of the murderer that night.

I knew by then that Michael had an alcohol-induced alter ego. If he had too much to drink at a party, he would take it on himself to provide the entertainment during a lull. One incident I will never forget happened during dinner at a restaurant with my mother and Lisa. The evening had gotten boring, and during a lull, Michael excused himself and went upstairs to the restroom. He was already pretty tipsy. A few minutes later, I became aware that people were laughing and looking at the stairs. There was Michael, stark naked and holding a napkin over his privates, coming down the stairs in time with the music on the sound system. My jaw dropped. Everyone at our table froze in horror. My mother was transfixed.

Lisa was pulling on my arm, saying, "Oh my God, Mommy! Mommy!" She wanted me to make it stop.

All I could think was, "Please don't drop the napkin!"

At the bottom of the stairs, mercifully, he turned and went back up, disappearing on the landing. He got a big round of applause and whistles from the other customers. *Oh God*, I thought, *don't encourage him*!

On the way home in the car with my mother and Lisa, no one said a word. I knew there was no point in talking to him while he was still drunk. But I laid into him the next day. How could he do that in front of Lisa and my mother?

He kept saying, "I'm so sorry. I'm sorry, I had too much to drink."

I could forgive a striptease, however embarrassing, but that turned out to be the tip of the iceberg. It was as if he had a double personality. He could be so sweet, so nice, so helpful. But there was this other persona lurking somewhere in the background—someone who emerged when he drank too much. This other person had a dark quality about him that I found disturbing.

I would ask myself, *Is it me? Am I imagining this?*

I was torn. I couldn't reconcile the two Michaels I knew. When I finally learned the depth of the problem, it was almost too late.

I knew that Lisa and Michael had a complicated relationship. Lisa was always intensely jealous if there was a man in my life, for she was very possessive of me. Since she'd lost her father, I was all she had. She had been jealous of Michael in the beginning. At Christmas, Michael had bought me a present, and naturally, I thanked him and gushed over the present. Lisa immediately got upset.

"What about my present? You like his better than the one I gave you!"

I had to reassure her, "No, I love your gift. I think it's beautiful. Why would you think that?"

If I held one of Michael's hands, she wanted to hold the other. If he and I sat close together, she wanted to sit between us. She loved spending time with him. They would swim and play together. It gradually dawned on me that she had developed a schoolgirl crush on him.

When I asked her about it many years later, she said it was true. "Yeah, I did. I really liked him. I thought he was kind."

At the time, I felt fortunate that Lisa had such a wonderful father figure. It is so painfully ironic in retrospect. For years, I had dedicated myself to keeping Lisa safe, protecting her from the dangers outside. Often, that meant keeping her at home. Home was the safe place. Except, as it turns out, it wasn't.

When Lisa was fourteen years old, the world as I knew it fell apart. I had just come home from a business trip when Lisa came to me and said that Michael had come into her room the night before while he thought she was asleep. Then he pulled back the covers to look at her in her nightgown. He was drunk, and it had made her feel very uncomfortable.

I asked her if he had done it before, and she said no, it was a onetime thing. I questioned her closely. I asked her if he had touched her in any way. She said no, he hadn't touched her that night. He had never touched her inappropriately. My mind was racing. I began to remember the times I had been away from home for work. *What if something had happened in one of my absences? Michelle was usually there, but still... Had she been there every time? Was Lisa telling me the whole extent of it?*

When I confronted Michael, he was quick with an explanation. He said he had just checked on Lisa and then pulled up the covers to tuck her in. It was plausible, and I wanted to believe him. I also knew that Lisa sometimes made up stories to get attention. But this felt different. Lisa had sensed that something was wrong, and I believed her. We had a family discussion about it, and there was a temporary truce, but I remained conflicted.

I kept a close eye on things while I was figuring out what I should do. I finally decided that I couldn't risk having Michael in the house with my daughter. I told Lisa that I was going to ask him to move out, that I no longer felt I could trust him. She began crying hysterically.

"No, Mom, no! Mom, nothing happened. Please!"

I replied, "Lisa, something did happen. He went into your room and pulled back the covers to look at you."

"No, Mom, please!"

Lisa was distraught that I was making him leave. She begged me not to do it. She even wrote me a letter supporting Michael while I was away on business and Michelle was staying with her. I still have it.

She told me, "You mustn't forget Michael Edwards, your 4-ever 2-b. I know you love him! Maybe not *all* the time but deep inside when you say you hate him, you really love him. Just like you really love me." And then she reassured me that I didn't need to worry, because everything was fine at home.

I was so confused. Lisa had told me that Michael had looked at her in a way that made her uncomfortable, but she was adamant that nothing else had happened. I didn't know what to do. But thank God, I did understand that something was very wrong with his feelings for Lisa. I could not take the risk that something had or would happen to my daughter.

It was difficult to get him to move out. He continued to deny Lisa's account. I had been with him for almost six years by then, and I had my own feelings for him. Our lives were intertwined. It took some time and a profound internal struggle on my part before he left. Throughout the ordeal, I had a guilty fear that I was being unfair, that I was doing the wrong thing. But I couldn't take the risk of letting him stay. I had to protect my child at all costs, and if I was making a mistake, so be it.

Four years after he moved out, Michael wrote a tell-all book about me. It was unkind and often fictitious. In his book, he openly admitted that he'd had a sexual obsession with Lisa since she was twelve years old. He described how he'd felt about Lisa when she was twelve: "[I'd] always thought of Lisa as a daughter, but now I was engulfed by a stronger emotion.... Like every father who has ever seen a beautiful daughter through puberty, I found it difficult to keep a grip on my emotions." When I'd asked him why he'd pulled up Lisa's sheets years earlier, he'd given me an innocent explanation. In his book, he admitted that he'd wanted to "pour my heart out to Lisa and beg Priscilla to understand how much I cared for Lisa. The feelings I had for her I knew I would never have for another.... I wanted to take her in my arms and love her right there in the bed her mother and I shared."

I was sickened. If I'd had any idea of his feelings, I'd have kicked him out years earlier. I also thought how out of touch with reality he was. He had openly written about his sexual obsession with a child. She was twelve; he was in his thirties at the time. There is no indication that he even realized how his confessions would be regarded. He seemed to believe that his feelings for Lisa were normal.

A couple of years after the book came out, he called me to say he wished he had never written it. I don't think he regretted his behavior, but he regretted admitting to it publicly. It's like the criminal who isn't sorry he did the crime but is very sorry he got caught. If he wanted my forgiveness, he didn't ask for it and wouldn't have gotten it. There are some things you can't unknow. One thing was certain. If Elvis had still been alive, Michael wouldn't have been calling me about his regrets. Elvis would have shot him.

I thought that phone call was the end to a painful chapter in our lives. I was wrong. Forty years later, in her memoir, Lisa wrote that Michael Edwards had molested her for years while he lived with us. It was the first time I had heard her say that he sexually abused her. The graphic descriptions stunned me. But her revelation didn't make sense to me, either. She had told me something completely different at the time. And there were other people in our home that she could have confided in. My sister Michelle was living in the room next to Lisa during those years, and Michael's daughter, Caroline—who was like a sister to Lisa—had often stayed over in Lisa's room. Lisa never said anything to them, either. I couldn't understand why she had never told any of us. I struggle to make peace with Lisa's words. Because I didn't hear them until after her passing, we never got to talk about it together. I know I will never have closure.

CHAPTER 7

Acting Out

Changes are a-comin'
For these are changing days.

AFTER THE CHAOTIC AND EMOTIONAL END TO MY relationship with Michael Edwards, I had to reassess what was best for Lisa. I was aware by then that she was smoking cigarettes, and I suspected she had at least experimented with alcohol and pot. I also knew that cocaine and other serious drugs were readily available in her social circles. With Elvis's history of addiction, this easy access to narcotics worried me. I wanted to get her away from the environment we were living in. Too much money, too many drugs. So I enrolled her in a private boarding school in Ojai, a secluded, idyllic-looking town in the mountains north of Los Angeles. It was called Happy Valley School, and with a few children of celebrities attending, Lisa wouldn't attract attention. Ojai was only an hour and a half's drive from our home in Beverly Hills. I could go up every weekend if I wanted to, and Lisa could come home for visits. She wasn't happy with my decision, but she was resigned. School was her burden to bear. No matter which school she attended, she hated it. To my surprise, however, she turned out to like Happy Valley fairly well. She made friends and was happier there. Of course, she continued to complain every chance she got, but I was used to that. I missed seeing her every day, but I had to do what I thought was best for her.

Meanwhile, I was exploring the next steps for myself. Representing Wella Balsam required me to do an increasing amount of camera work, something I was uncomfortable doing. I decided that some training might help me deal with my stage fright, so I enrolled in an acting class with the highly respected acting coach Milton Katselas. I had no clear goal; I was just feeling it out. The other students in the class were a mixture of beginners like me and established actors keeping their craft fresh. Because it was LA, there were several award-winning actors in the class. It was intimidating. I attended four or five sessions but never once went on stage. Scared to death to participate, I just sat and watched.

Finally, Milton called me out. "Priscilla, you come to these classes, but you're not contributing anything. You're just watching." Clearly, this would no longer be an option.

Milton told me to get up on the stage, so I did. I stood there, too shy to say a word, dreading whatever was coming next. To my surprise, he told me to skip around the stage. Just skip like a little girl.

Milton kept saying, "Loosen up, Priscilla, loosen up! Keep skipping."

I'd say okay and skip some more.

After a while, he said, "Hop now. That's good. Now do hopscotch. Hopscotch!"

The entire time, I was being watched by the whole class, including some of the who's who in Hollywood. I was a nervous wreck. I kept thinking, *I'm making a complete fool of myself.* The class would clap after my "performances." I was so embarrassed. To my surprise, though, after about fifteen minutes, my anxiety began to dissipate. I felt freer and stopped caring about what people were thinking about me. By the time I sat down, I was feeling good. All of that hopping and skipping had prepared me for whatever came next. Who'd have thought?

Everyone was being assigned scenes with a partner, and Milton chose a challenging scene for me to prepare and rehearse. My partner and I were to do a scene from *Who's Afraid of Virginia Woolf?* It was a heavy, demanding piece, and performing it before an audience was nerve-racking. But the scene was fairly short, and it went well. When the audience applauded, I realized that actually doing it wasn't nearly as frightening as imagining it.

That scene became a turning point for me. I began to feel like part of the class. I realized that we were all working hard to meet a certain standard for auditioning and performing. I had begun the class to cope with stage fright, but my goals had been transformed. The experience had broken me out of my shyness, my fear of being watched. I had learned to stand up in front of an audience without experiencing crippling stage fright, and it felt wonderful. For the first time, I began thinking seriously about acting as a profession. Not long afterward, I was introduced to an agent from William Morris and soon had representation.

One of the first real television opportunities offered through my agent was one of the lead roles in *Charlie's Angels*. Farrah Fawcett had recently left the show, and the producers were looking for a replacement. To my agent's surprise, I turned it down without hesitation. It was a bold move from an inexperienced actress. I understood what a compliment it was to be asked, but I had to decline. Being an "angel" simply wasn't the image I wanted for myself. I had worked hard to become an independent woman. I didn't want to play a character who lived to please a man, even on a television program. If I was going to pursue a career in television and movies, I wanted to do something more substantive. I had learned that lesson from Elvis. Once he made his first hit movie with a bevy of girls and a medley of mediocre love songs, there was no turning back. He was stereotyped, and his lucrative contract became a sort of indentured servitude. He was miserable. *Charlie's Angels* was a hugely popular show, and the women in it were household names. I applaud them for it. But it wasn't for me. Instead, I went in a completely different direction.

By then I was gaining a reputation for my interest in animal rescue. I think that was one reason I was offered a role on *Those Amazing Animals*. The show was a spin-off of a popular television program called *That's Incredible!*, which focused mainly on unusual and gifted people. *Those Amazing Animals* featured the animal kingdom. The show premiered in August 1980 and ran weekly for a year. It was aimed at younger viewers, and though some episodes were dangerous (like the shark encounter) or funny (like the opera-singing parrot), the thrust of the show was educational.

There were three of us humans in the cast, two of whom had some pretty funny animal connections of their own. My cohosts were Burgess Meredith, who had famously played the Penguin on the *Batman* TV series, and Jim Stafford, a popular singer whose biggest hit was "Spiders and Snakes." I loved doing the show and liked both of my cohosts, though I had a particular soft spot for Burgess Meredith. I loved Burgess, who was in his seventies when he did the show. He was so kind and so interested in the animals. No matter what the creature was, he would be gentle and sweet and pet it until it relaxed. I still miss Burgess, who passed in 1997.

Our "special guests" ranged from the creepy-crawly to the too-cute-for-words: spiders, seals, skunks, bobcats, raccoons, baby deer, gerbils, snakes, an armadillo, ponies, and many more. I am proud to say that with the exception of the rattlesnakes, I handled everything that came on set. Some of the episodes were shot on location for practical reasons. The aquatic sequences were shot underwater, sometimes under the supervision of famed oceanographer Jacques Cousteau, who consulted on the series. The sequence with our divers in a school of sharks was terrifying and nearly fatal. Surprisingly, though, one of the more dangerous episodes was shot in the studio with a live audience.

The guests, members of a snake handlers club, brought with them a large number of rattlesnakes. There were piles of snakes crawling around center stage, with a group of booted, bearded men handling them. One of the men kissed a rattlesnake—very, very carefully. The most harrowing bit was when one of the handlers crawled into a sleeping bag that the other men then filled with snakes. I watched in fascination as he slowly made his way out of the sleeping bag without getting bitten. I was very uncomfortable, but the snake handlers were reassuring. They assured me that all would be well if I moved slowly and didn't scare the snakes.

They told me, "Priscilla, you'll be fine. Don't worry. Just be careful."

I learned a lot about fear on that show, mine and the animals'. I was taught that animals react primarily to scent, the smell of fear. As long as I could manage my own anxiety, all would be well. I knew I needed to remain calm. I learned that animals could feel my fear, and I didn't want to have that in my body or my mind. I knew the animal could react if I communicated any distress, and I learned not to.

Animals, I discovered, become dangerous out of their own fear. We are bigger than most of them, and if we approach quickly or unexpectedly, they react. We have to give them time to adjust, and we have to reassure them. It is up to us to handle them delicately and, before picking them up, to let them know that we're there. It was all common sense to me. On one episode, I talked soothingly to a real-life boa that was wrapped around my neck. I'm not sure which of us was more nervous, but we both got through the episode without panicking. It was all fascinating to me. I was disappointed when the show wasn't renewed for a second year. I loved every minute of doing it. In the current cultural climate, a show like this might be picked up, but at the time, there wasn't the interest in animals there is now.

When the show wasn't renewed, my agency put me up for a very different kind of role: Jenna Wade on *Dallas*.

The character had been played by two previous actresses over the years but had served only a minor role in the plot line. The producers were looking for someone to bring the character back. Norman Brokaw, the top guy at William Morris, became my cheerleader. *Dallas* was the most popular show on television at the time, so this was a huge opportunity for me. The first audition went well, and they called me back for a second one. When they cast me as Jenna, I was thrilled. It was an incredible opportunity that became an amazing experience. My years on *Dallas* were some of the best of my life.

Despite my euphoria, I was apprehensive about taking on the series. I had never done a dramatic role before, much less on such a high-profile show. Gathering around the television to watch *Dallas* every Friday night at nine had become an American ritual. I didn't want to let the rest of the cast down. And I was worried about stepping back into the spotlight. I knew it meant being in the rumor mill, something I'd experienced for years with Elvis. Rumors were already floating around that I was feuding with Linda Gray, one of the lead actors on the series. I hadn't even met her yet, but apparently, we were in a feud. I was also concerned about losing my anonymity again. True, I was still recognized regularly as Elvis's ex, but now I would be front and center in the spotlight as myself. Millions of people would be tuning in to the show every week, and I knew it would mean a huge loss of privacy.

Despite the changes I was facing, I never second-guessed my decision. For one thing, I was excited to take on the role of Jenna Wade. I liked her, and I identified with her. She was her own person, a self-reliant woman who was raising a daughter by herself. She had integrity. I had been hoping for a meaningful part since I'd turned down *Charlie's Angels*. I felt I was enough like the character to portray her well, and, apparently, audiences agreed. My temporary contract turned into five years on the show, with Jenna becoming a major character in the saga.

Ironically, the rumor mill I feared soon found me. As my first day on set loomed closer, people began to warn me about the show. They told me to watch out for Victoria Principal in particular. I remembered her from my years at Bis and Beau, but I didn't know her well. I was told to remind myself that it was really her show, hers and Larry Hagman's. She was the lead. It was about the Ewing family, and my character wasn't part of that family. Victoria probably would not be accepting of me, and I should be prepared for that. I needed to be very careful about how I interacted with her. I listened to all this advice and became anxious about how I would fit in. It wasn't so much stage fright as stage concern. This was a major series, and the standard would be high. I had never done a dramatic scene on camera before, and on my first day, I was scheduled to shoot a scene with Patrick Duffy, who played Jenna's love interest, Bobby Ewing. I learned my lines backward and forward and ran the scene in my head so many times, it was dizzying. I had many sleepless nights in the lead-up to my first day at MGM, where *Dallas* was filmed.

I was a nervous wreck when I arrived at the studio. After hair and makeup, I made my way to the set where I would be shooting my first scene. I wondered the whole time how I'd have the nerve to step out on cue when the cameras started. The cameras would roll, and I would say my first line. It was jumping into the deep end of the pool. Sink or swim.

After all the anxiety and the long buildup, it turned out that I had worried for nothing. None of the things I had been warned about were true. Patrick couldn't have been kinder or more supportive. He reassured me that everyone understood my anxiety—that they'd all been through first-day nerves and would help me in any way they could.

He asked me, "Do you want to rehearse the scene? Do you want to go over the lines with me first?"

His warmth was incredibly freeing. I felt myself relax into the moment. And it wasn't just Patrick. The whole cast was warm and welcoming—even Victoria! They accepted me on the spot, and I was able to let go of the fact that this was my first big part, and in a hugely popular show. Everybody welcomed me.

"Hi, Priscilla!"

"It's such a pleasure having you with us."

"You're going to be a wonderful Jenna Wade."

What a great group of people! Not only great at what they did, but also great human beings. Everyone was surprisingly down-to-earth, including Linda Gray, who was lovely. She was welcoming and put me at my ease. They were all huge stars at the time, but they didn't behave that way. I was a newcomer, yet they accepted me without question. I will always be grateful for that. We became friends. Contrary to rumor, there were no romances but some wonderful friendships. I had lunch with some of the cast from the first day, and we hung out on the set. It was one of the best professional experiences of my life.

Larry Hagman was amazing. He was truly so funny. Every day, he'd bring a bottle of champagne with him to work. He carried it everywhere on set, and he'd sip it throughout the day. Even during breaks in scenes, and between scenes. It was never enough to get drunk, just little sips all day long.

When we all sat down for lunch, he'd plunk the bottle on the table and ask, "Anybody want champagne?" with that big grin of his.

And then there were the Sundays at Larry's house on the beach in Malibu. He was a fixture in Malibu, walking most places and greeting passersby with a smile and a cheerful word. Every Sunday, he would invite the cast to his place. On my first Sunday there, we all walked on Surfrider Beach together, enjoying one another's company, and then went back to his house. His wife Maj would be there to greet us. We all laughed and discussed the week together. Well, most of us did. Larry didn't talk. At all. The first Sunday I went, I was baffled. Larry was usually chatty. That day, he walked with us and laughed with us, but he didn't say a word. I thought, *What?*

It was Linda who explained to me what was going on. She told me, "You know, this is Larry's day off talking."

I said, "Really? He doesn't talk on Sundays?"

Linda explained that Sunday was the day he rested his voice. He had the most demanding role on the show, with a lot of dialogue. He was in nearly every scene, every day. Larry coped with the show's demands by making Sunday his day of rest. Laughing, socializing, communing were all restorative for him, but he didn't need to use his voice to do those things. So he just enjoyed our company in companionable silence. It worked for him.

Both Larry and Patrick loved to pull pranks. One day, we all thought we were having a glass of water in a scene. But when we took a sip, it turned out to be vodka. Everyone had to blink back their reactions and go on like it really was water. I don't know whether it was Larry or Patrick who did it, but it was one of them. Sometimes they worked together. I was rushing to get ready for a scene in a bowling alley for one shoot. I was trying to adjust my dress and fix my hair quickly so I could make my entrance on time. Larry and Patrick noticed and put a bowling ball in the path I had to take to make my entrance. They correctly guessed that I would be in a hurry and wouldn't be paying attention to where I was walking. Sure enough, I tripped right over the bowling ball. I didn't hurt myself, but it wasn't exactly graceful! They were like mischievous little boys. It wasn't just me; they pulled pranks on everyone. Nobody was safe.

It was easier to shoot on weekdays, because Lisa wasn't home when I started the show. When I'd sent Lisa to school in Ojai, I'd done it in hopes of moving her to a safer environment. What I didn't know was that underneath the small-town charm, Ojai had a thriving drug subculture that rivaled the one in Beverly Hills. Only this time, I wasn't with Lisa every day to monitor her well-being. She began experimenting with more serious drugs. I eventually found out she was using pot, cocaine, alcohol, and sedatives while she was in school there.

In the middle of Lisa's junior year, she reached a low point. Lisa was oversleeping and missing classes. In every way possible, she made it clear that she did not want to be in school. At the end of fall semester, she had all F's. I didn't want her to know this, and I didn't want the information to leak to the press. I asked the school to give me her report card directly, before Lisa saw it. I knew that her failing grades would hit her self-esteem and reinforce her idea that school was the wrong place for her. Sending her away to school hadn't achieved what I'd hoped. I thought she would be safer and perhaps even happier there, away from the temptations in LA. It proved to be an unrealistic goal. So I packed her up and brought her home.

I briefly enrolled her in a local private school, but she found ways to get drugs there, too. Changing locations wasn't solving the drug problem. They were available everywhere, and I finally realized that I was in denial about the problem. I didn't want to believe my child was taking serious drugs. I told myself she had been taught better, both by me personally and by Scientology, which is fiercely antidrug. Now I became fearful for her safety. I worried about their effect on her health and future and what they could do to her reputation. Part of the price of celebrity is that your children can't make their mistakes in private. If the press gets a hold of damaging information, they exaggerate and repeat it. The rumors become lies, and the lies proliferate. No matter what I did, Lisa Marie would always be Elvis's daughter, and because of his struggles with addiction, the press would pounce on the news that Lisa had drug problems. I had to protect her, and the only way to do that was to address the problem head-on.

I knew that the Scientology Celebrity Centre had an active drug rehabilitation program called Narconon, and I enrolled Lisa in it. I was desperate to save my daughter from herself. I couldn't lose her, too. We packed some clothes, and one evening, I took her to the center and checked her in. It was a residential program where she would be staying for several weeks. She didn't want to go, of course, but she was seventeen, and I didn't need her permission to enroll her. The people running the program put her through a detox purification program to get the drugs out of her system, and she began the drug education process. She was also taught communication skills that improved life for both of us. Fortunately, she made a few friends there fairly quickly, and that made a big difference. The biggest difference, though, came when she met Danny Keough, whose mother was high up in Scientology. Danny was a tall, kind, very good-looking musician who was devoted to Scientology. Lisa was smitten, and drugs quickly became less attractive to her than Danny and Scientology. For me, it was a win-win situation.

Not long afterward, Lisa came to me and said, "Mom, I was really rough on you. I did get some things from Scientology that I liked." She even added, "And I just like giving you trouble." This wasn't news to me, but it was nice to hear her say it. She became dedicated to Scientology for years afterward.

I did not reenroll her in school when she finished rehab. I saw no reason to return her to an environment filled with unhappiness and temptation. Lisa was nearly eighteen by then, and she was clean, sober, and happy. That was more than enough for me. It was time to let go and let her live on her own terms.

When Lisa turned eighteen, I got her an apartment of her own in Westwood, a few miles from home. Westwood is a college town, home to UCLA, and it was pretty, interesting, and safe in those days. Lisa could walk to restaurants or the local movie theater safely, even at night. I got her a cute little two-bedroom apartment that she shared with a roommate. Danny was a frequent visitor. I paid the expenses directly, as Lisa hadn't yet learned to write a check, much less deal with the ins and outs of leasing an apartment. She was over the moon about the move. The freedom that had eluded her for so many years was finally hers. For better or for worse, she could make her own decisions, choose her own schedule, decide for herself how she wanted to spend her days. Thank God, she had never really been a partier, so I didn't worry about that. As long as she remained safe and happy, I was happy for her.

Not that I quit worrying about her. She called me regularly and kept me up on what was happening in her life. Now that she didn't have to tell me, keeping me posted on her life didn't seem to bother her as much.

I still asked her, "Where are you going? Who are you going with?" We were close, and she put up with it.

We talked frequently, and I kept my ear to the ground in between. I quickly became expert at gleaning information from her unsuspecting friends, and a casual phone call could tell me if she had arrived safely at a destination. I knew she wouldn't like my checking up on her, and I didn't blame her, so I was discreet. I just needed to be sure my girl was safe.

I missed her terribly. There is a special bond between a daughter and a mother who raises her alone. Letting go was hard. I missed saying prayers with her and kissing her good night. I missed having her around the house. Her room felt empty. I continually reminded myself of how it felt to be eighteen. Did I want my mother around all the time when I was that age? Of course not. I had a new appreciation for what my parents had gone through when they let me move to Memphis at about the same age as Lisa. They worried constantly, they wondered if they had done the right thing, and they missed me. And they had Elvis to contend with. He took over the decision-making for me, and I let him. My parents lost control of me. I marveled now at how they'd done it. Lisa was just across town from me, and I was struggling.

It's hard for other people to understand what a heavy responsibility it was to raise Elvis Presley's daughter, and to do it without him. His early death had given him an almost-godlike status in the public eye and in that of his daughter. Lisa was the only surviving link between Elvis and his fans. They were fascinated with her, searching her face for her likeness to her father, following her life as closely as they could. I had protected her from that for eighteen years, and now I had to let her go. I've been considered overprotective by some in the public, but to me, I was just being a mother to a very special child. The paparazzi were lined up with cameras at Lisa's birth, and they would line up again at her passing. My job was to keep her safe in between.

CHAPTER 8
Love Me Tender

Love me tender, love me true
All my dreams fulfill.

About the time I joined the *Dallas* cast, I began dating Marco Garibaldi. A few months into our relationship, he moved in with me. We remained together for twenty-two years.

Shortly after Lisa moved out on her own, I became pregnant. I was thrilled. I never thought I'd have another child. And this time, I wasn't under the same pressures I'd been when I was pregnant with Lisa Marie. I had conceived her on my wedding night, and neither Elvis nor I had been ready for the sudden change in our lives. It hadn't helped that as the wife of one of the most famous men in the world, my pregnancy was under a microscope. There had been little privacy. This time around was much more relaxed.

My only concern was Lisa. I wasn't sure how she would take the news. She had always been very possessive of me. But when I told her, she was excited at the prospect of having a baby brother or sister. She did ask me if I was going to get married now and if my last name would still be Presley. Lisa had always been concerned about me marrying again. The prospect of me taking a new last name bothered her. I assured her I wasn't. The only thing that would change was that she would be a big sister.

I joyfully embraced the pregnancy. I read baby books voraciously, as I'd done waiting for Lisa. I wanted to give this baby the healthiest food and raise him or her with all the care I had lavished on my daughter. This time, I didn't have the anxiety that I'd had the first time. I was no longer a young wife who didn't know what to expect. I wanted to savor this experience.

I hid the pregnancy for as long as I could, and the press didn't get wind of it. Because I am thin, I could wear looser blouses and not give the secret away. I did get bigger, of course, and I had to tell the wardrobe mistress for *Dallas*. She carefully adjusted my costumes to hide my condition as long as possible. It wasn't long before I had to confide in the producers as well, for my pregnancy would be Jenna's when it became impossible to hide. To my relief, they decided to embrace the change rather than hide it. I had already been on the show years longer than my original contract, and they could easily have created a dramatic departure for Jenna. Instead, the writers rose to the occasion. They were so gifted, the real heart of the show, and they seamlessly blended Jenna's pregnancy into the narrative. Most viewers didn't realize the pregnancy was real until the baby was born and it made the papers.

I had already arranged with my doctors to have a natural birth. When I'd had Lisa, they gave me so many drugs that I don't even remember the actual birth. They had to wake me up to show me my baby girl. I didn't want to go through that again. I wanted to be present for the birth, mentally as well as physically. I had always felt a little cheated to have missed that moment with my daughter.

On March 1, 1987, I gave birth to my son. It was one of the most thrilling experiences of my eventful life. I was fully conscious as he emerged and the doctor placed him in my arms. A healthy childbirth creates an intense joy, a natural high that is unparalleled in a woman's life. It is completely different from giving birth in a drugged, semiconscious state. I gazed in awe at my beautiful baby, with his large dark eyes and the little fuzz of soft hair covering his head. We named him Navarone, after the movie *The Guns of Navarone*. For me, Navarone's birth was my second miracle. I was ecstatic. I couldn't believe that another precious human being had come from my body. I had wanted one of each, a girl and a boy, and now I had them. The fans were wonderful. Once word got out, I was flooded with congratulations, cards, and flowers. Their support was sweet.

It was difficult to adjust when I first went back to work, but once again, the *Dallas* team couldn't have been better. I was allowed to take Navarone to the studio, where my fellow actors oohed and aahed over him to my heart's content. I hired a nanny, Vikki, who brought Navarone to the studio every day

I was shooting. I kept him in my dressing room to nurse and care for him so he wouldn't disturb the recording process. Vikki took care of him while I was on the set. I still marvel at what a forward-thinking company Warner Brothers was. At the time, it was unheard-of to be allowed to bring your baby to work.

At the end of the 1988 season, Jenna's story arc had played itself out, and my part came to an end. Jenna left Texas to move to Europe with Ray Krebbs (played by Steve Kanaly), never to return. It was time for me to leave the show. My last day on the set was bittersweet. Patrick, Larry, Charlene Tilton, and Steve were all shooting that day, so they were there to say goodbye. It was sad to leave behind people I cared for so much. Everyone said kind things, how much they'd miss me, and what a good sport I'd been. Larry and Patrick had played so many pranks on me, and I'd always been good-humored about it. I'd been working with these people several days a week for five years, and that period was now ending. I would no longer be part of this group I loved. No more pranks, no more quiet Sundays at the beach with Larry. I wondered if I'd see them again. Letting go was hard.

Of course, I did see them again. We remained friends. It's like your family when they move away.

Each time you cross paths, you say, "Oh my God, what are you doing now? Where are you living? How's your family?" Those conversations that are nothing and everything.

Patrick still refers to me as "our beautiful Priscilla." So sweet of him. I recently saw him at an autograph event, and it was as if no time had passed. He still beams when he smiles, and he radiates affection for those he cares about. Larry is gone now, of course, but what a wonderful life he had. Rest in peace, my friend.

Life is about beginnings and endings. My time with my *Dallas* family had ended, but my life with my baby son was just beginning. And I was not surprised when Lisa told me she and Danny were getting married. They were clearly in love, and they wanted to be together. Lisa was eager to marry him, in part because she didn't want Danny to be unmarried. She wanted him to belong to her; she wanted to be able to say, "Stay away. He's mine!" I was happy for them. I hoped Lisa would find the constancy, the security she so badly needed in her life.

The wedding was a small ceremony at the Scientology Celebrity Centre. It was very private. Only nine of us were there. No press. The office was filled with pink star lilies and white tulips for the occasion, and Lisa looked beautiful. She wore a lovely traditional white dress of crocheted lace, with her curly blonde hair swept up and back. She reminded me of an old-fashioned porcelain doll. In the picture, which I still keep on my shelf, she looks so young, so vulnerable, so hopeful. Danny is tall and handsome in his formal black suit. What a good-looking couple they made! Though they would divorce in a few years, Danny was Lisa's first love and perhaps her only lasting love. He was there for her the rest of her life, not quite lover, not quite brother, but always her best friend. Danny was the one who held Lisa in his arms when he found her lifeless on the floor. On their wedding day, he promised to love her until death did them part, and he kept that promise.

That same year, a woman calling herself Deborah Presley inserted herself into our lives. Growing up, she had been told that her parents were college sweethearts. But about ten years after Elvis's death, her mother, Barbara, told Deborah that she, Deborah, was Elvis's daughter, the result of an affair when Barbara was fourteen. She took her mother at her word and legally changed her last name to Presley. In 1988, before Lisa Marie had come into her inheritance, Deborah filed a petition in the probate court asking for half of Elvis's estate, claiming that she was his daughter. The court ruled against her, but she continued to regard herself as Lisa's half sister and periodically reached out to her. It made Lisa very uncomfortable. Deborah even came to the hospital when Lisa was dying, asking to be allowed to see her "sister." I found the whole episode disturbing.

Deborah is one of many people who over the years have claimed to be Elvis's illegitimate child. These assertions were typically made after Elvis's death, when he couldn't deny or confirm them. I am very doubtful about them for several reasons. The first and most important reason is that none of those claiming Elvis as their father have produced any proof. There is nothing factual, such as DNA or written evidence, to back up their stories. I am also skeptical because I know how Elvis thought. Though he fooled around with many women, he rarely had intercourse with them. He was terrified of having an illegitimate child. And if he'd had a child out of wedlock, he would have provided for it. Elvis was generous and financially responsible. He would never have let a child of his go without, whether or not he was married to the mother.

I view people claiming to be Elvis's children as falling into two categories: the con artists and the true believers. The con artists know Elvis is not their father, but they want the attention, career advancement, or wealth that could come from being Elvis's child. The true believers are a different thing. They genuinely believe that Elvis is their father, either because they believe their mothers or because being a Presley fills a psychological need for them. It makes them feel special to be related to Elvis. It is a way to bring some of the magic surrounding Elvis into their lives.

My career took an exciting turn shortly after I left *Dallas*. To my astonishment, David and Jerry Zucker contacted my agency, William Morris, saying they wanted to meet me. The Zucker brothers were famous for writing and producing slapstick comedies like the huge 1980 hit *Airplane!* They were interested in having me play Leslie Nielsen's love interest in a new series of films called *The Naked Gun* and based on the hit TV show *Police Squad!* I was astonished. I had never done a comedy, and I didn't even know who Leslie Nielsen was. When I met them and they outlined the part they wanted me to play, I had to tell them the truth.

"I have to share something with you. I'm not a comedian. I'm not even funny."

They quickly reassured me. "Don't even worry about it. You don't need to be. We just want you to be you."

I nodded my head blankly, all the time thinking, *This is a comedy. How am I going to pull this off?* I just didn't get it, but my agent seemed to consider it a good opportunity, so I agreed.

The day I met Leslie was memorable, to say the least.

We introduced ourselves, and Leslie said, "Let's go sit down." As he sat down, I heard a loud sound of passing gas. He said, "Oh, excuse me."

I couldn't believe it. I thought, *My God, this is so embarrassing.*

He broke out laughing and said, "Priscilla..." Then he pulled a whoopee cushion out from the seat of his chair. I had no idea what it was. I didn't even know what it was called. Leslie explained how it worked and said he carried it with him all the time. He used it as an icebreaker for awkward social interactions. He did the routine so smoothly that people never guessed what he was up to until they heard it. It certainly broke the ice with us. We became friends from that moment forward. You hear stories about legendary comedians being sour or bad-tempered in real life. Not Leslie. He was good-humored, kind, professional, and very, very funny. The only problem I ever had working with Leslie was keeping a straight face. He played a bumbling idiot so earnestly that sometimes, I couldn't help laughing. What a precious soul he was. We lost him in 2010, and he is one of the people I still miss. He was one of a kind.

I enjoyed all the regular cast members, with one exception: O. J. Simpson. I vividly remembered the encounter with Michael Edwards and me years before. O. J. did nothing to redeem himself on the *Naked Gun* set. He was arrogant, hostile, and threatening. I avoided him as much as possible. Luckily, we were rarely in the same scenes, so I seldom saw him.

My first scene, in the first film, required me to climb up a library ladder while Leslie stood below, looking up.

I got halfway up and thought, *Oh my God, Leslie's right down there, and he can see everything if he wants to. I hope he's not looking up my dress.* Then I thought, *Okay, I'm not going to worry about it. I'm going to play it straight and pretend I don't realize he's down there. I'll just let him be funny.*

Leslie's expression as he struggled with temptation was priceless, and when he reached up out of camera range and pulled down a stuffed beaver, the symbolic taxidermy said it all. It set the tone for the remainder of the film. For the rest of the film, I played Jane with a straight face and an earnest expression. I remained blissfully unaware of the ridiculous behavior of the man Jane loved. Leslie was equally oblivious to his own behavior. When I saw the film the first time, I burst out laughing because the moment on the ladder was so funny. Together, our chemistry was perfect. I let Leslie carry the comedy, and it was pure gold.

The physical comedy was priceless, Luckily, though I look fragile, I'm actually very strong, so I enjoyed the challenge. One of the scenes involved a folding bed. Leslie's character, Police Lieutenant Frank Drebin, and I were trying to have a passionate romantic interlude. But every time we tried to lie down, the bed snapped shut and blew us out.

Leslie said, "Can you imagine this actually happening?"

I said, "Well, I can imagine it happening to you. I'll just sit here and let it happen."

Fortunately, the mattress was thick, so it didn't hurt when it closed on us. It took only one or two practice runs to get the timing down. In the movie, the scene seems to go on forever, but it didn't really take long to shoot. I felt like the *Naked Gun* movies should all have an advisory saying, "No humans were hurt in the making of this film"!

Another memorable scene was a parody of *Ghost*, the hugely popular drama made shortly before the second *Naked Gun* film. It starred Demi Moore as a woman whose boyfriend, played by Patrick Swayze, is murdered. He remains near her as a ghost, protecting her from the people who murdered him. The best-known scene in *Ghost* takes place at a pottery wheel. Demi is casting a sculpture out of wet clay on a spinning wheel. Patrick stands behind her, shirtless, encircling her with his bare arms. As he plunges his hands into the wet clay with hers, they coat each other's hands and arms with the clay, and the sculpture is shaped into an erect phallus. In their film, it is an intensely sensual scene.

In our film, Leslie and I reenact the scene, with a bare-chested Leslie wrapping his arms around me as we slowly become covered with clay. The effect is hilarious. The clay was wet and sticky and very uncomfortable, but we played the scene straight. For the camera, that is. We ended up doing multiple takes because we couldn't quit laughing at how ludicrous it was. Leslie always broke first, but his laughter was contagious, and soon we were both laughing. It took forever to wash the stuff off my skin and out of my hair, but it was worth it.

Perhaps the most iconic bit of physical comedy we did was the condom scene. It was a time when there was a lot of talk about safe sex in the wake of the HIV/AIDS epidemic, and condoms were being made available at some high schools. My character and Leslie's solemnly agree that when having sex, we must be sure to use a condom. The scene then cuts to us, gazing longingly at each other while covered from head to toe in plastic. We were wearing full-body condoms. Eventually, we fall into bed together to make love inside the plastic. The scene was one of the funniest I have ever seen, and the Zucker brothers get the credit for that. I have no idea what made them think of a full-body condom. But shooting the scene was a challenge. It took several people to get me into the costume, and once they did, I couldn't breathe. There was a little valve, but I could barely get air. Thank heaven I'm not claustrophobic.

Once I was in the costume, I had to walk toward Leslie. I initially thought that if I moved, I would fall over, but I told myself, *Don't think about it. Just do it.* I began moving toward Leslie, taking little bitty baby steps. It took forever for me to advance a few inches.

Leslie looked at me with a comically perplexed expression and said, "Are you going to get here? Or are you going to keep taking these baby steps?"

I was just proud of myself for not falling down. I looked preposterous walking around in that thing, and we kept laughing. We couldn't help it.

It took a lot of takes to get that scene. We could only shoot it a little at a time. In some movies, you can do a scene in one take, and somebody will say, "Okay, that's a wrap." Not these movies. The kind of physical comedy we did was difficult and time-consuming. But it was so completely worth it. Leslie and I had the time of our lives.

We laughed so much that the director said, "Okay, we only have so much time. Let's get this over with!"

Sometimes the humor was sly and situational. I had a reputation as an animal lover in the wake of *Those Amazing Animals* and in real life. So the writers gave my character a menagerie of pets. When Jane gets home and feeds her cat, she doesn't stop there. She keeps putting down bowls of food in her kitchen, for a dog, a chicken, several baby pigs, and a large grunting sow.

The moment is funny in itself, but for those who knew me, it was hilarious.

The third film in the series was classic Zucker brothers. The whole premise was geared toward those who knew the inside story. The supervillain was played by Robert Goulet. As anybody familiar with Elvis stories already knew, he couldn't stand Robert Goulet. Elvis was all about singing from the heart, not the head, and he thought Goulet's performances were technically good but mechanical. They lacked heart. Elvis had famously shot the television set whenever Robert Goulet was on-screen, whether or not Robert was singing. We went through a lot of TVs that way.

So the Zucker brothers cast Goulet as the villain opposite, of course, Elvis's ex-wife. I felt a little uncomfortable, and I even apologized to Robert because I thought he'd been put in an awkward position. He was aware of the Elvis stories but good-naturedly told me not to worry about it. I think he recognized that the comedic value of the situation was spot-on. And just to rub it in, at a villains' meeting, one man passes a newspaper to Robert's character, telling him to take a look at the headline. The main headline is about the villains' target, a scientist named Meinheimer. But right underneath is a slightly smaller headline that reads "Elvis Spotted Buying a Condo in Aspen." For audience members paying attention, it is a very funny moment.

Elvis would have loved the *Naked Gun* movies, especially Leslie Nielsen's performance, and he would have been proud of me for tackling the scenes I was given. I can almost hear his laughter as I minced slowly along in the full-body condom. With the scenes featuring both Robert Goulet and me, however, he would have had a dilemma. To shoot or not to shoot? I like to think he would have held his fire for my sake!

The one casting decision I thought was a little odd was Anna Nicole Smith, who appeared in the last of the films. Anna was famous for her image as a clueless blonde, but she was most famous for her unnaturally large bosom. Not that she pretended it was real. Real breasts don't look like that. She knew how to use them, too, to draw attention to herself. On set, though, they didn't inspire lust as much as incredulity.

She had several scenes with Leslie, and for one of them, the camera wasn't ready yet. So she put her arms around Leslie and began jumping up and down, with her bosom bouncing against Leslie's chest.

She kept exclaiming, "This is going to be so much fun!" over and over again.

The crew was staring in fascination and looking at each other as if to say, "What the...?"

Leslie's face was priceless. He alternately glanced down at her bosom and up at the rest of us with one of those classic Leslie Nielsen expressions on his face. It was a cross between "Look at those!" and "Save me!"

Anna had a trailer like we all did, and she sometimes brought a puppy to work. One day, she was sitting outside her trailer with the puppy, bent over so that her bosom was basically falling out of her dress. The puppy was licking her face, then her neck, and was gradually working its way downward. Leslie and I couldn't tear our eyes away.

He kept murmuring to me, "How low is that puppy going to go?"

I don't know why she did things like that. I think it was the only way she knew how to get attention. It was sad. Anna died young, a little more than ten years later, of an overdose after her son's sudden death. God rest her soul.

I had a ball making the *Naked Gun* movies. Working with David and Jerry Zucker was like a master class in the art of comedy. They were wonderful to work with, funny and flexible. If a scene wasn't working, they would change it. There was so much laughter on that set that it wasn't like work at all. Spending your days with Leslie Nielsen and the Zucker brothers. It doesn't get much better than that.

As for me, I'm still looking for the address of that condo in Aspen.

CHAPTER 9

Coming of Age

There's a brand new day on the horizon
Everything's gonna be just fine.

T HE EARLY 1990S WERE SOMETHING OF A GOLDEN time for our family. My professional life was rewarding, psychologically and financially. I had a young son whom I adored. My daughter was happily married to a son-in-law I respected and loved. And just when it couldn't get any better, Lisa gave birth to a daughter of her own. Danielle Riley Keough was born on May 29, 1989, in Saint John's Hospital in Santa Monica, California—the same hospital where Navarone had been born. At two years old, Navarone was an uncle. Three years later, on October 21, 1992, my grandson,

Benjamin Storm Keough, was born. Between us, Lisa and I now had three beautiful young children. How I wished Elvis could have been here to see his grandchildren.

Not that I was eager to label myself as a grandmother. Much as I loved my grandchildren, I couldn't quite wrap my head around being a grandmother at forty-four. I was still the mother of a toddler myself. To me, "Grandma" evoked Minnie Mae, who looked old by the time she was in her thirties. Grandmas didn't go anywhere. They sat in their bedrooms all day, talked about their no-good husbands, and watched soap operas. They had hairdos that were never in style in the first place. I had adored Grandma, but she didn't bear any resemblance to my self-image. And Grandpa Elvis? What's wrong with that picture? Yes, I can be vain, and on this occasion, vanity briefly raised its ugly head. But no temporary weakness on my part could eclipse the joy I felt in those children.

Riley and Benjamin brought Lisa and me even closer. As a new mom, Lisa had all the usual insecurities and questions, and she turned to me for advice.

She would call me and say, "Riley just did this. Is this okay?" Or, "Something is happening with Benjamin. Should I be worried?"

Lisa was a good mom, a really good mom, fiercely devoted to her children. She would do anything to keep them happy and safe. Her parenting style was different from mine, of course. She was as much a friend as a parent. Lisa held her children close. With Riley and Benjamin, there weren't that many trips to see Nona (as they referred to me). Lisa was jealous of anybody being too close to the children, even me. They were her babies. But

I understood, and I couldn't have asked for a more loving and committed mother for my grandchildren.

This was also a busy time for me professionally. In addition to my acting career, I continued to develop business opportunities. When I was approached by a German company that asked me if I would like to develop my own fragrance line, I was delighted. I became involved in both developing and marketing the product.

I found the process of creating the scents fascinating. The perfumers would line up a series of scents on a table for me. I limited my sampling to three at a time so that the scents wouldn't overpower me or confuse my senses. I would smell each one and comment on it. Some of the scents were too delicate. Others were too harsh. My first time through, the choices were a process of elimination.

"This one is a definite no. This one is a maybe. I like this one."

We would continue to narrow down the scents to my favorites, which could be modified or blended if necessary. The perfumers were very respectful of my opinions. They listened to me; they truly cared about what I thought. The end product reflected my taste and personality. I loved the fragrances we created together, and I wore them myself. We named the first perfume we developed Moments, and it enjoyed nice commercial success.

Over the years, Moments was followed by Experiences, then Indian Summer, and, finally, Roses and More. I was the face of the product line, the one who represented it publicly. There was only one drawback, and it eventually caused me to end my involvement with the company. It was an era when American products were strongly promoted, and my fragrance line was with a German company. The fact that, as a Presley, I was associated with an American icon complicated things further. Though we eventually parted ways, I am grateful for my time with the company. The people there treated me well, and I am proud of what we created together.

I remained busy and involved as the trustee for Graceland and Elvis's estate as well. For this work, I received a salary but did not receive any portion of his assets. Under the terms of Elvis's will, my financial duty as trustee consisted of two responsibilities. First, until she came of age at twenty-five, I could distribute funds for Lisa's Marie's support, welfare, and education. My second responsibility was to continue to accumulate income for the trust. That income came from Graceland after we opened it to the public and from Elvis Presley Enterprises. I am proud that I played a key role in saving not only Graceland but also Lisa's inheritance. Her inheritance had gone from less than half a million dollars to multiple millions of dollars by the time she received it. I didn't oversee the funds personally; that was done by the trust's accountant and bank. Elvis's will provided that when Lisa Marie was of age, if her grandfather Vernon and great-grandmother Minnie Mae were both deceased, she would receive all assets of the trust "outright and free of further oversight." I would continue as trustee for Graceland, but I would no longer oversee Lisa's inheritance once Lisa turned twenty-five.

Two weeks before Lisa's twenty-fifth birthday, we traveled to Memphis for a special celebration. The US Postal Service had chosen Elvis as the first honoree in a collection of stamps titled

Legends of American Music. Both Lisa and I were extremely excited about the honor that Elvis was receiving. The post office had originally suggested two stamps with Elvis's image, one nicknamed the young Elvis stamp, and the other, the old Elvis stamp, though Elvis certainly wasn't old in either image. They then held an election to let the public decide which one people liked better. It was the first time in history the postal service had let the public vote on a stamp design. Since stamps are official government documents, it was unheard-of to let people choose the version they wanted. Over a million people voted, and young Elvis won by a landslide. The winning version (a twenty-nine-cent stamp!) shows Elvis in a yellow-gold jacket against a vivid pink background, singing into a microphone. The post office printed five hundred million stamps before the first one was even sold. They are bright and eye-catching and are still the best-selling commemorative stamps in the history of the US Postal Service.

The stamp was scheduled to be unveiled at Graceland at midnight on January 8, 1993, what would have been Elvis's fifty-eighth birthday. The planning that went into that night was extensive. We were given plenty of notice, and our staff at Graceland outdid themselves preparing for the event. The house and grounds were lined with strings of lights that formed a beautiful outline against the night sky. I kept in close touch with the Graceland staff and the post office representatives in the weeks leading up to the stamp's release. Four satellite post offices were set up on the grounds at Graceland to sell the first Elvis stamps, starting at exactly midnight on the eighth. Stamps purchased that night would be postmarked with the date, time, and place of their purchase. Some three hundred thousand stamps would be sold that night, and the only way to get them was to stand in line. The lines were officially opened at nine that morning, and by midnight, there were over five thousand people waiting in them. People had come from around the world—Europe, Asia, South America, and all over the United States—to be there for the occasion.

And Jerry Lee Lewis was there. Jerry had become popular even before Elvis had, and he knew what the stamp meant. When Jerry and Elvis started, nobody took rock and roll seriously. Now even the post office was acknowledging it. Like Elvis, Jerry was from Memphis. He was a wildcat, but I liked him a lot.

Festivities had been going on for days by the time the big night arrived. The atmosphere was like a giant party. Elvis's old friend, radio host George Klein, broadcast live on television all evening. Local radio stations played Elvis's music, and the cable station TNT ran Elvis movies nonstop all weekend. It was almost the perfect launch. There was one small problem. It was an outdoor event, and by evening, it was pouring rain. The fans were undeterred. They just put up their umbrellas and stayed, and a canopy was erected for the presentation. All of us who were speaking that night did so with the sound of pouring rain threatening to drown us out, literally and figuratively.

The emotion of the event was overpowering. What an honor for Elvis! He would never have believed that it was happening. As honored as I was to be accepting it on his behalf, I kept wishing he were alive to accept it himself. He would have understood what it meant to have a US stamp in his honor. Elvis was so American, so patriotic, and so proud of his country. I don't think he ever realized how important he was to our country.

He would have tried to joke about the stamp to hide his emotion. *Well, of course I could get it, I'm Elvis Presley.* When he said those sorts of things, it was always in jest. His gratitude and humility ran deep.

William Morris, the mayor of Memphis, was the first to speak. He talked about how Elvis and Graceland had transformed the city economy, bringing in tourists year-round. He praised Elvis for his generosity and his patriotism and talked about how much the city loved him. Then the postal representative came up to the mic for the official presentation, and I had the amazing honor of receiving the first Elvis stamps. He presented me with stamp albums designated for me, Lisa Marie, and her children, Danielle Riley and Benjamin. The crowd welcomed me, but they knew I was coming, so they weren't surprised. I had often spoken at Graceland on occasions honoring Elvis. But what they didn't know was that I had a very big surprise in store for them.

Lisa had come to Graceland countless times since Elvis's passing, but she had never felt comfortable appearing at a public event. Representing her dad was emotional for her, and underneath the surface, she was deeply shy in ways people didn't expect. That night, though, she felt she owed it to her father to thank everyone on his behalf. So we had all come—Lisa, three-year-old Riley, and two-month-old Benjamin—to show our appreciation for the great honor Elvis had been given. When I introduced Lisa to the crowd and she walked out that night, there was an audible reaction and an outpouring of applause.

To the people there that night, Lisa's appearance must have been magical. Few of them had seen her in person, and then not for many years. Her hair was dyed black by then, teased up above her eyes, and at almost twenty-five years old, her resemblance to her father was uncanny. I could hear the murmur run through the crowd, but all I could think about was how nervous she was. She got through three or four sentences expressing how grateful and honored she was; thanked the crowd on behalf of Elvis, herself, and our family; and came to stand next to me with an air of relief. I handed her the albums and then put my arms around her as she smiled shyly at the crowd. We were both brimming with emotion. All I could think of was how proud Elvis would have been of the evening, of the honor, and, most of all, of his baby girl.

Three weeks later, on February 1, Lisa officially came of age. I was not involved in the financial transfer that took place; that was handled by Lisa's attorney and by her business manager, Barry Siegel. It was essential for me to stay out of Lisa's financial affairs. I was her mother, not her business manager. It is never a good idea to confuse those two roles. I don't know exactly how much she inherited, but suffice it to say, Lisa became a very rich woman.

I will admit that I was a little concerned about how Lisa's windfall would affect her. For one thing, expecting a twenty-something woman to handle a huge influx of cash isn't entirely realistic. Lisa had always been impulsive and changeable; she wasn't a planner. She did things on the spur of the moment. I could only hope she was getting good financial advice and would follow it. But most of all, I worried that her sudden wealth could make Lisa a target. She was already vulnerable to predators because of who her father was. With her inheritance, she went from being Elvis Presley's daughter to Elvis Presley's wealthy heir. I kept my thoughts to myself, but I worried.

In retrospect, Lisa's change in fortune seems like the beginning of a whole new life. It was not, however, the life I would have chosen for her. There had always been an economic disparity between Lisa and Danny—what was once called a difference in station. Lisa was the daughter of a man who is sometimes called American royalty. Her family had money and fame. That situation hadn't mattered when Danny and Lisa had met. They were young, just starting their life journeys. At the time, Danny had career aspirations of his own. He was a talented musician who had a good work ethic and who painted houses on the side. But he had no desire to spend his life painting houses. He worked as a house musician at Mad Hatter Studios in LA and played guitar with an up-and-coming band. As the band did more and more gigs, though, there was a problem. Lisa would go with him and see the pretty girls competing for Danny's attention. He was handsome, and the girls noticed. Having grown up watching girls throw themselves at her father, she knew it was one of the things that had broken up our marriage. She was eaten up with jealousy.

Marrying Danny was, in part, her way of telling the girls to keep away. But of course, they didn't. Just when success was in reach for Danny, Lisa asked him to quit the band. She didn't want him to travel anymore. Danny, who would have done anything to make her happy, reluctantly agreed. The decision was the beginning of the end for them. Losing his livelihood is difficult for a man; losing his calling is even harder. Leaving the band meant leaving his dreams behind. I don't think Danny ever got over it, but he remained committed to Lisa and the children despite his disappointment.

Inevitably, giving up his music created an even bigger gap between them. Now Danny had no job and no income. Lisa's inheritance was the breaking point. As Lisa herself put it, referring to Danny in a *Marie Claire* interview years later, it is hard for a man to be with a woman who is wealthier and stronger than he is. I'm not sure anyone was stronger than Lisa, and she was certainly wealthier. She wanted to be with a man who was on the same level she was. In the spring of 1994, she divorced Danny. Three weeks later, on May 26, 1994, she married Michael Jackson in a secret ceremony in the Dominican Republic. She told me it was happening, but I was clearly not invited. My lack of enthusiasm was obvious.

When she said she was marrying Michael, all I said was, "*Really?*"

I was appalled by the marriage. I knew in my bones that Michael wasn't marrying Lisa Marie; he was marrying the Presley dynasty. The King of Pop was allying himself with the King of Rock and Roll. I didn't believe he loved her. He married her at a time when he desperately needed good publicity that depicted him as a desirable heterosexual man. It was one thing to legally fight the child molestation charges against him. There was no way to come out of that looking good. But photos of him with Elvis's daughter wearing the huge diamond engagement ring he'd had made for her? That image was pure gold.

I said to Lisa, "You know Michael's a huge fan of your dad's. Did you ever think about the fact that now he's married to Elvis Presley's daughter?"

She replied, "Oh Mom, come on. You worry too much."

I said, "Yeah, I do. I do worry. I don't want you being used."

I had met Michael Jackson before, of course. Lisa had first met him in Las Vegas as a child and reconnected years later. He was ten years older than she was, the same age difference there had been between Elvis and me. Michael had started reaching out to her when the child abuse charges went public. I think that's how he hooked her in the beginning. She felt sorry for him, and naturally, she believed in his innocence. Nobody wants to believe those kinds of allegations against someone they know. They began talking on the phone regularly, and she was gradually drawn in. Michael was a manipulative man, and I think he had his sights set on her long before she realized it. The childlike innocence he projected was part of his public mask. She learned this early on, and it bothered her, but she didn't see it for the warning sign it was.

My relationship with Michael was bizarre from the beginning. Not long after Lisa started dating him, she invited me to a party that he was attending at her house. She'd invited a group of people over to eat, and Michael was included. I thought it might be a good chance for me to get to know him a little and see if my concerns were valid. I was prepared to be pleasant, but he wanted nothing to do with me. He stayed as far away from me as possible. In fact, he stayed far away from all the adults.

The adults were sitting up near the house, and there was a field below where children were playing ball. Michael was down below, playing with them. The adults were all chitchatting away, watching them play, but he stayed away from everyone. I don't know if he didn't want to answer questions about the court cases or if he simply preferred playing with the children. I thought maybe he was just very shy. He had that reputation, of course, the childlike shyness and tiny voice. I watched him and tried to figure out what was going on. He was courting my daughter, and I wanted to know who he was as a person.

I asked Lisa, "Doesn't he talk?"

She said, "Yeah."

"In that little voice?"

"Yeah. Well, no, not when we're alone. Then he talks normally. He's different when it's just us. He acts, you know, normal. Not like he is the rest of the time."

I thought, *What?*

The news of their marriage leaked out the second week of August.

I found out when I heard the news helicopters circling my house. I called Lisa to say, "Is there something you want to tell me?"

The marriage went truly public, of course, at the MTV Video Music Awards, when Michael brought Lisa onstage and gave her the infamous passionate kiss. It was awkward and embarrassing, and no one was more uncomfortable with it than Lisa. I was angry with him for ambushing Lisa like that in public. When I asked her about it, she cringed.

He continued to go to great lengths to avoid me. My only actual contact with him was during an Elvis event in Memphis. I think it was a tribute concert. Michael showed up at Lisa's hotel unexpectedly, planning to sit with her at the concert, and his plans bothered me. His appearance was guaranteed to draw a great deal of attention, which would detract from the focus on honoring Elvis. It felt almost like another publicity stunt. I went by the hotel beforehand to meet up with Lisa and asked her where Michael was. She said he was in the other room. He didn't come out to greet me. A few minutes after I arrived, the door down the hall opened, and Michael popped out. He grabbed his hat off the table where he'd left it, sort of smiled, and then popped back in the room and shut the door. He said nothing to me on the way to the show. Lisa and I were appearing in the show, so there was no opportunity to talk to him when we arrived. Early the next morning, he was gone. That was the sum total of my direct interactions with my son-in-law during the marriage.

We were on vacation in Hawaii not long after they married when Lisa told me, "Mom, Michael wants us to have a child."

We were walking down the beach alone, and it was clear that Lisa wanted to talk.

I said, "I think it's too soon, Lisa. I don't think you should have a child with him."

She said, "What do you mean?"

I told her, "Well, you just got married. You need to work out the marriage first." I reminded her that she'd been with a lot of guys over the years and then broken up with them. I told her that I thought she needed to put some time in first and make sure the relationship worked out before bringing a child into it. I was privately wondering why the hurry. I didn't trust his motives. A child would be a proof of virility. And I couldn't help wondering if he wanted to have Elvis's grandchild.

"Michael says that if I don't want to have a baby, Debbie Rowe will have one with him."

Oh, boy. Big red flag. Thank God, Lisa agreed with me that it was better to wait.

I asked her if they had a physical relationship. Like so many people, I wasn't sure.

She said yeah. There was a pause, and then she said, "But I hardly ever see him, Mom."

I said, "What do you mean, you hardly ever see him?"

"I don't see him. He'll come for a couple of days, and then he leaves again. I don't know where he goes."

"Do you ask him where he's going?"

"Yeah. He just says he'll be back in a couple of days."

I thought that was odd, quite odd. It was a very strange relationship. He'd come and go for days at a time, and she was always wondering where he was. I don't think she ever found out.

Lisa was very unhappy. Michael was never around. She knew that sometimes when he was gone, he was at his ranch with the kids. It bothered her that he would rather be with them than with her. I think that eventually, the allegations ate away at her. Both of them were so famous, and Michael had such a huge fan base, that she felt as though they were constantly under a microscope. She didn't feel comfortable criticizing him publicly, because she would come out of it the culprit. Her words would spread like wildfire, and she was the one who would look bad.

Finally, she'd had enough. She called to tell me she wanted a divorce. She had begun to feel like the marriage was a setup. He didn't want to be with her; he wanted to be with Elvis Presley's daughter. If he'd wanted to be with her, he wouldn't have been gone for most of their marriage.

On January 18, 1996, Lisa filed for divorce. I could practically hear Elvis sigh with relief.

CHAPTER 10

Memories

Memories, pressed between the pages of my mind.
Memories sweeten through the ages just like wine.

Naming my son after ***The Guns of Navarone*** was a fortuitous choice because, from the beginning, he was a little pistol. Like his sister before him, he was the center of my life from the day he was born. Yes, I was busy with movies and perfumes and Elvis Presley Enterprises. But nothing has ever mattered to me more than my children. There is a reason **Mother** is the first word I chose to describe myself on my Instagram page.

Navarone always said that his first word was *flower*. I said his first word was *more* because he always wanted more food. He loved to eat. And no wonder, for he was introduced to good food early. Not that I cooked it. Eating something I cooked might have qualified as child abuse. Elvis could have told you that. But Navarone was surrounded by women who cooked well. Marta, his nanny, came in the mornings and made his breakfast. When my assistant, Vikki, or I picked him up from school, we always brought a snack that Vikki had prepared for him. Depending on the day, we brought everything from vegetables to salad to homemade madeleines. Sometimes, Vikki would fix little chicken legs or apple tarts. Whatever it was, Navarone happily gobbled it down. He wasn't picky like most kids are.

I sometimes brought him with me when I traveled, and the rule was, he always had to eat what they ate in that country. Even when he was little. He ate everything, even frog legs, because I never made a fuss about it. He would try something, and he usually liked it. If he was with another kid, they'd go, "Ewww..." Not Navarone. He has an international palate. If it's well prepared, he'll essentially eat anything. We had a little vegetable garden in the backyard when he was about three years old. Navarone would pull up the carrots and pick the tomatoes to eat. What kid loves vegetables? Mine did.

Because he was constantly surrounded by adults, he talked like one, even when he was little. Lisa, his only sibling, was nineteen years older than he was. At home, he was the only child. I still remember taking him to school for the first day of kindergarten. There was a little boy there named Joey, whose parents were also somewhat famous, and he was sitting at a table talking to another kindergartner. Navarone was so happy to see two other boys.

He ran up to them and said, "Hi! How was your day?"

The two boys looked at each other and then looked at him like he was from another planet. What five-year-old opens a conversation by saying "How was your day?" But that's what people said at home to express friendly interest. Adult people. It was too mature for Joey and his friend, so they turned away from him. Navarone was crushed. I didn't much like Joey after that. He was just a child, of course, but he had hurt my son, who was only trying to be friendly. Navarone had no idea that he didn't talk like a child. He spoke like a forty-year-old in a five-year-old's body.

He didn't like school. What child does? But he didn't hate it as much as his sister had. He stuck to it and got by. Vikki and I both saw to it that he did his homework.

Vikki would make him do his spelling words over and over until he'd complain, "Stop bugging me!"

It worked, though. He aced his spelling tests. Vikki still has a note from Navarone telling her he got an A because of her constant bugging. So he did all right academically. Lisa had to cope with unwanted attention at school because she was Elvis's daughter. Navarone had to deal with it because he was my son. The other kids didn't realize it at first, because he wasn't a Presley. But word got around, and kids—or their parents—would start seeking his attention because they wanted to meet me. He hated it and sometimes got into fights over it.

Just getting him to school could be an adventure. One day I was driving him to school when we saw a chicken in the road. (Apparently trying to cross it!) It was running around a busy Beverly Hills street, scared and confused, and I knew it was almost certain to get run over. Both Navarone and I are animal lovers, so I decided to try to get it to safety. I pulled over to the curb and got out just as the chicken cleared the street and went into an alley. I began chasing after it like a wild woman while it ran away from me. Can you imagine the pictures the paparazzi would have taken? I can just see the tabloid headline: "Priscilla Presley Running Around Like a Headless Chicken!" Navarone just watched. He didn't even try to help me. I never did catch that chicken. After a while, I gave up, and we went back to the car. I was feeling pretty proud of myself for trying to save the poor creature, but Navarone was unimpressed.

"It's just a chicken, Mommy."

Some animal lover.

Despite his dislike of academics, Navarone had a remarkable ability to learn languages. When he traveled with me, he quickly picked up the local phrases and began understanding some of what people were saying. He used to tell me that where he came from, they didn't speak the way people spoke at home. He liked to say that he was from a different planet, and he even created his own interplanetary language. My son could have entire conversations in this invented language, and if you didn't know better, you would think it was real. It sounded real. When he grew up and met his relatives in Brazil, he was speaking beautiful Portuguese within six months. His uncle couldn't believe it. "You speak like you were born here," he told Navarone.

Navarone was a happy-go-lucky child and a mischievous one. Very mischievous. He learned early how to push adults' buttons. He would lift up Vikki's and Marta's skirts and peer underneath. At first, it was curiosity, but it caused such a commotion that he did it again. Every time he did it, he would laugh gleefully. He pulled up little girls' skirts, too, just to make them mad. It's a wonder that none of the girls smacked him. It got so bad that Vikki and Marta had to stop wearing skirts around Navarone. Naturally, I tried to put a stop to it, but it was hard to get mad at him. He was a little bitty kid with a big grin and a twinkle in his eyes. Navarone was a different kind of troublemaker than his sister, but both of them were little scamps. Clearly, they got this impish trait from their fathers. I had been a well-behaved, eager-to-please child. At least that was the story I went with, and I'm sticking to it.

Navarone was also an independent child, and on one occasion, he scared me to death by going off on his own. He was only about four or five, and we were at Disneyland. I was buying souvenirs and had taken him into the store with me. I let go of his hand to pay, and when I looked down a moment later, he was gone. He had just disappeared.

I panicked. I started calling him, "Navarone! Navarone! Where are you?"

I was looking around, but he was nowhere in sight. By then I was crying, calling out, "Navarone! Oh my God! Somebody help me!"

A hundred things flashed through my head—he had gotten lost, he had been kidnapped. Kidnapping was always a fear for me with both of my children. Navarone wasn't a target like Lisa had been, but I was. I represented a potential ransom.

He wasn't in the store, so I ran outside and started looking down the street. It was crowded with clusters of people, and all I could see were tourists and Disney characters. Finally, I spotted a small, curly head about a block away. There he was, weaving calmly through the crowds as if he did it every day. It was pure luck that I saw him. I ran after him and grabbed him up in my arms. I don't think I had ever been that frightened in my life.

I held him tight, then looked intently into his face and said, "Don't ever do that again! Don't ever do that! You scared Mommy!" I didn't want to make him feel bad, but I wanted him to understand that without me, he might not be safe. I think he understood, as he never did it again.

After that, I didn't take him with me in public unless I surrounded him with people. Vikki, Marta, or my sister would go with me, and we would hold hands with Navarone. If I let go of his hand for a moment, someone else would be holding the other one. The little stinker. I don't think he ever realized how much he'd scared me.

Getting him dressed every day was a challenge. Like Lisa at Graceland when she was little, if he wasn't in the mood to get dressed, he balked. He wanted to wear his pajamas and slipper socks all the time. Once, he stubbornly refused to cooperate, and I took him to school in his pajamas. I thought it would teach him a lesson, but his attire didn't embarrass him a bit. Online, there are still paparazzi photos of me carrying Navarone on a shopping trip, dressed in his pj's and slippers. Vikki came up with a solution that worked some of the time. She would put his clothes in the dryer to warm them up before we got him dressed. He liked the feel of warm clothing, especially in chilly weather, and would usually put them on willingly. They had to be comfortable, though. Unlike his father, who liked to be dressed to the nines, Navarone would only wear comfortable clothes.

He adored Vikki and Marta. If I left him alone in the playroom when he was little, he would immediately start calling, "Wiki! Tata!"—his nicknames for them. It was hard for them to get anything done, because he wanted them there constantly as his playmates.

When it was time for Marta or Vikki to leave, he never wanted them to go.

He would ask, "Can you stay extra? Can you stay?" He didn't see them as my employees. To him, they were playmates and unofficial aunties. He loved them, and they loved him back. For grown women, they were remarkably good playmates.

He loved to wear costumes. What an imagination that boy had! He would glue beads on T-shirts so he could pretend to be a Native American. And he loved to dress up like a cowboy, complete with a cowboy hat and pistols. He took the role-playing very seriously. I had a place in Montecito, California, at the time, and we would go walking together around the nearby Montecito Ranch. Navarone liked to dress like a cowboy when we went there. There was a path around the ranch where you could walk or ride horses, and we would walk down the path and watch the horses go by.

One day I asked him, "Navarone, what do you think of the place?"

He looked up at me and said, "Shh! Cowboys don't talk!"

If it wasn't a cowboy, he would dress up like a Ninja Turtle or a pirate and act out the role. He loved to play make-believe.

Sometimes he'd climb the neighbors' wall and call out, "Mommy, Wiki, Tata, guess where I am! I'm in El Salvador!" Marta was from El Salvador and had told him stories about it.

He especially liked acting out movies. One of his favorites was *The Princess Bride*. We watched that over and over, and he liked to play the six-fingered man. And he loved *The Wizard of Oz*.

He'd pretend to be the Cowardly Lion and say, "Put 'em up! Put 'em up!"

I would pretend to be the Scarecrow. One time, Vikki played the Wicked Witch of the West. He acted out the whole last scene with her, complete with throwing her on the grass and dumping a bucket of water on her. She is a very patient woman.

Halloween was a special favorite. We would decorate the ceiling of his room with spiderwebs. We had a big party for him on the tennis court once. I would go trick-or-treating with him, too, for nobody recognized me in costume. One year, we went as mad scientists. I had fake blood all over my face. And we didn't have to worry about paparazzi. Vikki was the only one there taking pictures.

Navarone was so active. Lisa had never been very active. She swam in the pool at home, but she never did sports. Navarone loved sports. He went to the batting cage in Sherman Oaks, about half an hour's drive from our house. And I took him to Lake Arrowhead in the San Bernardino mountains for his soccer games. I had a house there in a gated property with only six homes, so it was very safe for Navarone to play there. Some of my neighbors had kids he could play with. There was a baseball field on the property, and he and the neighborhood kids played all the time. He also joined a soccer team while we were there. I made sure he didn't miss his games. Even if we were back home in Beverly Hills, I drove him up for his games. I also put him in karate lessons with Jenny Lee, his best friend, so he could learn the sport that Elvis and I had loved. The constant activities burned off a lot of his energy.

I did things I would never have done without him. When he was about eight years old, I took him, his cousins, and a couple of his friends to the Grand Canyon for a river rafting trip. Of all the many places I've been, the Grand Canyon is one of the most amazing. Photos don't do it justice. It's **huge**, almost two thousand square miles. The pale orange and sandstone cliffs tower above the Colorado River, which flows almost a mile below the canyon rim. The river itself flows for almost three hundred miles. The canyon is truly awe-inspiring. It's hard to believe a river could carve out something that big. The river alternates between a steady current and white-water rapids, and I'll admit, I had some doubts about going down it in a raft full of kids. We had a guide, of course, to steer the raft and tell us about what we saw along the way. I knew we were in good hands, but still...Yikes! It really was one of the adventures of a lifetime. We were exhilarated going down the river and relieved to arrive safely back at the campsite. It wasn't often that Navarone got as filthy as he got that day. So did the other kids. So did I.

Being Navarone's mom was an adventure. I got drawn into situations I would never have imagined. Navarone loved living creatures. So did I, and I'd encountered a lot of them on *Those Amazing Animals*. But whereas I was drawn to dogs and horses, he was fascinated by bugs and reptiles. Just what every mother wants in her house. We had a bug box that he kept in his room, and we used a magnifying glass to check on the insects.

Navarone loved insects, but reptiles were his favorite. I got a reptile tank for his room, and he filled it with frogs, lizards, and snakes. His first lizard was a small one that he named Susie. I hadn't yet learned that much about reptiles, so I'd had the tank put in a sunny area. It was a mistake. The light made the tank far too hot, and Susie's tail fried. The poor thing died. Navarone was heartbroken. When he got his first iguana, he named it Iggy. Marta would tell him stories about her and Andreas (Marta's husband) growing up in El Salvador, where they eat iguanas. This terrified Navarone.

He told us, "Don't let Andreas come in the house! He's going to eat Iggy!"

Navarone had a little garden snake that he'd found in the yard, and one day, the snake got away while he was at school. It was dead when we found it. We didn't have the heart to tell him his snake had died. So Vikki, Marta, and I went hunting through the yard, crawling around and searching through bushes and other plants. What I wouldn't do for my son. Finally, we found another snake in a bush. It was about the same size, so we put it in the tank with the other reptiles. Thank God, Navarone didn't notice the switch.

And then there were the "fire belly frogs," which Vikki was squeamish about.

One afternoon after school, Navarone told her, "Vikki, close your eyes and put out your hands." And he filled them with fire belly frogs.

Making my first dog rescue at age five, 1950. *Photo courtesy of Priscilla Presley's personal collection*

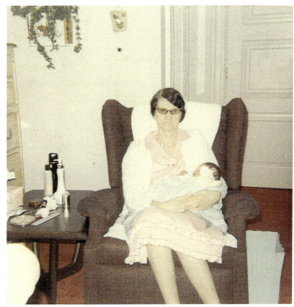

Grandma Minnie Mae with newborn Lisa Marie in her bedroom at Graceland, 1968. *Photo courtesy of Priscilla Presley's personal collection*

Elvis and me in the den at Graceland, holding newborn Lisa Marie, 1968. *Photo courtesy of Priscilla Presley's personal collection*

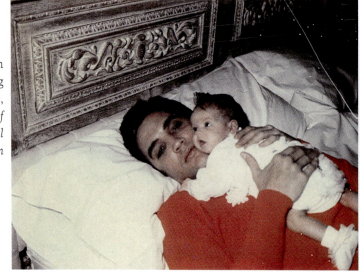

Elvis in our bedroom at Graceland, cuddling newborn Lisa Marie, 1968. *Photo courtesy of Priscilla Presley's personal collection*

Lisa with Snoopy and Brutus, her personal canine statues. *Photo courtesy of Priscilla Presley's personal collection*

Bathing beauty. *Photo courtesy of Priscilla Presley's personal collection*

Lisa Marie's first birthday party, at our home in LA, 1969. *Photo courtesy of Priscilla Presley's personal collection*

Born to be wild—Lisa Marie on my motorcycle, 1970. *Photo courtesy of Priscilla Presley's personal collection*

Elvis "helping" Lisa Marie hunt for Easter eggs at our LA home, 1972. *Photo courtesy of Priscilla Presley's personal collection*

Mirror images—Lisa and me posing at home in LA, 1972. *Photo courtesy of Priscilla Presley's personal collection*

Lisa and me in Bis and Beau mother-daughter outfits, 1973. *Photo courtesy of Priscilla Presley's personal collection*

Lisa Marie in Paris on our trip abroad following Elvis's passing, 1977. *Photo courtesy of Priscilla Presley's personal collection*

Snuggling with my girl in Grandma's room at Graceland, 1979. *Photo courtesy of Priscilla Presley's personal collection*

Me and Lisa celebrating Christmas at home, 1981. *Photo courtesy of Priscilla Presley's personal collection*

Lisa and me at my sister Michelle's condo, 1984. *Photo courtesy of Priscilla Presley's personal collection*

Four generations of Iversen women: Michelle, Mom, our grandmother, me, and Lisa, 1986. *Photo courtesy of Priscilla Presley's personal collection*

Lisa and me rocking the babies, Navarone and Riley, 1989. *Photo courtesy of Priscilla Presley's personal collection*

Baby Riley playing with Uncle Navarone, 1990. *Photo courtesy of Priscilla Presley's personal collection*

Me and three-year-old Navarone, 1991. *Photo courtesy of Berne Boehm*

Family love—Navarone kissing Riley, 1990. *Photo courtesy of Priscilla Presley's personal collection*

All he wants for Christmas is his four front teeth, 1993. *Photo courtesy of Priscilla Presley's personal collection*

Navarone visiting Colonel Parker at his house in Palm Springs, 1993. *Photo courtesy of Priscilla Presley's personal collection*

On one of my adventures with Navarone, 1998. *Photo courtesy of Priscilla Presley's personal collection*

On vacation in Hawaii with Navarone, 2002. *Photo courtesy of Priscilla Presley's personal collection*

Riley, Lisa, me, and Benjamin in Tokyo, 2004. *Photo courtesy of Priscilla Presley's personal collection*

Riley, Lisa, me, and my beautiful mother, 2006. *Photo courtesy of Priscilla Presley's personal collection*

With Navarone, Lisa, and the newborn twins, 2008. *Photo courtesy of Christopher Ameruoso*

With my son, the snake whisperer, 2014. *Photo courtesy of Christopher Ameruoso*

Trick or treating with Harper and Finley, 2016. *Photo courtesy of Christopher Ameruoso*

Navarone preparing for a show with his band, 2019.
Photo courtesy of Christopher Ameruoso

With Navarone and Riley at my surprise birthday party, 2024.
Photo courtesy of Christopher Ameruoso

My family: Michael Lockwood, Danny Keough, Finley, me, Riley, and Harper, 2024. *Photo courtesy of Christopher Ameruoso*

Me and Ridley at home with my collaborator, Mary Jane Ross, 2025. *Photo courtesy of Christopher Ameruoso*

She jumped out of her skin and dropped them on the floor. He loved to get a big reaction, and he knew exactly which of his pet reptiles people were afraid of. He never outgrew this prank. To this day, if you go to his house, he might surprise you by putting a snake on your head. He's done it to me. He thinks it's hilarious.

He has always loved geckos. When we went to Hawaii on vacation, he went around outside, collecting geckos. Geckos are relatively small lizards, and they have feet like suction cups. Soon the walls and ceiling of the place I was renting were covered with geckos. While I was packing to go home to LA, there were geckos everywhere. I couldn't reach any of them. I kept thinking about the guests who were checking in after us. What would they do when they found a ceiling covered with lizards? And what would the management say? It's not like I'd paid a gecko deposit!

His favorite reptile was the water monitor. These large lizards look a little like alligators. They are very small when they're born, but the problem is, they grow to be huge. They're the second-largest lizard species in the world, reaching seven feet long or more. Navarone carried his water monitor everywhere, like you might carry a puppy, but as they both grew over the years, he would drape the thing around his neck. He tried to drape it around my neck, but I wasn't having it. Water monitors put us into a whole new category of pet owners. We had gone from a bug box to a tank in his room, to a bigger tank in his room, and now we had the equivalent of a baby alligator. No tank would hold it as it grew, and I wasn't willing to have a water monitor habitat in my house. So I moved it to the big dog run by the side of the house. During good weather, when it was just the family, we'd let it out, where it would lounge happily by the pool, taking a dip whenever it wanted to. When guests came or the weather got cold, we'd put it back in the cage.

Navarone was a joyous child, an adventurous spirit who thoroughly enjoyed life. Part of the reason was his nature: He was born happy and mischievous. Part of the reason was the environment he grew up in, surrounded by loving adults who encouraged his interests—even when those interests were reptilian. But an important part of the reason was that, unlike his sister, he did not grow up in the public eye. I carefully avoided taking him places where there might be paparazzi. Much of the public didn't realize he existed. All the attention went to Lisa Marie because she was Elvis's daughter and a dead ringer for him. I couldn't protect her from that reality. But people had never heard of Navarone's father, and except for his eyes, Navarone didn't look like me. We could be seen together without people realizing he was my son.

Most of all, Navarone was kind. I sometimes took him to New York at Christmastime to see the decorations and go shopping. One Christmas when he was about five, we were walking toward a toy store when he noticed a man on the sidewalk. The man looked poor and tattered, and Navarone noticed him immediately. My son had never seen someone like that before, propped up against the wall as people walked by. You don't see that in Beverly Hills. A man walking ahead of us stopped when he saw the man, dug into his pocket for change, and gave the man some money. Navarone had stopped walking as well and stood there watching, taking in the situation with a serious look on his face. Then he reached into his own pocket. I had given him a five-dollar bill so he could buy himself a treat or a small toy, and he was excited to have his own money. He looked at the money for a moment, then walked over and handed it to the man before taking my hand again. My heart swelled as I watched my son's act of kindness.

Navarone was more outgoing and gregarious than Lisa had ever been, and he made friends easily. His ability to make friends was hard on Lisa. When Navarone was born, Lisa adored him at first. He was a cute little baby, and she loved being his sister. But as he got older, things gradually changed. By the time he was seven or eight, she regarded him as competition. She accused me of loving him more than her, which, of course, wasn't true. I don't look that way at my babies, my children. She resented the time I spent with him. He was at the age when kids demand a lot of time: taking him to school, picking him up, taking him to soccer and baseball, going to all the places kids that age go. I took him and his cousins and friends to Disneyland and Knott's Berry Farm—all the places I'd taken Lisa Marie as a kid. The problem was, she didn't remember much of that. She was always peppering me with resentful questions.

"Did you take *me* to school?"

"Yes, unless I was working."

"Did you pick me up?"

"Yes, unless I was working. Remember, we used to get ice cream after school."

"You're always taking him to Disneyland."

"I took you, too. Lots of times. Don't you remember?"

And so on and so on. It became exhausting. I knew she'd always been possessive of me, and I was sorry she felt threatened by Navarone. But there was nothing I could do about it. They were both my children. Besides, she was an adult. It's not like they were siblings living at home and fighting over their room. Lisa was almost twenty years older than Navarone. She had her own life and her own children.

Despite the bumps in the road, Lisa and I remained close. In August 1997, the two of us prepared to go to Memphis for a solemn yet joyous gathering. August 16 of that year was the twentieth anniversary of Elvis's passing. He would have been sixty-two. The gathering was a marriage of two traditions. The first was the annual candlelight vigil at Graceland, a moving ceremony that had originated with Elvis's fans. On the first anniversary of his death, a large crowd of mourners had spontaneously shown up at night to commemorate his passing, many of them carrying lights. Our family was amazed and deeply moved by their demonstration of loyalty and love. Since that first year, the tradition has grown beyond the original candlelight vigil. It continues to this day, with nearly a week dedicated to Elvis's remembrance. The other, newer tradition was made possible by the technological advances that had occurred since his passing. Technicians were now able to separate the background noise from Elvis's concert vocals and produce videos of Elvis in a performance that evoked the original concerts. For the twentieth anniversary tribute, a small army of musicians and technicians put together footage for a virtual concert in his honor. It would be the highlight of the annual remembrance.

The concert took place in the Mid-South Coliseum in Memphis, known as the "Entertainment Capital of the Mid-South." The venue, which seats ten thousand people, sold out almost immediately. The concept was unique and compelling. Elvis's concert images and vocals would be combined with a live orchestra and singers. Nearly all the remaining members of Elvis's band and backup singers would be performing. We had even booked Al Dvorin, Elvis's former announcer, to end the evening by announcing over the PA, "Elvis has left the building." It was a huge and thrilling undertaking, and it could not have gone off better despite the intricate performance challenges.

The opening was dramatic. The arena was pitch black, with searchlights overhead, as the orchestra began to play "If I Can Dream," followed by the theme from *2001: A Space Odyssey*, which opened all of Elvis's concerts. The effect was electric. When the curtain came up, Elvis's image flickered onto three huge screens in the darkness, with a full array of performers filling the stage. The illusion was amazing. Elvis would be on-screen talking to his musicians by name, and as he introduced them, they would stand onstage in real life and acknowledge Elvis. The longer the concert went on, the more the past and present blended so seamlessly that it felt like a live performance. Even I was caught up in the illusion.

Lisa and I were there to close out the concert. As the video flickered out, I walked to center stage and thanked the audience for coming, telling them that Lisa and I had been looking forward to this evening for months. I told them that of all his accomplishments, Elvis's proudest one was not his performances, but his daughter. Lisa had spent the weeks before the concert working on an original idea to show her appreciation to the fans for their years of devotion to her father. Then I left the stage and stood in the wings as yet another video filled the screen behind me.

Once again, Elvis's image flickered into sight, this time singing "Don't Cry, Daddy." As Elvis came to the end of the first verse, a new image appeared on-screen—Lisa Marie, singing the chorus. She was dressed in a loose white shirt that mirrored Elvis's white costume. As she began the next stanza, Elvis's image returned, his voice now blended with Lisa's in a duet. This time, though, the video was interspersed with family pictures of Elvis, baby Lisa, and me. It was the first time Lisa had sung in public, and as I watched her sing with her father, I was overwhelmed with emotion. In that moment, I could feel him there with us, still present in the darkness. As the song ended, the virtual Lisa threw back her head and smiled with such joy that it was tangible.

Then the real Lisa, my beautiful daughter, walked onstage as the lights came up, head held high, and thanked the audience for their dedication to her father's memory for so many years. Afterward she walked back across the stage and held her hand out to me, where I was waiting by the stairs. She led me onstage as the audience's love washed over us. A few moments later, our arms encircling each other, we walked back into the darkness together as Elvis's voice filled the arena one last time: *Memories sweeten through the ages just like wine...*

CHAPTER 11
Leaving Las Vegas

Go on dry your eyes
You know that I've forgiven you and I'm sorry

Call it destiny or genetics, Lisa Marie was born to be a musician. I knew it from the time she was a child. She would listen to music for hours in her room. It was her solace. Sometimes she'd crank up the volume and lip-sync to a song. Other times she'd sing along with it. By the time she was eleven or twelve, she was practicing songs in front of the mirror. If I walked by her room and she saw me, she would immediately become shy and stop singing. I would smile or say "Nice" but keep going. I didn't want to make a fuss encouraging her, but I didn't want to discourage her, either, so I kept my mouth shut. She knew the stakes were high for her because she was Elvis's daughter. Terrified of failure, she was afraid she would embarrass herself. If Lisa was going to be a musician, she had to find that path on her own.

Eventually, she did. By the time she was eighteen or nineteen, she was singing more often and learning to play the guitar. I think being with Danny, who was a talented musician himself, was a big part of that. By her early twenties, she was writing songs. She didn't share much about it, and I didn't intrude. It all had to be in her own good time.

The turning point was the duet with her father that she videotaped for the virtual concert. I think that debuting with a videotape, instead of singing live onstage, was less intimidating for her. Most of all, however, I believe that singing with her father gave her courage. Elvis was gone physically, but he was very much present spiritually when she recorded her first duet with him. The images of him on the screen, the sound of his voice, the photos of him smiling at her—all these things contributed to the illusion that she wasn't singing alone. He was there with her. And in a sense, he was.

She wouldn't let anyone, including me, see the duet while she was rehearsing it. She didn't want me to see it until it was perfect. When I saw it for the first time with her, I was blown away. It was so beautiful—beautifully felt, beautifully delivered. Like her father had, she was living the song, not just singing it. Hearing the duet was very emotional for me. It brought tears to my eyes that first time. It was so rewarding to have her share the song with me. I'd been waiting for that for years, waiting for her to break out. I felt like she was finally doing what she was meant to do. She was so talented. I hoped it would be only the beginning of a career in music, and it was.

Five years later, in 2003, her first album debuted. I knew she was writing music for an album and that it was autobiographical. It was in a very real sense Lisa Marie's coming-out party. After years of avoiding the press and hearing tabloid stories about herself, she was ready to say, "This is me. This record is me." She wanted the public to finally see who she really was, not who others claimed she was. Lisa liked honest, sometimes dark music that communicated the truth about the human soul. This was the truth about her soul. She wrote or cowrote everything on the album, including the liner notes.

Some of the songs were about her father. "Nobody Noticed" is about her love for Elvis and her resemblance to him:

> *You made me. I love you and*
> *Did you know nothing has changed*
> *And now everyone they notice it*
> *Everyone notices.*

The standout track, "Lights Out," about Elvis's passing, is also a chillingly prophetic song about her own mortality:

> *Someone turned the lights out there in Memphis.*
> *That's where my family's buried and gone.*
> *Last time I was there I noticed a space left*
> *Next to them there in Memphis in the damn back lawn.*

Not all of the songs are sad or angry. "So Lovely" is a love song written for "her sweet little babies," Riley and Benjamin. The album is raw and edgy, obscene and tender, powerful and evocative. In other words, the album is the conundrum that was Lisa Marie. She references herself on the album as LMFP, and the tape on her tambourine identifies her that way. When she did *Late Night with Conan O'Brien* as part of the publicity tour for the album, Conan asked what the initials meant.

She immediately became shy and asked, "Can I say this on air?" Then Lisa rather sheepishly answered the question: "Lisa Marie F***ing Presley."

Conan comically cringed, saying, "No, you can't say that on the air!" It was bleeped out. Yep, that was my daughter.

Lisa was very worried about performing in her first big concert, scheduled at the Rose Bowl on May 17, 2003. She was one of a long list of performers at Wango Tango, a wildly popular daylong concert sponsored by radio station KIIS-FM, which is iconic in LA. That year, the lineup included Kiss, Sting, and Santana, so Lisa would be performing with some real heavyweights. She was very anxious. I wanted to watch her rehearse, but she wouldn't let me. She told me it would make her even more nervous. I told her I understood. I'm the same way. I don't like anyone seeing me rehearsing. That's the time to test things out, to make mistakes, to improve. She wanted it to be perfect before I saw it, and I think she also wanted to surprise me.

She told me, "Mom, I'm really nervous."

I reassured her, "You got it. You got it, girl. You're going to be amazing. Don't be nervous."

She said, "I know, I know." I wanted so much to support her through it, to ease her fears, but of course, she didn't entirely believe me. After all, I was her mother. Maybe so, but I was certain she would step up when the time came. Or as Lisa would have put it, she had the balls to come through when it counted.

And she did. When the time finally arrived late that afternoon, she came on like the powerhouse she was. With her denim vest and violet-streaked hair, she looked like a rock star. Her voice was strong and sultry singing "Lights Out," her body moving as she sang, feeling every poignant, ironic lyric. And I was blown away. Tears filled my eyes as I watched her overcome her anxiety and sing like she was born to. The audience loved it, and as they cheered at the end, she looked directly at me and gave me a big smile. She had taken an important step forward on her chosen path, and she knew it.

Afterward, she kept saying, "I'm so glad it's over. I'm so glad it's over."

And I kept telling her, "You did amazing. You were amazing."

She said, "Yeah, but you're my mom."

I told her, "You did a great job, Lisa. Look at the audience. They loved you. I'm so proud of you. I'm *so* proud of you."

I think going onstage got a little easier after that. Having a successful first show helped. But she never completely got over her stage fright. She was always nervous before she went on. She wanted me to go on tour with her for company and moral support, and when I could, I went. It was so rewarding to sit in the audience and watch my daughter pursuing her dream.

Her second album, *Now What*, came out two years later. By then she was a full-time musician, and her life centered on writing, recording, and touring (and always, of course, her children). She cowrote all but one of the songs, writing several with Linda Perry. Most of the songs were, like her first album, autobiographical. One day, Lisa told me that she was writing a song about me. I was a little anxious. Would it be about our struggles, or would it be about our love for one another? As it turned out, it was about both. When she was satisfied she'd gotten it right, she played it for me. The title was "Raven," and it told the story of our journey together:

> *Hold your head up high,*
> *I know that I've been ruthless*
> *I've been ruthless.*
> *Go on dry your eyes*
> *You know that I've forgiven you and I'm sorry*
> *And everything till now*
> *It wasn't that bad really*
> *Beautiful lady...*
> *And you'll finally be okay with me*
> *And I'll hear your stories*
> *That fill your sad eyes*
> *When you had raven hair...*

I was so touched. Her honesty and the bond we shared despite the struggles shone through. By the time she finished, I was in tears.

My daughter often came across in her music as dark and brooding, but there was another side to her. In some respects, she was the eternal optimist. After her disastrous marriage to Michael Jackson, she focused on raising her children, and though she dated, she kept it casual at first. But in the summer of 2001, that changed. She met Nicolas Cage, and their meeting was like a clap of thunder. She had recently gotten engaged to musician-songwriter John Oszajca, and Nick was still married to his estranged wife, Patricia Arquette. But those relationships went out the window when Nick and Lisa set eyes on each other at Johnny Ramone's birthday party. Nick described his reaction to seeing Lisa as life-changing. The world stopped spinning, and there was no going back for him. Within a short time, both of them had left their exes in the dust. Lisa was all in. The two of them had tremendous chemistry.

They also had a great deal in common. Both came from famous show business families. Nick's real last name is Coppola; he is the nephew of iconic director Francis Ford Coppola. With the Coppola name proving a liability when Nick started his acting career, he changed his professional name to Nicolas Cage. He and Lisa knew what it was like to continually be judged by a family name. Nick also fit Lisa's image of a man who was on the same level she was. He was successful in his own right, and heaven knows, he was strong enough for her, as would soon become apparent.

I liked Nicolas Cage from the beginning. Despite his stormy temper (which my daughter shared), he has a good heart and a great capacity for love. He faced considerable opposition in the media when he first fell for Lisa. Because he was an Elvis fan who had gained critical acclaim with the film *Leaving Las Vegas*, people assumed he was with Lisa because she was a Presley. *Honeymoon in Vegas*, where he briefly played an Elvis impersonator, only made the rumors worse. Ridiculous stories filled the tabloids about Nick's supposed Elvis obsession. If you got to know him, though, it was clear that the stories were fabrications. After the Michael Jackson marriage, I was particularly sensitive to men pursuing Lisa because she was Elvis's daughter. But I never got that sense with Nick. He was clearly and passionately in love with Lisa.

Unfortunately, the kinetic attraction that drew them together also made it difficult for them to stay together. They were not only romantically passionate but also passionate, period. Lisa had inherited Elvis's temper along with his good looks, and Nicolas could match her in a fight toe to toe. And oh my gosh, how they fought. They screamed and they yelled, they threw things, and sometimes they broke things. They broke up. And the next day, or pretty close to it, they made up. Lisa and Nick broke up and made up so many times, it was dizzying. The relationship was like the old saying about the little girl who had a little curl, right in the middle of her forehead. When it was good, it was very, very good. And when it was bad, it was horrid. Their solution to the chaos and instability in their relationship? They decided to get married. Oh, boy.

Nick presented her with a six-carat, $65,000 diamond ring. It was stunning, but it didn't last long. One afternoon, they went sailing off the coast of Catalina Island on Nick's yacht, the *Weston*. Something set off another of their epic fights, and Lisa pulled off her engagement ring and threw it at Nick. Furious, Nick threw the ring overboard. Almost as soon as the ring hit the water, Nick went into panic mode and hired divers to try to find it. A thorough search of the ocean floor resulted in nothing.

As far as I know, the ring is still there. So what did Nicolas do? Two days later, he bought Lisa an even bigger diamond (ten carats), and they got engaged all over again.

Watching the relationship was like watching a soap opera. I was not surprised when they proceeded with plans for their wedding. Though I had little hope that the marriage would last, I did my best to be optimistic. The wedding was a small family-and-friends affair at the Mauna Lani Bay Hotel on the Big Island of Hawaii. It took place on August 10, 2002, six days before the twenty-fifth anniversary of Elvis's death. Her third wedding, and again no father to walk her down the aisle. My father did the honors, escorting her down an outdoor path to where Nicolas waited. Riley and Benjamin were both attendants. Lisa looked beautiful in a traditional wedding dress with a long train and a white flower garland in her hair. We all embraced them and hoped for the best.

Three months later, Nicolas filed for divorce. Lisa called to tell me it was happening. She later described their relationship by saying she and Nick were like tyrannical pirates. When one pirate marries another, they sink the ship. It was an apt description. Though their parting was tumultuous and hard on both of them, they got past the initial trauma and remained friends. Nick later told Barbara Walters that he still missed Lisa every day, but if they got back together, things would end the same way. They were better off as friends. I think they both gained a little wisdom from the relationship.

Meanwhile, Navarone was growing up. Outwardly, things didn't seem to change. Navarone got taller, and the snakes got bigger, and the water monitor looked like an alligator, but

Leaving Las Vegas | **163**

Navarone remained my sweet boy. What I didn't know was that when he started high school, he began experimenting with drugs. I knew it was likely he would try pot. Many of the people I knew used it recreationally, and though I didn't use it myself, it was part of the environment he grew up in. Celebrity kids kind of took it for granted. But it didn't occur to me that he would try anything else.

Given my antidrug activism as both my children were growing up, it was ironic that both of them developed an unhealthy relationship with drugs. I think their reasons were a little different. Lisa turned to drugs out of angst and rebellion. She didn't fit in. She felt different from other kids, and drugs were a refuge. Navarone, on the other hand, was outgoing and adventurous. He was the kid who would try any food and get into everything. When his friends tried drugs, he wanted to try them, too. Both Lisa and Navarone knew I was adamantly opposed to drugs because of my experiences with Elvis. But instead of stopping my children from using, that knowledge just made them good at hiding what they were doing. They knew I would be angry and deeply worried if I found out. So they went to great lengths to keep me in the dark. Navarone knew I had no clue he was experimenting with heroin by the time he was fifteen. He intended to keep it that way, and for a long time, he did.

I also think that, like his sister, he struggled with the family legacy when he reached his teens. Our family was divided into Presleys and non-Presleys, and he wasn't a Presley. He didn't want to be, but he still felt the pressure. Though he kept out of the spotlight, he was acutely aware that Lisa and I were in it. It was odd for him to know that Lisa was publicly perceived as an only child. People were always surprised to learn I had a son. On the rare occasions that we were in a public setting with Lisa, everyone gravitated to her. They didn't even notice Navarone. Sometimes I would go stand next to him to demonstrate that he was with me, and he would reassure me.

"It's okay, Mom. You don't have to stand here. I know I'm your son. It doesn't bother me what other people think."

But I think it did bother him. He and Lisa had opposite ends of the same stick, and it was hard on both of them.

I was careful not to bring Elvis up at home while I was living with a man. And I rarely played his music if other people were around. It often triggered emotions for me, and I usually played it when I was alone. But I remained a public figure who personified the Elvis legacy. I was actively involved in Elvis Presley Enterprises. I made public appearances at Elvis legacy events. I was most decidedly a Presley. Navarone had to deal with people who befriended him in an effort to get to me. He always knew how deeply I loved him and that being his mom was one of the two great joys of my life. But still, it was sometimes hard for him.

In 2005, our family had a personal and financial crisis. Lisa had never been very good at handling money, and twelve years after coming into her inheritance, she was broke. I was pretty sure that she wasn't receiving good financial advice, but I couldn't do anything about it. And talking to her about it was very, very delicate. What I didn't see coming was her solution to the problem. In August of that year, she sold 85 percent of her inheritance, including Graceland. She would retain the mansion and grounds, as well as Elvis's personal effects within the house, but she would no longer have control of Elvis's legacy. I was devastated. I thought it was a bad financial decision, because Graceland and Elvis Presley Enterprises generated ongoing income for her. But more important, I felt gutted to lose what was still my emotional home, not to mention losing control of Elvis's legacy. I was heartbroken.

I had poured so much of my heart and energy into creating a legacy at Graceland that Elvis would be proud of. I had opened the Annex there, and Lisa and I had set up exhibits of some of Elvis's belongings. One of the most impressive was the exhibit of Elvis's gold records. The Recording Industry Association of America awarded him a total of 117 gold, 67 platinum, and 27 multi-platinum album awards during his lifetime. The display I helped create was stunning. Each record is like a little work of art, and walking into the exhibit for the first time is jaw-dropping. The records gleam like a gold mine all around you. The first time you see the exhibit, it stops you in your tracks. Even other artists walk in and say, "Whoa! I had no idea!"

Now Joel Weinshanker, a man who had never even met Elvis, was majority owner of Graceland. A company called Authentic Brands took over Elvis Presley Enterprises. I could still visit Graceland, but I had no say about what happened there. I struggled to make peace with the new reality, and eventually I did, because I knew I had to.

That same year, Lisa Marie married again, this time to her music producer and guitarist, Michael Lockwood. She met Michael shortly after she completed her first album. He became lead guitarist and producer for *Now What*. By 2005, they were spending most of their time together working on the album. They became close friends and soon fell in love. Maybe she had learned with Nick that jumping in the deep end immediately after meeting someone might not be the best course of action. Even I had taken my time falling in love with Elvis, despite his legendary charm. Lisa and Michael were joined at the hip musically well before they married.

I met Michael after one of Lisa's concerts in Nashville, about a year after her divorce from Nick. He was playing guitar in her band. When I went backstage after the concert, Lisa introduced us. It was apparent that she was falling in love with him. She raved about how great he was and told me she really, really liked him. Liking him was a good sign. It implied respect and friendship and not just attraction. I liked him immediately. Michael is a very nice man, a patient man who cared about my daughter.

They waited three years before marrying, another good sign. On January 22, 2006, they got married in a traditional Japanese ceremony in Kyoto, Japan. It was a small, private service. Lisa had custom kimonos made for all of us. She wore a brilliant red flowered kimono over a white dress, with her black hair swept up. Michael dressed in a black kimono, and I wore a beautiful black kimono with a floral print around the bottom and a gold sash. Riley was Lisa's maid of honor, and Benjamin was a groomsman. Danny, Lisa's first husband and still best friend, was Michael's best man. I had the honor of walking her down the aisle and giving her away. I fervently hoped this was the last wedding she would ever have. Afterward, there was a reception with a traditional tea ceremony. It was a simple but elegant event. Once again, I was hopeful that the marriage would prosper.

As Lisa experienced another beginning, I was experiencing another ending. After almost twenty-two years together, Navarone's father and I parted ways. The relationship had run its course.

Lisa Marie was still young, still hoping she'd found true love. I myself no longer hoped for that. There were many reasons, including the fact that I had not always made good choices. Like my daughter, I had been a target of flattery and greed for many years, from both men and women, because I was Priscilla Presley, with all that this name entailed in the public perception. People gravitated to me for many reasons, including money. I think of my house as home, but for some, it was desirable real estate, a chance for free rent. I am also well connected, an access point for prestigious positions and people. I have been approached and sometimes used to gain access to A-list personalities and entities. In some cases, "friends" have claimed my accomplishments as their own.

There is also the inevitable Elvis factor. People sometimes wanted to get close to Lisa because she was Elvis's daughter. People sometimes want to get close to me because I was Elvis's wife. The name Presley has a certain magic to it, and people sometimes want to bask in the glow. Like my daughter, I am a living link to an idol who was lost too soon. The flip side of that is that men often feel they are living in Elvis's shadow when they are with me. They compare themselves with Elvis and feel resentful or inadequate. I used to think I had some control over that. Contrary to allegations from some exes, I was careful not to bring Elvis into the lives of the men I dated. I rarely took his calls when he was alive or played his music when other men were around. I didn't talk about him to them, except as it related to business decisions for Elvis Presley Enterprises. My son can attest to that, as my daughter could have, too.

My personality contributes to the problem. Friends say that in some ways, I am still the fourteen-year-old girl Elvis met. In business, I am cautious, but in my personal life, I can be naive. I have been caught off guard by people I trusted. I tend to assume that people are who they seem to be. If they are friendly and nice, I take that at face value until I have reason to believe otherwise. If a man is charming and kind to me, I assume he's a nice guy. Maybe I am a slow learner, but ultimately, it is a choice. I choose not to be a cynic. Living my life suspecting everyone's motives, thinking the worst of people, is no life at all. Letting people get close to you is always a risk. Though I have learned to be careful, I am unwilling to shut myself off completely.

By the time I emerged from my relationship with Navarone's father, I was sixty years old. Like so many women as they grow older, I had learned a great deal about myself. I knew I was stronger than I had ever imagined. I knew I was a good businesswoman. I knew I could rise to the occasion when life presented me with challenges. And when I was once more on my own, I rediscovered the joy of independence, of freedom. I was no longer the young wife who had been ready to dedicate her life to pleasing her man. I still want to please those I love, but to focus all my energies on pleasing a man? I'd rather please myself, thank you very much. I no longer have the desire to fall in love with someone. I have continued to date occasionally, and I have formed and nurtured close friendships with men, but I have kept my independence. It was hard-earned.

Elvis unquestionably lies at the heart of my reluctance to marry again or to find another serious long-term relationship. People long for true love, the kind where you fall deeper and deeper until you realize it is bottomless. I found it before I was old enough to understand it. I lost the chance to find it again with Elvis, because he never had the chance to grow old. Once, when Lisa and I were visiting Graceland after the divorce, we sat in Grandma's room with Elvis and Grandma, chatting. Somehow, we got talking about our old age. Elvis said that he'd be gray by then and have a beard. Then he said, "We'd probably be old by the time we got back together. Imagine us racing around in golf carts then. You'd be sixty, and I'd be seventy!" And we all laughed.

Elvis never got the privilege of turning sixty or seventy. I did. I was sixty when my last serious relationship ended. I have left seventy behind me. So what would I say to Elvis's comment now?

"Fire up the golf cart, Sattnin'! I'll even let you drive."

CHAPTER 12

Guest Star

Flaming star, keep behind me...
Give me time to make a few dreams come true.

Whʜᴇɴ I ꜰɪɴɪsʜᴇᴅ ᴛʜᴇ ʟᴀsᴛ *Nᴀᴋᴇᴅ Gᴜɴ* ᴍᴏᴠɪᴇ, I pretty much retired from acting. I enjoyed the work, but I didn't have a burning desire to be an actress. All the work I'd done had come through approaches to my agent at William Morris. I didn't actively seek out roles. Navarone had just turned seven when I did my last movie, and I wanted to focus on being a hands-on mother. I didn't want to be at the studio every day while he was growing up. Every now and then, though, my agency would reach out with an offer of a guest starring role, and I would take it just to keep my hand in.

Guest starring is different from being a regular on a show. You aren't familiar with the culture of the show and usually don't know any of the cast. It was especially tricky for me because I attract publicity, and people who have never met me will often have a preconceived opinion of me. I knew if I kept to myself on a new show, I ran the risk of being considered conceited or self-important. I paid close attention to my surroundings and people's reactions to me. Realizing that people were kind of feeling me out when I came on set, I made a point to be friendly and accessible. I would quietly watch the scenes that everyone else was doing, to indicate interest and learn a little about the show. I chatted with the cameramen or the makeup artists so people knew I was approachable. Usually someone would bring me a chair so I could watch in comfort. People could see that I was interested, and though there was never time to form relationships with anyone, I was treated well. Everyone was very nice, and I appreciated it.

My first guest starring role was on **Melrose Place**. I did three episodes, and oddly enough, my billing in each episode was "Cameo by Priscilla Presley." Cameos are usually very brief appearances where people are playing themselves. This wasn't a cameo. I was part of the main plotline and did several scenes. I played the head nurse at a creepy psychiatric hospital right out of **One Flew over the Cuckoo's Nest**. I even assisted with a lobotomy! Equally strangely, the first episode I did was titled "Peter's Excellent Adventure" (Peter being the show's star, Jack Wagner), which referred to a popular screwball comedy of the time. There was nothing remotely funny about the episode. Apparently, these things were part of the culture of the show.

Unfortunately, I was one of the few people who didn't watch the program back then. In fact, I had never seen it. It was a slick soap opera for young people with major television stars, sort of a *Dallas* for twentysomethings. Naturally, I didn't admit to my ignorance. I pretended that I knew the show and tried to fit in. I suspect that Jack Wagner wondered what the heck I was doing there. People thought of me as a celebrity more than as an actress. My credits were respectable, but I wasn't Meryl Streep. Everyone was pleasant to me but rather indifferent. I was only on for a few episodes. It wasn't my best work. I played a one-dimensional, love-starved psychiatric nurse who instantly falls under Peter's spell. My performance came out fine, everything considered. I did the best I could with the material they gave me.

A year later, I was offered a lovely part on *Touched by an Angel*, playing an ob-gyn who has to deliver her husband's child by his mistress. The character, Meg Saulter, was written with depth and sensitivity. A plot that could have been cliché was instead compelling. And I got to show my acting chops in the dramatic scenes. I had the advantage this time of not only watching the show but also having rehearsal time. We did table reads of the whole show. I loved that. And the cast was wonderful, very welcoming. Della Reese was just lovely, sweet and kind. My only disappointment was that I didn't get to hear her sing. It was a good ensemble, the kind of people viewers hoped for when they imagined the *Angel* cast in real life. Doing the show could have been disillusioning, but it wasn't. Like the show's viewers,

I hoped that in real life, the actors would reflect the kindness of the characters they played. They didn't disappoint me. It was a good set, and it's not always like that. I am proud of my work on that show.

I also enjoyed doing two episodes of *Spin City*, the popular sitcom starring Michael J. Fox at the peak of his popularity. It was my first comedy since *Naked Gun*, and it was so much fun to do. I played Aunt Marie Paterno, aunt of Stacey (played by Jennifer Esposito) visiting from out of town. Aunt Marie is kind of a small-town Mrs. Robinson, out to seduce James (Alexander Chaplin), a shy, geeky young man who works with her niece. Aunt Marie, as we eventually learn, is not a serial predator. She is instead a frustrated spinster fourth-grade teacher who is tired of saving her virginity for the right man. I watched *The Graduate* to prepare and get ideas for playing the role. I didn't want to copy the role, but I sought a little inspiration before making it my own.

They gave me great material to work with, and Alexander, the young actor playing the object of my desire, was wonderful. His character seeks advice from his more sexually experienced colleagues when Aunt Marie asks him to teach her about making love. His colleagues advise him to rent the romantic comedy *Nine Months* and use it to get my character in the mood. He accidentally brings home the soundtrack for *How to Learn the Banjo in Nine Weeks*. His attempt to do a striptease for me to "Dueling Banjos" was hilarious. I sat on the bed watching him, and I have to admit it wasn't just good acting on my part. I could hardly keep a straight face.

And though I didn't get to do any scenes with him, I got to meet Christopher Lloyd, who was there to play a character based on Doc in *Back to the Future*. He is one of the funniest actors of his generation, usually playing bizarre characters like Jim on *Taxi*. He turned out to be a very nice, welcoming man, and it was a pleasure meeting him. My only regret on the show was not doing any scenes with the geriatric dog. It would have been my first animal scene since *Those Amazing Animals*!

Perhaps the most challenging thing I've done on television is *Dancing with the Stars*. The show approached me in 2008, when I was sixty-two years old. If I accepted, I would be the oldest dancer on the program that season. I was intimidated by the prospect, and I hesitated at first. After all, it would mean performing on live television while doing something I'd never done professionally before. But I do love a challenge, and I liked the idea of testing and toning my body. I had always been strong physically, and I hoped my background in ballet and karate would help me. So I agreed. The moment I did, I began to have doubts, and by the first day of rehearsal, I was a nervous wreck.

If you don't watch the show, the setup is that twelve celebrities are invited to participate in a dance competition. None of them are dancers, so they're each paired with a professional dancer who will teach them the basics of a dozen dances. Each week is a different challenge. The contestants are given five days to learn a dance that they then perform live on the sixth night. Three judges score them, and the home audience does call-in scoring. The two scores are combined, and each week, the couple with the lowest score is eliminated. The performances are quite elaborate, beautifully costumed, and performed before a studio and television audience. It was one of the most exhilarating and terrifying experiences of my performing life.

When I walked into the practice studio the first day to meet my partner, Louis van Amstel, I was nervous but determined. I told Louis I felt like a kid on the first day of school, and it was true. I also told him, though, that I wanted him to be tough with me. I didn't want him to hold back because of my age or image, for I look far more fragile than I am. Louis replied that we were going to learn the foxtrot for our first competition and that he planned to challenge me from the beginning. He told me we were going to do the death spiral the first week. In ice skating, the man spins his partner around him by the ankle. For the foxtrot, Louis spun me by the hand. In both the skating and dance spins, the woman's head barely clears the floor.

I thought, *Oh God*, and responded, "What have I got myself into?"

My opinion didn't change over the following days of rehearsal. It took all of my physical and psychological strength to master the routine. When I'd started *Naked Gun*, I thought comedy would be the hardest thing I'd ever do. When I'd begun making speeches around the country, I thought public speaking would be the hardest thing I'd ever do. But I was wrong. That first performance on *DWTS* was the hardest thing I'd ever done.

I was lucky in that I had a wonderful support system. Each contestant is given a group of front-row seats for friends and family on performance night. My family showed up in numbers, with Lisa Marie and Navarone in the front row and my parents cheering behind them. My mom was especially excited. She loved dancing and was thrilled that I was participating. Even my dad got into it, cheering excitedly as Louis and I fox-trotted around the dance floor. To my intense relief, I neither tripped nor forgot my choreography. The judges were kind and encouraging, giving us three 8s on a scale of 10, the second-highest score of the evening. I was thrilled. I got an ovation backstage, too, for the contestants were all supportive of each other. We were in the same boat, with the same challenges, and we cheered one another on. Of course, we all wanted to win, but we wanted to do it by being the best, not by seeing our fellow dancers fall on their faces!

I hoped it would get easier after the first week, but it didn't. We moved from the foxtrot to the mamba, from the mamba to the tango, and from there to the waltz and the rumba. Each dance required completely different tempos, movements, and skills, so success in one dance didn't necessarily translate into success in the next. The one skill that I was commended on and that remained consistent from week to week was my acting ability. My time in front of the camera in acting roles paid off. I could project a sexy, sensuous, or elegant persona as the dance called for it. The male judges described me as very sexy but never trashy, a compliment I thoroughly enjoyed. What sixty-something woman wouldn't enjoy hearing that?

It was fun to get into character for some of the dances. For the mamba, for instance, they dressed me in a leopard print. At the end of the dance, Louis "threw" me onto the floor, where I pulled myself sensuously across the dance floor like a cat. By far my favorite dance, though, was the Viennese waltz. Louis very cleverly taught me the rhythm and flow by taking me rollerblading along the harbor. The long, gliding movements of the skates mirrored the glide of the waltz. On performance night, I wore a gorgeous pale aqua chiffon gown that draped over my arms and swirled and floated around my legs as I moved. The waltz is intrinsically romantic, and I embraced the dance that expressed the romance in me. Unfortunately, though, we were so caught up in the moment that when Louis spun me around his legs, my feet lifted slightly off the floor. Lifts are not allowed in the waltz, so we received point deductions that put us near the bottom of the scores.

Although I was proud of my achievements, as the weeks went by, I found myself getting frustrated. Louis was talented, a perfectionist with high expectations for me. He pushed me to my limits; his multiple directives for the same moves were sometimes overwhelming.

"Be more precise," he'd urge. "Focus! Relax! Speed up here! Now slow it down!"

I felt as if my head would blow up, and I sometimes vented my frustrations on him. But I had asked to be pushed, and I wouldn't have changed that. The hardest part for me was the time factor. Louis overestimated my learning curve. We typically practiced three hours a day, which wasn't enough for me to perfect the routines. Every couple was scheduled for a few hours in a rehearsal room each weekday, but Louis and I only averaged three hours of practice. Some of the other dance teams reported practicing up to six hours at a time. I needed more time practicing. I would be up practicing at home until three or four in the morning, talking myself through the routines, but I still felt unprepared by performance night.

By week five, the frustration had caught up to me. The rumba that we were performing included several challenging moves that I didn't feel fully prepared for. I went all out on performance night, even doing the splits twice. The audience erupted in cheers as I slid into splits on the floor, clearly surprised that I was able to do it, and to do it well. I received a standing ovation, but the judges weren't impressed. I was under-rehearsed, and it showed. I had never achieved the level of mastery needed to lose myself in the dance. The home audience apparently agreed, and Louis and I were eliminated from the competition.

Was I disappointed? Maybe a little. Mostly, though, I was relieved. My first thought was, **Thank God.** I had reached the point by then that I was literally praying not to make it to the next week. On performance nights, when they announced who was going home, I had begun thinking, **Please, God, let it be me.** The pressure, the exhaustion, and, most of all, the gnawing feeling of being constantly underprepared, had eaten away at me. It was nerve-racking. I had spent many sleepless nights worrying about my ability to measure up. My only real disappointment was letting down my parents, who came every week and loved every minute of watching me perform. Still, I meant it when I thanked the judges and told them what an incredible experience it had been for me. I had learned that I was capable of doing things I had considered beyond my reach, and I had held my own against contestants half my age. I had shown people that for the fortunate among us, age really is just a number.

And I had made a new friend in the show's producer, Nigel Lythgoe. Contrary to belief, I never became romantically involved with Nigel, but he has been a good friend and companion over the years. Our friendship has endured.

Keeping a toehold in the entertainment industry led me to other opportunities. My old friend Kirk Kerkorian invited me to serve on the board of MGM. I was proud to be asked. The board is a prestigious group that wields a great deal of power in Hollywood. Being on the board means being with the who's who, hearing the back stories of the latest movies. I got to see preview showings of the films and discuss them afterward. We tracked earnings and losses. Was the movie a success? A failure? Should we pull it from the theaters or extend its run? I was more of a listener than anything else, for these issues were way out of my area of expertise. Eventually, I started to get a little bored with the constant discussion of profit and loss. It's important work, just not my work. Some of my acquaintances were incredulous when I gracefully exited. They would have given anything to have a seat at that table.

I continued to enjoy the role of businesswoman and creator. From designing my home with Elvis, to my days at Bis and Beau, to my fragrance collection, I had loved designing items that expressed my taste. So when the opportunity arose to partner with Australian fashion designer Bruno Schiavi in developing a line of linens, I jumped at the chance. I have always loved fine linens, especially bed linens, because the bedroom is my sanctuary away from the world. It is an intimate place, whether you share it with a partner or revel in the peace that solitude can bring. When I was a child, my bedroom was the only place where I could get away from my five siblings for a while. I loved snuggling down on fresh sheets and temporarily shutting out the world.

I have always been highly sensitive to texture, and I had learned a great deal about fabrics at Bis and Beau. No matter how visually appealing bed linens are, unless they are also soft against the skin, they don't belong on your bed. All the sheets we made had high thread counts and had to pass the touch test. Bruno and I also agreed to prioritize colors and trims that appealed to both sexes in our designs. So many bed linens cater to female tastes, with florals and pastels, yet half the population that sleeps in a bed is male. We created unisex designs, crisp whites with blue trim and burgundy sheets with black stitching. They looked and felt wonderful. Because details are important to me, we even designed beautiful, reusable bags to hold the linens. We premiered the line in Canada, the United Kingdom, and Australia to an enthusiastic response.

Despite our successful designs, however, sales began to decline. The problem was not with the product; the problem was with the publicity. I had worked successfully on publicity campaigns promoting both Wella Balsam and my fragrance line. But this company seemed to think that putting my name on the collection was enough. They wanted me to be the face of the company, but they expected me to do that by myself. An effective publicity campaign needs an infrastructure. You have to create a network of contacts, coordinate a complicated schedule, and hire people to make all these things happen. All these steps are labor-intensive and expensive. I couldn't market the product effectively without a team supporting me. We needed an aggressive, well-funded campaign. Although I worked effectively with HSN (formerly called the Home Shopping Network) to sell the linens, that wasn't nearly enough. The partnership with the company died a slow but inevitable death. I was sorry to see it happen. I had hoped to expand the line to candles, bathrobes, towels, and other complementary items, but it wasn't to be.

Throughout these years, I continued to support Elvis's legacy. Each year, I joined the celebration at Graceland commemorating Elvis's birth. I remained active in Memphis events. I served as an adviser with my daughter as Graceland underwent ongoing additions. Keeping involved grounded me. In keeping Elvis's memory alive, I remained connected to him. Embracing my past enabled me to face the future.

I've never lacked opportunities. I receive a lot of invitations, but I'm selective about what I accept. When I was asked to be godmother to a steamboat, however, I couldn't resist. I wasn't quite sure what it would entail. The christening part was easy to picture, but I didn't know a thing about piloting it through life. Luckily, the primary requirement was breaking a bottle of champagne on the boat at the launch and posing for the occasional picture. That I could do.

I was honored to be asked. The invitation was done as a show of appreciation for my work in support of the city of Memphis, which would be the boat's home port. The steamboat evoked memories of the past, when these watercraft were the main carriers down the great river. The *American Queen* was a Mississippi steamboat believed to be the largest steamboat in the world. At over four hundred feet long, it has rooms for 436 passengers to take long-distance trips down the Mississippi River. After some earlier incarnations, it had been refurbished and relaunched, to great enthusiasm. At the launch event, I managed to smash the champagne bottle on the first swing, but I got quite a bit of blowback in my face. Oh well. If you're going to get soaked, it might as well be with champagne.

It's fun and flattering to be made the godmother of a riverboat or to sit on the board of a major movie studio. But in the end, life isn't about boats or movies. Our lives have meaning only when we bring meaning to the lives of others. My work as ambassador for the Dream Foundation has been some of the most moving, challenging, and fulfilling work of my life.

The Dream Foundation was started in 1994 in Montecito, California, by Tom Rollerson, whose partner, Scott Palmer, had died of a catastrophic illness in 1993. When Scott became ill, Tom discovered that though there were many organizations supporting the wishes and needs of terminally ill children, there were no comparable organizations for adults. Tom used his grief to motivate him in creating the Dream Foundation, which seeks to grant wishes to terminally ill adults with less than twelve months to live. It grants a myriad of wishes, such as going to a Yankees game, reuniting with a childhood friend, or meeting a favorite celebrity. The foundation is privately funded, with no government support, and relies on the work of many volunteers to make the wishes come true.

I got involved with the Dream Foundation when Tom called me to say someone had requested to see me. I had never heard of the group, so I looked it up to see what it was all about. I loved what it did, and I immediately volunteered to help. If the person wanted to meet me, or I could arrange a meeting with a celebrity they wanted to meet, I would try to do it. If there was a way I could help, I wanted to.

Most of the time, I visited people in the hospital, spent time talking with them, and then had lunch with them. It was a huge learning curve for me. They were all close to death, and they knew it, yet how strong they were. They were still living their lives, in some cases still clinging to hope. Not knowing how to act at first, I learned to let them take the lead while I went with the flow. Were they depressed? Were they withdrawn? Resigned? Frightened? Cheerful? Living in the moment? Everyone reacted differently, but they all had one thing in common: Their days were numbered, and they knew it. We all know that we're going to die, but for most of us, we keep the knowledge abstract. We mentally add the word *someday* to the acknowledgment of our own mortality. There was no *someday* for the people I met.

I had a very hard time being with them at first. The whole time I talked with them, all I could think about was that they were going to pass soon. The normal conventions of conversation felt trite. I would fill the void by saying whatever came into my head.

"How are you? It's so nice to meet you. Do you live here in Montecito? Do you like it?"

I would try to get to know them a bit. I had nothing really interesting to say, but it didn't seem to matter. They were so happy to be with a celebrity that just talking to me lifted their spirits. I was making a difference in their lives. Their last wish was to meet me. It was incredibly humbling.

Sometimes their wish was to do something, often for the first time. One man had always wanted to ride a horse. He loved horses, but he'd never been on one. So we took him to the stable and helped him on a horse so he could ride around. His face lit up with joy. When you see people smile who haven't smiled in a long time, that's a gift. It reminds us of how lucky we are.

Sometimes they just wanted to take a walk, and I would walk with them, holding their hand and listening to them. They'd talk about their lives or the people they love. Getting to know them, caring about them, all the time knowing what the future held for them. It was hard to keep my composure.

I walked with one woman who was dying of cancer. We walked around the town together, holding hands like children, as she talked about her childhood dream. She'd wanted to be a doctor. That would never happen now. She was courageously preparing for the end. Sometimes, people wanted to talk about Elvis. How they'd idolized him, had a crush on him when they were teens. I would tell them stories about Elvis, and their eyes would light up. They were hearing about their idol, hearing it directly from me. It was easier for me when they asked about Elvis. It gave me something to talk about that I knew would make them happy.

For many years, I would keep up with the people I had met through Tom. He would tell me when they went back into the hospital. I'd ask questions.

"Will they get a chance to go home? How many days do they have left? How are they doing? Are they in pain? Afraid?"

Eventually, I couldn't take it anymore. I would tell Tom not to tell me. It was just too hard. The burden of so many people's pain became crushing. I already carried so many people with me. Vernon. Grandma. Elvis. And all too soon, I would be carrying more pain than I ever could have imagined.

CHAPTER 13

Second Thoughts

I gotta follow that dream
Keep a-movin', move along.

On October 7, 2008, I was blessed with another grandchild—twice blessed, in fact. Lisa gave birth to twin girls. It had been a long road for Lisa. She and Michael had been trying to get pregnant for two years, and she had suffered through several miscarriages. When she conceived the twins, she was naturally hesitant to announce it until she felt certain she could carry the babies to term. The tabloids were cruel. Noticing her weight gain, they began criticizing her appearance and "unhealthy" eating habits. Naturally, when she did announce the pregnancy, there was no apology from the tabloids. The pregnancy was healthy but exhausting for my daughter. Carrying twins at forty years old was hard on her body.

We were all excited to have twins, but after the initial shock, we weren't really surprised. Twins ran in the family. Elvis, of course, had a twin brother, Jesse, who was stillborn. Two of my brothers were twins. The whole family was thrilled by the prospect of having twin girls.

On the morning of the seventh, Lisa called me to say she was in labor.

She said, "It's time, Mom." I told her I would meet her at the hospital as soon as I could.

The drive to Los Robles Hospital in Thousand Oaks took about forty-five minutes, and by the time I got there, Lisa was on the table. I was a nervous wreck. She was clearly in a lot of pain.

She told me, "I want you with me, Mommy," and I reassured her I'd stay with her. Michael was there, with Riley and Ben, all of us awaiting the big moment. The doctors put her partway under, into twilight sleep, before performing a cesarean section. She had a tough time with the first twin, who, at five pounds, fifteen ounces, was the bigger of the two. The second, smaller baby, was a little easier. She weighed five pounds, two ounces. It was such a joy to see them. I couldn't believe how tiny they were. And how perfect.

I kept thinking, *Oh my God, these are my grandchildren. Twins.* I was ecstatic.

They named the girls Harper Vivienne Ann Lockwood and Finley Aaron Love Lockwood. They are fraternal twins.

Harper's third name is in honor of me, and Finley's second and third names are in honor of Elvis and his mother. I think Finley was born first, but I'm not certain. They looked so much alike as newborns. I was just glad my daughter and the babies were all right.

The nurse put the babies into Lisa's arms. She was thankful the pain was over and joyous to hold her girls. Michael got to hold them next. He was so nervous. They were his first children. It was endearing to see how delicately he held and carried them. He had wanted children for a long time, and now they were here. Then the babies were handed to us, one at a time. I realized that Riley was nineteen years older than her baby sisters, the identical age gap to the one between Lisa and Navarone. History repeating itself.

Lisa doted on those girls, and Michael couldn't have been a more loving, committed father. They took turns with the babies to make sure both parents bonded equally with each girl. It was exhausting but joyous, what Lisa described as chaotic bliss.

It would be a long time before I found out, but there was a worm hidden in the bud of our joy. The birth had been hard on Lisa, and she was in considerable pain afterward. Her doctors gave her opiates to cope. Ordinarily, this wouldn't be a problem, but Lisa had inherited Elvis's vulnerability to opioid addiction. By the time she was released from the hospital, she was already addicted. She continued to renew her prescription. It was the beginning of a yearslong battle with addiction that took her to the edge. I was blissfully unaware of what was happening. For a long time, I didn't know she was taking painkillers. The only thing I noticed was that Lisa seemed more docile than usual, and Lisa is normally anything but docile. I thought at first that she was just tired or simply content with her beautiful girls. It never crossed my mind that she would go back into the darkness of drugs again. I thought she had left that far behind her.

A few months after the twins were born, Lisa and Michael decided to look for a place in England. They wanted a retreat where they could get away from the pressures and glare of Hollywood. Both Lisa and I had always loved England. The landscape is beautiful, and the British treat us like people, not like celebrities. Lisa wanted an estate in the countryside where she could care for her girls, reflect on her life, and write music. In retrospect, I also realize she wanted a place to deal with her addiction. She rented a house in the countryside in Kent while she looked for a place to buy. Navarone and I flew over to visit her.

It was an old house with an eerie feeling about it. I chalked the feeling up to my imagination. When it was time for bed, Lisa showed me what room I'd be sleeping in.

I said, "Oh, great. This is nice," and didn't give it a second thought.

Just as I was about to drift off to sleep, I heard somebody turning the knob on my door. Thinking it was Navarone, I got out of bed and opened the door, expecting to see my son. I caught a glimpse of something, but it was so fast that I couldn't identify it. It wasn't Navarone. It wasn't anyone. The doorway was empty. I felt chills go down my spine. I slept very little that night.

The next morning, when I joined the others, they said, "So how was it?"

I told them what had happened. Then Lisa said, "Yeah, that's the ghost room. It's haunted. We didn't want to tell you. We wanted to see if anything happened."

Thanks a lot, guys. I get the ghost room? Very funny.

Then they began telling me the story. Lisa explained that everybody in the neighborhood said the house was haunted. People claimed to have seen the ghost, usually in the room I'd slept in or on the stairs. It was an old-fashioned figure. People thought it was someone who had once lived there. A friend of Lisa's who was staying with us told me that she had seen something coming down the stairs. None of us knew what to think about it, but it was eerie.

That night, we stayed up late, talking. I think we were all putting off bedtime. Lisa had put the twins to bed early, and they were sleeping peacefully. We could hear them on the baby monitor. Finally, we all decided to turn in, and Navarone walked me to my room. Afterward, he went to the kitchen to make a snack. The twins were in the room directly above the kitchen. The house was quiet by then; everyone had gone to bed. Suddenly, Navarone heard something coming from the baby monitor. He listened more closely and heard heavy, slow footsteps. He ran up the stairs to check on the girls, but there was no one in the babies' room. The hall was empty. Everyone was apparently sleeping peacefully. By then he was panic-stricken. The first I knew about it was when he burst into my room and crawled into bed with me.

"Mom! Mom! I heard the ghost!"

He stayed with me the rest of the night. We were both glad to have the company.

At the risk of becoming tabloid fodder, I will admit that this was not our family's first experience with the unexplainable. Every summer, we used to go to Hawaii, where we would swim and snorkel and breathe in the tropical winds to clear the LA smog out of our lungs. We usually stayed at the same hotel where Lisa got married. On one trip, when Navarone was about fourteen, the woman who set up our Hawaiian itinerary every summer told us a strange tale. There were ponds on the property, a historic site where rituals were performed in the days of King Kamehameha. She said that for many years, there had been stories of unusual sightings at the ponds. That year, a group of guests had told her that one evening, they had seen warrior ghosts performing a ceremony at the ponds. The guests claimed that when they tried to take pictures, the ghosts had chased them and destroyed their camera. The story was far-fetched, but it piqued our curiosity. After that, when we went for an evening stroll, we would go by the ponds to see if there was anything unusual.

Late one evening, we decided to take a walk down to the ponds just for something to do. Navarone, his friend, and my cousin Ivy walked with me. It was a typical Hawaiian evening, warm and aromatic with a light breeze. As we stood there talking, we noticed a small ring of orange light on the water. We started looking around to see where it was coming from, but there were no nearby lights that could have been causing a reflection. As we watched, four more circles of light appeared on the water. That was odd but not remarkable. And then, everything got very strange. The circles of orange light began to emanate what looked like a cloud of orange gas rising up. The gas thickened into columns, and images of Hawaiian warriors began to form. We were transfixed. The figures seemed to undulate backward and forward. Suddenly, one of the figures began moving forward. It sped up and rushed directly toward us. We turned and ran all the way back to our rooms. By the time we got there, the figure was gone. I have no explanation for what we saw that night, but we all saw it. We were all sober and, I like to think, relatively sane. Whatever it was, we did not go back to the ponds at night again.

As harrowing as that experience was, my most disturbing experience with the supernatural was also in Hawaii, alone on the beach one night. I woke up at about two in the morning, unable to sleep. It was a beautiful evening, and our place was on the beach, so I went outside. I stood on the sand just yards from the water, breathing the fresh salt air and enjoying the beauty and the sound of the waves. Suddenly, I heard a faint pounding noise. I looked toward the noise and saw a troop of ancient warriors in full Hawaiian garb. They were marching in formation to the pounding of a drum. I froze. I couldn't believe what I was seeing. There have been stories of the night marchers, the huaka'i pō, in Hawaii for centuries. Hundreds of people have claimed to see them, and locals who haven't seen them still believe in them. They are considered dangerous. Local people warn that if you see them, you should never look in their faces, which is a sign of disrespect. You should take cover and try not to let them see you.

I kept thinking, *Oh my God, oh my God, am I dreaming this? Is this real?*

They were headed down the beach along the waterline, and my first impulse was to hide before they saw me. I hid behind a small tree for a few moments, but the nervous strain was unbearable. I ran back to the house and went inside. I could hear them marching past me. I was trembling, and I kept repeating, "Oh my God" over and over. I didn't want to believe it was happening. It was like a nightmare. It's one thing to hear the stories; it's something else entirely to experience it. I almost preferred to think I was crazy, that I had imagined the whole thing. It was less frightening than believing it was real. It took me a long time to make peace with what I saw that night.

While Lisa and her family were settling into the beautiful English estate she had purchased (which was not haunted!), I was adjusting to my youngest "baby" leaving the nest. Navarone had moved out on his own to the beautiful seaside city of Santa Cruz, California. His girlfriend had wanted to move away from the city, and they decided to move together. They found a house in a beautiful, isolated spot in the forest. It was as far from the lights of Hollywood as you could get. He was down to only one snake at that point, and he took it with him. I gave him a rescue French bulldog that Navarone named Jerry Garcia, and the dog became part of the new household.

Navarone loved being independent, away from the glare of celebrity surrounding our family. Nobody he met up there had any idea he was my son, and he planned to keep it that way. When I went up to see his new place, I found rows of pots in his backyard. Pots of pot, to be exact. He was growing marijuana. Hmm. Well, I couldn't pretend that I was really surprised. I think it was a sign that he was claiming his identity and making his own choices now. I could only hope he would make good ones. I missed him, though. I did my best to support his move, to let him grow up, but his absence left a lonely place in my house and my heart.

He had been interested in music for a while by then, what he thought of as the family business. He played the guitar and sang very well. And he was a good songwriter. He tried forming a band, but it took some time. It was difficult to find talented musicians with the same taste in music to begin with, and it was even harder to keep them. They would stay awhile and then take other jobs or otherwise move on. Finally, he met a keyboardist named Kyle Hamood. By a strange coincidence, it wasn't their first meeting.

When Kyle told his mom about meeting Navarone, she said, "You mean Priscilla Presley's son? Navarone Garibaldi?"

It turned out that our families had met one summer while we were on vacation in Hawaii, and our baby boys had played together. Navarone had been only one year old at the time. Now here they were, twenty years later, meeting by chance in Santa Cruz. They had musical chemistry and similar ambitions, so together they formed a synth rock group called Them Guns. It was an homage to *The Guns of Navarone*, the movie Navarone was named after. Finding a good drummer who would stay took some time, but when they did, they were in business. Navarone was naively hopeful. He'd been around successful performers all his life, so in his mind, they would do an album and then tour it. He had no concept of how hard that was to achieve. But he was committed to the task, and he worked steadily at writing lyrics, rehearsing the band, and looking for gigs.

Lisa was also hard at work on her own music. The stay in England proved fruitful. Songs seemed to pour out of her, and within two years, she was ready to do another album. She worked with T-Bone Burnett to create what critics agreed was the best work of her career. Online music service Spinner described the album as a "moody masterpiece," and *Rolling Stone* called it "the album she was born to make." It was titled *Storm and Grace*, and it was autobiographical like her previous albums but with a new maturity and less anger.

The title track is a love song to her son, Benjamin Storm Keough. The storm, of course, is a reference to both his middle name and the storms of life she'd weathered. Grace is a reference not only to Ben's grace but also to the grace she'd been afforded by having him for a son. Her previous songs focused on darkness. This song is filled with light.

Lisa had put her whole heart into the album, which is a small masterpiece. She put her whole heart into promoting it as well. She returned to the United States to tour with it, making a meaningful stop at Sun Records in Memphis, where Elvis had recorded his first record, "That's All Right, Mama." I came to watch her when I could or took care of the four-year-old twins when I was needed. Lisa did the whole circuit of talk shows: *Oprah* and *Jimmy Kimmel* and so forth, despite the fact that she had never enjoyed doing talk shows. The shows made her nervous. Despite her nerves, audiences gave her a warm reception. By the time the 2012 Grammy nominations were announced, Lisa's hopes were high. This was the best work she would ever do. The album was her heart and soul. Recognition by the music industry would be validation that she was worthy of being Elvis's daughter.

She wasn't nominated. Lisa was devastated. Michael, Riley, and I did everything we could to comfort and reassure her, but nothing we said helped. She said she was finished. She would never write another song, and she never did. Her decision still breaks my heart. She did, however, make one last recording.

Lisa had continued to do duets with her father since 1997, when she had first sung publicly for the twentieth anniversary of Elvis's passing. The duets became a tradition. On the thirtieth anniversary, she recorded a haunting version of "In the Ghetto" with Elvis. "I Love You Because" honored the thirty-fifth year. And in 2018, she recorded the powerfully moving "Where No One Stands Alone." For me, it was a painful reminder of what was lost when she stopped recording albums. But I was grateful that her last song was a tribute to her father. It would have meant so much to Elvis.

Of all the songs on *Storm and Grace*, though, one song attracted a different kind of attention. It was titled "You Ain't Seen Nothin' Yet," and it is about Scientology. For those who knew the church, it was a protest song announcing Lisa's departure. She defiantly referred to herself in the lyrics as "transgressive and suppressive," Scientology terms for negative people. Church teaching requires faithful members to "disconnect" from these negative influences, the equivalent of shunning in some faith traditions. Unbeknownst to me, Lisa had been investigating rumors about Scientology for years before she released her song.

I found this very surprising. Although she had resisted church membership as a child, she had become a more dedicated member than I was, working tirelessly in support of Scientology causes. Gradually, though, she became disillusioned with it. Her misgivings reached a crisis when the head of Scientology,

David Miscavige, disconnected from his father and put him in the equivalent of a Scientology prison at a secluded location in the San Bernardino Mountains. Lisa had had enough. Fearless and angry, my daughter walked into the eye of the storm, Scientology headquarters in Clearwater, Florida, and confronted David directly. She told him with great anger and passion just how she felt about him disconnecting from his father. Lisa was never subtle when she was angry.

The aftermath was frightening for her. She called me from Florida after her visit to headquarters and said, "Mom, I'm so scared. I gave it to David, and now they're following me. There are black limos parked outside my house and following me around. This is real. This is what they do."

When Lisa took such a firm stand against the church, it forced me to reexamine my own relationship with it. With the passage of time, I had begun to feel increasing pressure from the church. In the early years of Scientology, the expectations for me had been moderate. But as I went up levels on the "bridge to total freedom," the demands increased exponentially. Members are expected to commit more and more time to their personal growth on the higher levels, up to six hours per day. Financial commitment increases, too, as you are expected to help the church grow. The church must come first in your life, ahead of everything else. For a long time, I was able to cope successfully with the church's expectations. The problem I eventually confronted, though, wasn't time or money or even the church's philosophy. It was my family.

The first consideration was Lisa. She had taken a courageous and risky stand against the church, and I wanted to support her. My parents also became an issue. Mom and Dad were faithful Catholics, and I was asked to disclose this when auditing. Scientologists consider people who belong to other religions, especially those that are critical of Scientology, negative influences who might lead members away from the philosophy Hubbard taught. To prevent that from happening, I was subtly encouraged to loosen ties with my parents. That wasn't going to happen. I loved my parents deeply and had no intention of distancing myself from them. If I had to choose, I would choose my family every time.

Ultimately, Lisa and I left the church at about the same time. She went out with a bang and a lot of headlines. I chose to go quietly. It was hard to leave. There were things about Scientology that I loved. I still miss it sometimes. I miss the auditing, which lifted some of my burdens. And I miss being part of a community with people like John Travolta, who first got me into Scientology. John remains my friend. He was one of the first to call when my daughter passed away. I wish him well, along with the many good souls who pursue the same ideals I once hoped would help the world.

CHAPTER 14
Raise Your Voice

A little less conversation,
A little more action.

When Navarone grew up and moved out, I began to consider what I wanted to do next. I did not want to pursue a full-time professional career. I would continue to be there for my family; that was a given. But it wasn't enough. In what seemed like the twinkling of an eye, I was in my seventh decade, and I didn't want to waste the coming years. I knew I wanted to make a difference. Scientology was right about one thing: Celebrities have a unique ability to attract attention for causes they believe in. They have a voice, a public voice that will be heard and often listened to. I wanted to use my voice on behalf of those who could not speak for themselves, for celebrity has obligations as well as privileges. I continued to work for Dream Foundation, but there had to be more I could do. The question was, *what?*

In retrospect, it seems inevitable that I became an animal advocate. Animals are living beings with thoughts and emotions, but they cannot speak for themselves. We must speak— and act—for them. From the time I hid a homeless puppy in my closet as a little girl, animal rescue has been important to me. That day, I saw a small, frightened creature who was alone, without a "mommy," as I thought of it at the time. My vocabulary has changed, but my impulse has not. Every domesticated animal needs a caretaker, a "mom." We have made entire animal species dependent on us, and we profit from them in countless ways. For that, we owe them care and consideration. Our pets need security and affection as well as food. If they know that they are loved, they will return that love tenfold. Our moral obligation extends to wild species as well. We need to protect their habitats. We need to ensure they are not abused, for profit or for our convenience. Elephants almost disappeared from the wild because of human greed for ivory. We cannot stand by and let that happen. These beliefs have motivated me to commit my time, effort, and money to protecting all God's creatures, great and small.

The easiest form of commitment for me was donating money and goods. When you go to a lot of animal advocacy events, as I do, you learn who's doing really good work. I help with money, with food and blankets, with collars and beds, and with whatever else they need. I'll call and say, "What do you need?"

And then provide it. Groups I work closely with call me to tell me when they have an urgent need. Sometimes I'll hear about a need or read about it in the paper and reach out to them. That used to be my primary way of helping, but over the years, I have become more actively involved.

My commitment has included legislative advocacy. I lobbied to prevent California's Hayden Law from being repealed. The law protects shelter animals, giving them reasonable time to be found or adopted and ensuring humane care while they wait. I campaigned against the Tennessee anti-whistleblower bill that would criminalize investigations into animal cruelty. I advocated for a Tennessee bill to protect Tennessee Walking Horses from soring, a cruel practice of putting caustic chemicals on the horses' legs to train them to lift their legs unnaturally high. Sometimes my advocacy extends to direct protest, which has occasionally drawn criticism from the public.

For example, I have worked extensively with Chris DeRose at Last Chance for Animals for years now. In 2018, we took up the cause of dog eating in South Korea. The practice included acquiring dogs, some of them pets, then killing and butchering them in the cruelest possible manner for human consumption. When advocacy seemed to foster little progress, we held a controversial protest in front of the South Korean Consulate in Los Angeles. Some of us held up signs; others of us held dead dogs that had been euthanized at a local shelter. I was one of those who cradled a dead dog in their arms. Some people called me out, outraged by what they considered a tasteless celebrity stunt. But it wasn't a stunt for me. I held that dog on behalf of the thousands of dogs that were being slaughtered in Seoul, many of them without ever being held. The important thing is that we finally got people's attention. Thanks to our efforts, and particularly to Chris, South Korea has passed a law banning the killing of dogs for human consumption. Sometimes, you just have to get people's attention.

When Graceland was in danger of being liquidated after Vernon's death, the horses could have been sold to raise cash. They were purebred horses, valuable in their own right, but as Elvis Presley's horses, they would have fetched a small fortune. Elvis had famously showed off his Tennessee Walking Horse, Bear, to admiring fans at Graceland's gates. They also watched him, dressed like a cowboy, racing his palomino, Rising Sun, back and forth across the Graceland pasture. Imagine how much a bidder would have paid for either horse. But we did not sell them. I made sure they and other horses, including Domino, the quarter horse Elvis gave me, were well cared for at Graceland through their old age. Since then, the Graceland stable has become a shelter for rescue horses. They receive the same luxury treatment the purebreds once enjoyed. There is always, by the way, one palomino in residence in honor of Elvis's beloved Rising Sun.

Adopting dogs has become a way of life for me. If I can't take them, I will find someone who can. At one point, I had six rescue dogs in my family. These days, I try to limit it to three at a time, but my passion for giving them homes has never waned. I was still living with Elvis when I started adopting rescue dogs. I already had Honey, the little honey-colored poodle Elvis gave me. I loved the name because I thought it was cute and funny. I'd call, "I'm home, Honey," when I walked in the door. I had a

German shepherd named Haji, too, when I got a call from someone at a Memphis rescue. They had a collie they were going to put down, and I took him. I named him Baba so that I could call the dogs "Haji Baba." I thought it was hilarious. I also rescued Brutus and Snoopy, two beautiful Great Danes, a brother and sister that used to be show dogs. They were so regal, they could have sat on either side of the stone steps of an Egyptian library.

Years later, when I was visiting Memphis, I heard about a woman who was hoarding goods and dogs. It was the worst hoarding case in the state of Mississippi, and the police had to go in. They were looking for people to take the dogs.

My cousin Ivy and I drove out to where the woman was living. It was a run-down lot with clotheslines and chains where dogs had once been tied. She was living in an old trailer stacked to the ceiling with unopened boxes, and the smell was overpowering. On top of the boxes, huddled in the corner and looking down at me, was a little Boston terrier puppy. I already had a Boston terrier at home and have a soft spot for the breed.

I asked her, "Is this puppy taken?" She said no, so I told her I'd take him. Then I asked her, "What do you have left?"

She said she had a pit bull mix that was leashed to a tree in the back. He was nine months old and had been tied to the tree all his life. I said, "Oh my God," and went looking for him.

I found a sad little puppy with a light brindle coat. Pit bulls have bad reputations, and nobody could have blamed this one for having a bad temperament after being tied to a tree from birth. But looking up at me was one of the sweetest faces I've ever seen. I named him Boz and introduced him to his new brother. When I brought them to my car, they both jumped in and settled down together like they'd known me all their lives. Ivy and I drove them back to LA because I didn't want to put them on a plane, and they were little angels all the way. Whenever we got to a hotel and settled them in, they'd go right to sleep. It was as if they'd been waiting for me. They knew they were going home.

That was fourteen years ago. Boz is sleeping near my feet as I tell this story. His muzzle is gray now, and he moves slowly. I suspect he is deaf. But he is still the same sweet puppy I unhooked from the tree in the dirty yard near a dilapidated trailer so long ago.

Helping animals has been incredibly rewarding. Elvis loved animals. And if I've learned one thing by now, it's this: If a man doesn't like animals, he's out. I'll choose the dog every time.

I have provided a voice for animals for many years now. Elvis, in contrast, was famous for his voice. But it was silenced long before he could say so much of what he thought and felt. Worse yet, his story has often been told by people who never knew him. At worst, they magnify and focus on his failures and shortcomings; at best, they stereotype him. This distortion of his character is partly due to the manner of his passing. If Elvis had died in bed at ninety, surrounded by his daughter, grandchildren, and great-grandchildren, his last years would have been treated with respect. But instead, he died face down on the bathroom carpet with an overload of drugs in his system. That reality has colored the public understanding of him ever since. It created a false perception. Elvis was a remarkable human being. Yes, he was flawed, as all of us are, but he was a flawed diamond. He was passionate, loving, generous, artistically brilliant, and utterly unique. I want the world to remember the man I remember, ever more clearly with the passage of time. I want to give Elvis a voice, to say the things he never got to. I want to represent him publicly for the man he was.

I got an opportunity to do that in 2015, when Elvis was honored with a second US postage stamp. The first stamp, issued twenty-two years earlier, remained the best-selling stamp in the history of the post office. The Forever stamp, part of the Music Icons series, was issued thirty-eight years after Elvis's passing. I traveled to Memphis to represent the family at the ceremony and to take part in Elvis Week, the annual event honoring his passing. Lisa Marie and the twins joined me later in the week.

As they had when the first stamp was issued, fans flocked to Graceland from all over the world to purchase the first stamps and to honor Elvis. The dedication ceremony was held in the late afternoon on the lawn in front of the mansion. It was a bright day, and I remember shading my eyes as the dignitaries spoke. Elvis would have been honored by the theme each speaker chose. The first speaker commended him for his patriotism and his military service. A small color guard took its place while the national anthem was played. Several ministers honored him for his religious dedication, reading one of Elvis's favorite scriptures, 1 Corinthians 13, often called the love chapter. The postmaster said we were there to honor the man, not the icon, who impacted so many lives with his passion, his music, and his voice. The mayor told a joke about etymology, saying the root of the word *Memphis* was "Elvis." He said it was difficult to find an honor big enough for a man who had brought so many people together. Then he introduced me, commending me for having the vision to open Graceland to Elvis's fans and referring to me as "the steward of the Elvis legacy." I was touched by his words.

I stood at the podium looking out at the assemblage, wishing as always that Elvis were there with me to experience the honor he was receiving. I told a personal story about the day that the highway in front of Graceland was renamed. As a teenager, I had addressed my letters to Elvis to Highway 51 South. Today, I would be addressing them to Elvis Presley Boulevard. Elvis and I had stood on the front porch that day as Elvis tried to take it in.

He looked at me and said in wonder, "My own street. My very own street."

He would have found it surreal to have his image on two stamps so many years after his passing. I told the crowd that a Forever stamp seemed fitting, as Elvis was forever in our hearts. Finally, I thanked the postmaster for this great honor for Elvis.

We brought the ceremony to a close with the unveiling of the stamp. A large, poster-sized image had been set on an easel nearly twice my height. The poster was covered by a blue drape with USPS written on it. The public had not seen the stamp yet. The postmaster and I stood on either side of the easel and did the honors of pulling down the drape to reveal the stamp. It was strikingly different from the first stamp, the older one with its vivid pink background that highlighted a singing Elvis. The newer one was more classic. It featured a 1955 black-and-white photograph of a very young, serious Elvis taken before he became a superstar. His vulnerability showed. To his left was his signature in gold. In the right bottom corner was a tiny gold crown, signaling his status as the King of Rock and Roll. The image was timeless.

The stamps officially went on sale that day, along with a compilation music album titled *Elvis Forever*. As they had with the first stamp, crowds lined up to buy them.

The rest of the week was filled with activities. There was a musical tribute at a packed Orpheum Theater in downtown Memphis, with Elvis impersonators performing. People of all ages came. My favorites were the small children dressed in Elvis costumes. So cute. I could not resist hugging some of them. I served on a Q and A panel with several others, including Mac Davis, the singer-songwriter who wrote "In the Ghetto." He shared for the first time publicly that Elvis had not sung the song the way Mac had written it. Mac had intended it to end with the words "in the ghetto." Elvis had added the refrain "and his mama cried." I have no doubt that Elvis was thinking of Gladys. Fittingly for the occasion, the Stamps Quartet sang, as they had sung with Elvis for so many years.

The week ended with the highlight for our family, the candlelight vigil. As the crowd waited silently in the dark, hundreds of candles flickering, Lisa Marie was escorted out with the twins. All three wore long white dresses with golden garlands in their hair as they walked across the front lawn of Graceland. Lisa was smiling slightly; the twins' faces showed wonder at the sight of so many candles in the darkness. When they reached the podium where a torchbearer stood, all three were given candles. Lisa's was lit with the torch. Then she used her candle to carefully light Harper and Finley's candles as they solemnly watched. It was a beautiful tableau. And it would have been Elvis's favorite moment of the week. Even more important than the accolades he never lived to see.

Though I had rarely been directly involved in Elvis's music while he was alive, it was time to try to make one of his musical dreams come true. He had always wanted to perform with a live orchestra. I was regularly going back and forth between the United States and England during the years that Lisa lived there. On one of my trips, I met someone whom I liked very much and who was part of an orchestra. Through him, I made contact with the Royal Philharmonic Orchestra. I pitched my idea there and was thrilled to get some interest. I knew I was more likely to succeed in getting an album done in England than here in the States because the British people love Elvis. They appreciate his music even more, I believe, than people do here. I worked with a British team to executive-produce an album with Sony Records and the Philharmonic. I was delighted; we were actually going to make something Elvis had always wanted.

Few people know that Elvis loved both opera and classical music. Whenever classical artists performed on television, Elvis sang along. Mario Lanza and Enrico Caruso were both heroes of his; he loved the drama and the power of their singing. He styled "Now or Never" after Mario Lanza's "O Solo Mio." Elvis also loved the opera *The Student Prince*. In fact, we connected over it when I first met him. My father had played opera all my life, and I loved it. I was familiar with the great operatic singers and productions, including *The Student Prince*. Elvis was fascinated that such a young girl had classical taste.

He loved classical orchestras and longed to perform with one. Colonel Parker, though, wasn't interested. From the first time the Colonel had seen Elvis perform live, he had seen the frenzy created among girls. He wanted to duplicate that response in the movies. The Colonel's unwillingness or inability to understand Elvis as an artist created tremendous stress for Elvis. The Colonel and the record company controlled the recordings he made, and they had no intention of funding a record of Elvis singing with an orchestra. Such an album would be expensive to produce and would deviate sharply from the style his fans had come to expect. These men were unwilling to take the risk. Because I had no doubt Elvis would have eventually taken that risk, I decided to take it for him.

We recorded the album at the famed Abbey Road Studios, where the Beatles had once recorded. I was very hands-on. I curated the album, carefully selecting both the songs and the singers who collaborated on two of them. I included some of the big hits, but I deliberately chose some lesser-known songs like "And the Grass Won't Pay No Mind." It was also essential to include gospel songs because they were especially precious to Elvis. He would warm up with them and sing them after the concerts. Sometimes he'd wander around the house at four in the morning, singing them. I chose "How Great Thou Art" because he loved it so much.

I chose "An American Trilogy" because it has special meaning for me. The first time I heard it, I was listening to the radio while driving down Sunset Boulevard in LA. I immediately turned around and drove straight back home to call Elvis. People rarely brought songs to Elvis. He chose them himself.

But when he heard "An American Trilogy," he said, "Damn, good song."

For Elvis's Philharmonic album, the producers and I searched carefully for artists who wouldn't compete with Elvis on the duets. We ended up choosing Michael Bublé to do a duet on "Fever," and Il Volo, an Italian operatic pop trio, on "Now or Never." All the singers were very professional and a pleasure to work with. I chose "If I Can Dream" because it is powerfully sung and as relevant today as it was fifty years ago. It became the title of the album.

The completed album was greeted with wonderful reviews. Rather than overshadowing Elvis, the orchestra made his voice sound sweeter and fuller. The force of his voice blending with the orchestra is exactly what he would have done. My risk had paid off. The album was released by RCA and Legacy Recordings on October 30, 2015, during the yearlong celebration of Elvis's eightieth birthday. It debuted at number one in the United Kingdom, selling 1.6 million copies in the first year. It was the first time Elvis was on a classical chart. It went to number one on the American charts for two weeks and remained in the top fifteen for almost a year. The album went platinum in the United Kingdom and Australia. The success of the first album led to the release of *The Wonder of You*, a second album with the Philharmonic, on October 21, 2016. Both carry the DNA of Elvis, and in a sometimes-confusing music industry, both keep him relevant.

We did two concert tours with the Royal Philharmonic in Great Britain, playing cities in England, Scotland, and Wales. Later we toured Europe and Scandinavia with the Czech

Philharmonic, stopping in the Netherlands, Sweden, Denmark, Germany, Switzerland, Belgium, and Austria. I traveled with them and greeted the audience at each performance. The format was much like the tribute concert in 1997, where Lisa Marie first sang in public, but the technology was much more sophisticated by then. Skilled musicians and technicians had synchronized archival concert footage and Elvis's vocals with the orchestra's score and the backup singers. The completed effect was thrilling. It felt as though Elvis was there in person.

We sold out everywhere we went, ending the British tour at the O2 Arena in London with a crowd of twenty thousand. It's the most prestigious concert arena in England, in part because the acoustics are so good. There is little to no echo from the music. The aesthetics were dramatic. The concert opened with a giant image of the gates of Graceland opening for the audience, then slowly swinging closed. A lone saxophonist began playing the melody of "If I Can Dream" while the lyrics were projected on a dark blue curtain. He was joined first by a few violinists, then gradually by the whole orchestra and the backup singers. Elvis's signature appeared on the curtain as the song ended.

As the last note sounded, I walked onstage. I was dressed as you do for a formal concert, as was appropriate for the Royal Philharmonic. My black satin gown fell to the floor. Then I greeted the audience with the words "Elvis is back!" and went on to tell them that they would see Elvis's connection to the audience and band members for themselves. I told them they'd see his personality, his sense of humor. I mentioned the phenomenon of Elvis still filling an arena nearly forty years after his passing. Finally, I reassured them that though Elvis could not be there in person that night, his spirit would definitely be there. I meant it. I could feel his presence, and my heart swelled with joy and pride that I had been able to make this dream come true for him. Elvis would have been so proud of me. I was proud of myself. The stadium was filled with people of all ages, including children. I was passing the legacy on to a new generation. I exited the stage as a video image of him flickered onto the screen like an old movie. Which, of course, it was.

We ended the tour at Graceland, with the Memphis Symphony Orchestra. Coming home. What a wonderful way to end this adventure.

The orchestra tour was fulfilling for me, but it didn't address one of my most important objectives: to show people who Elvis really was. People didn't know Elvis deeply. He wasn't just a singer. He wasn't just an entertainer, some popular guy in a bejeweled suit who performed in Vegas. A one-dimensional character, a caricature, really. He was so much more as a person. He was thoughtful, deep, introspective. Elvis was always searching for answers to the meaning of life, to his purpose on earth. He wanted so much to do what God intended for him.

Jerry Schilling and I used to talk about that so much. Jerry is one of my dearest friends, like a brother to me. I have known him since I was a teenager at Graceland. He was a young boy when he met Elvis. He knew the man, the real person behind the icon. Both Jerry and I were tired of the stereotypes, of the jokes, of the snobbery that some people directed at Elvis. I wanted to make a documentary about the real man. Elvis had longed to make serious films, movies that meant something. I wanted to fulfill that dream for him. So did Jerry. But it took us seven years to find the right production team.

In 2014, we approached Kary Antholis, the president of HBO miniseries, and talked with him about our vision for an Elvis documentary. He was immediately intrigued and reached out to producer Jon Landau to jump-start the process. Jon in turn contacted director Thom Zimny, whom he'd worked with on Bruce Springsteen documentaries for nearly twenty years. Jerry and I talked in depth with Thom and Jon, and during the discussions, I referred to Elvis as a searcher, a man who had spent his life searching for the truth. Jon was struck by the phrase and suggested we use *The Searcher* as the title of the film. I readily agreed. I was impressed by Thom's insights and sensitivity. He asked me penetrating questions about Elvis that no one had ever asked me before. I knew we had found the right team at last. Jerry and I came on as executive producers.

Making the film was a long labor of love. We were not shoved aside. We were consulted every step of the way. We wanted to make the definitive documentary about Elvis the artist, the musical genius. He wasn't just some good-looking Southern boy who stumbled on success. He knew exactly what he wanted to accomplish. Elvis was a producer of his recordings, not just the singer. He was so much more than a singer. He worked incredibly hard. He was not an overnight success. Just a year out of high school, he was a boy forging a path in a highly competitive world, enduring criticism and even ridicule from both the music and the religious establishments. The moralists saw him as a threat to decency. He hated the nickname "Elvis the Pelvis" and didn't understand it. Because he drew inspiration from everywhere, he didn't quite fit in anywhere. Elvis wanted to reach and feel what we all go through as human beings. In sharing his music, he was sharing his life. Elvis wanted to grow, to evolve as an artist. Instead, he was pushed into a kind of artistic prison. His management saw him simply as a moneymaker. He felt trapped. *The Searcher* showed his vulnerability, the ups and downs of what he went through. Thom was a brilliant director who used innovative techniques to get our message across.

The Searcher was divided into two parts. Part 1 premiered on March 14, 2018, at the South by Southwest Film Festival in Austin, Texas, and Part 2 showed the next day. On April 14, the documentary premiered on HBO. Thom, musical director David Porter, Jerry, and I walked the red carpet in Austin. Thom talked to the press about the intimate conversations he and I had had while making the film. I told them they would see stories previously known only to those closest to Elvis. After the showing and a standing ovation from the crowd, we did a panel discussion. Three days later, *The Searcher* was shown at Graceland's Guest House Auditorium. The place was packed. In addition to those of us who worked on the film, Jerry Phillips, son of Sam Phillips, who did Elvis's first recording at Sun Studio, attended on his late father's behalf.

The response from viewers and critics alike was everything Jerry and I could have hoped for. They understood that the film was the real deal. Audience members congratulated me, saying, "Oh my God, I had no idea. I had no idea who Elvis really was." They described the film as thoughtful, sensitive, and spellbinding. The film was referred to in the press as "the definitive film about Elvis Presley." *The Hollywood Reporter* called the film "probing and thoughtful." Praise for the film was almost universal, with a 96 percent score on **Rotten Tomatoes**. Tom Petty commented, "He was a light for all of us. . . . We should dwell on what was so beautiful and everlasting, . . . that great, great music."

We could not have asked for a better team. I am forever grateful for the gift they gave us in making the film. I like to think that somewhere, somehow, Elvis is grateful, too. It is a wonderful thing to make someone's dream come true. It was a wonderful thing to have mine come true in the process.

CHAPTER 15

Poison Apples

My middle name is misery...
So don't you mess around with me.

England has long been a magical place for me. I love the people, the traditions, and the green meadows in spring. My frequent trips to Britain to visit my daughter brought me into contact with many warmly creative people. I'd had the opportunity to help create the recordings of Elvis with the Royal Philharmonic, an orchestra long associated with the British musical elite. But England also brought me a very different kind of opportunity, one that has been thriving in British villages and towns, inns and theaters, for hundreds of years. It crosses all classes and is as English as

Yorkshire pudding. The British panto, short for pantomime, has been around since the first Queen Elizabeth of England. It is a staple of the yuletide season; an English Christmas isn't Christmas at all without it. Many Americans have never heard of it. So how did a retired American actress and grandmother of four end up starring in one? Father Christmas?

No, my agents at William Morris. I had made friends in England while working on projects there. The word was out that I was frequently in Britain, and word eventually reached the people staging the Wimbledon Panto. They contacted my agents, who in turn told me it was a good opportunity. As with the initial offer to do *Naked Gun*, my reaction was "Why me? I'm an American who's never even done a stage play!" The thought of working before a live audience terrified me. British panto isn't what Americans call pantomime. The characters speak. I would have to learn lines and hope I didn't forget them. But my agents persisted and convinced me that it was a wonderful opportunity for me, one they were confident I'd enjoy. They were right.

I couldn't have had a better opportunity for my first venture into pantomime. It was scheduled for a month in the 2012–2013 Christmas season in the New Wimbledon Theater. The Wimbledon is a beautiful Edwardian baroque theater that simply drips character. It was built in southwestern London a century ago. With a capacity of over sixteen hundred people, it is sort of a stopping-off point on the way to the West End for new musicals, in addition to a repertory of its own. I had the honor of starring as the evil queen in *Snow White* opposite Warwick Davis. Warwick, a wonderfully warm and talented actor with dwarfism, is well known to viewers through his roles in the *Star Wars* films and *Harry Potter* and as the title character in *Willow*. The only challenge in working with Warwick was in not letting him steal the show!

Panto is known for its brilliant costumes and fairy-tale flair. I got to wear gorgeous velvet and brocade dresses and headpieces that ranged from jeweled crowns to devil's horns. It was like being a child playing dress-up. I was terrified the first time I faced a pantomime audience, which was seated only a few feet in front of me. I kept thinking, *What if I don't remember my lines? It's not like they can stop the cameras and do another take. What if no one laughs? What if they laugh when I'm not trying to be funny? What if they don't like me?* But I soon relaxed into the moment. Few things are more fun than being wicked in a beautiful gown. I got to interact with the audiences in ways I'd never done before. In British panto, the audience is so interactive that the members are like part of the cast. They are not only expected to cheer and boo but also expected to shout warnings. "Look behind you!" "She's over there!" I was deliciously booed, for I had the pleasure of playing the wickedest of them all.

Perhaps the very best part was that Lisa's twins were just four years old and living in England when my pantomime career started. They were so excited to see their Nona onstage as one of their favorite fairy-tale characters. Best of all, they didn't have to sit still and be quiet. They could wiggle and talk all they wanted. I enjoyed my first pantomime experience so much that I've continued performing in them whenever I can for the last ten years. It's been one of the most festive and fulfilling experiences of my career. I feel honored that the British public has welcomed me so warmly.

Wickedness on a pantomime stage wielding a poison apple is one thing. In real life, it's entirely another. The malignancy that seeped into my family during those same years slowly began to poison our lives.

Rarely does trouble come out of nowhere. It starts when small streams eventually come together and form a deluge that leaves all involved struggling to keep their heads above water. My daughter inherited a powerful legacy. Lisa's traumatic loss of her father at such a young age left her with a longing for what she'd once had. Every man she loved was subconsciously compared with her father, and none of them could match the exciting, adoring man she'd lost as a child. The pattern repeated itself over and over: hope, disappointment, restlessness, and moving on. As much as I wanted to believe Lisa's fourth marriage would last, I was not surprised to see warning signs that the relationship was deteriorating. Nor should I have been surprised when she succumbed to drugs for the second time in her life. It was in her genetic makeup. Her grandmother Gladys had depended on medication to get through the days, and of course, drugs played a strong role in Elvis's early death. I can still remember being a young teen and watching Elvis counting his medication into piles before he began swallowing them. I didn't understand the import of that behavior at the time, but it made me uncomfortable from the beginning.

What I didn't expect was for Navarone to follow a similar path, though for very different reasons. I didn't learn about his experiences until many years later, when Navarone confided his story, but he was fascinated by drugs from his teen years on. He was intrigued by the drug experimentation of the 1960s and

1970s and its relationship to creativity. As his interest in creating music began to grow, so did his interest in mind-altering substances. Another factor for him was his natural curiosity. From childhood, he had wanted to try new things, taste new foods, have new adventures. He has an adventurous, fearless spirit that sometimes overcomes common sense.

What made drugs really attractive to him was that for years, he'd never had a bad experience with them. My limited experience with the pills Elvis had given me had been unpleasant. They didn't make me feel good, so I soon declined to take them. Not so with my son. Every drug he tried made him feel great. When he took LSD with his friends, he had a euphoric experience. One of his friends did not, however. And thank God, Navarone noted the friend's bad reaction and didn't try to repeat the experiment. He tried almost everything else, though, including cocaine and heroin. He particularly liked the way heroin made him feel.

Once he moved out on his own, there were no real constraints on his usage. He became a regular heroin user but was convinced he was not addicted. His intake was stable: three times a day, rarely more. Unlike many users, he did not continually increase his intake in search of a bigger high, so he considered himself a recreational user instead of an addict. All the years I had spent raising him to lead a drug-free life were a failure. Like so many parents, I discovered that my guidance was in vain. He successfully hid his habit from me, and because I didn't see any personality changes, I remained in the dark. As far as I was concerned, Navarone was the same sweet, loving son he'd always been to me.

He felt safely anonymous living in Santa Cruz, but that anonymity didn't last long. In 2008, word got out that he was growing marijuana in his backyard, and the *National Enquirer* got a hold of the story. It ended up on the front page: Priscilla Presley's son was growing drugs at his house. So much for avoiding the spotlight. Suddenly, everyone knew who he was, and his beloved adopted town was no longer a refuge. He decided to return to LA to record music with Them Guns and prepare for a tour. Back in Beverly Hills, he had to be more vigilant about hiding his drug use. He brought his snakes and his water monitor back to LA with him, and once again, I had a reptile habitat in my backyard while he got settled.

Now, water monitors are cute when they're little. Navarone had raised one from a baby only a few inches long. His name was Stefan. By the time Stefan moved into my house, however, he was seven feet long, the size of a small alligator. Navarone usually fed him, but on one occasion, Navarone was out of town, and it fell to me to feed his pet. Water monitors are carnivores, so I took a steak outside to feed him. I didn't realize I was supposed to grip the meat with a pair of small tongs when I offered it to the animal. Stefan was hungry and eagerly grabbed the steak, sinking his teeth into the meat—and my right hand. It wasn't an attack, and as soon as he got the meat in his mouth, he let go of my hand. When I looked down at my hand, it was gushing blood. I ran into the house and put my hand under the kitchen faucet, running cold water over the wound, clenching my jaw with pain. My cousin Ivy happened to stroll into the kitchen right then and calmly began filling a glass with cold water.

I looked at her. "Are you kidding me?"

"What?" she said blankly.

"Haven't you noticed I'm bleeding all over the place?"

"Oh, yeah."

"Good grief!" I said in exasperation.

Luckily for me, Vikki drove me straight to the doctor. Stefan had almost severed my tendon. The injury required multiple stitches and took a while to heal. During that time, I was left physically awkward, since I'm right-handed. And yes, the injury left a permanent scar. Quite an impressive one. What a mother won't do for her son.

That wasn't the end of our adventures with Navarone's amazing animal. While Vikki and I were in England, Stefan escaped from his cage one day and began roaming the neighborhood. When Ivy saw he was gone, she panicked and called Marta, one of Navarone's "surrogate moms," to help her search. Marta raced to my house as police sirens began wailing. Ivy and Marta followed the sirens and found a police van and three Beverly Hills Police Department officers trying to capture a confused water monitor right in front of Sharon Stone's house. Sharon had called for help and then locked herself safely inside. Meanwhile, Ivy and Marta were calling around, trying to get hold of Navarone, who was back in town by then. They finally succeeded, and he rushed over to the "scene of the crime." I don't know who was more frightened by then, the police or Stefan. The situation wasn't going well. In the middle of all this chaos, Navarone walked over to Stefan, picked him up, and slung the lizard over his shoulder. Then he thanked the officers and calmly carried Stefan back home. Never a dull day in Beverly Hills.

Navarone was still taking drugs, but he considered himself a recreational user. He was well over a decade into heroin use before he really got into trouble. Suddenly, he began to crave more and more of it. The desire escalated until he was taking it every fifteen minutes or so. The craving was insatiable. What he didn't know was that the heroin he was taking by then wasn't the same drug. It was laced with fentanyl, a powerful opioid exponentially stronger than heroin. Fentanyl had hit the streets with a vengeance and has never gone away. It is the second-biggest killer of teens in the United States, and a single dose can hook or kill you. By that time, Navarone knew he was in trouble. The drug controlled every hour of his day, and if he missed a dose, he couldn't function; he immediately went into withdrawal. It became impossible for him to hide his use from anyone he was close to, including me.

Once I knew what he was facing, I went into rescue mode. I am a natural rescuer, so trying to save my son was my immediate response. My dear friend Jerry Schilling, Vikki and Marta (part of the "harem" that, along with me, Navarone fondly jokes, raised him), and my family joined in an intervention. Navarone knew he needed to get clean, and he wanted to please his loved ones—especially me—by doing as we asked. But as he will now tell you, getting clean for someone else never works. He checked himself into rehab and told the nurse he would test positive for heroin and cocaine because he'd just shot up. To his great surprise, the nurse reported back that he didn't have heroin in his system; he had fentanyl. The blood test was his first inkling of what he was really injecting into his body. Navarone lasted less than twenty-four hours in rehab that first time. In fact, he talked to another addict while there and got the contact information for another dealer. He walked out the door and went straight to his new dealer. He wasn't ready to face what rehab meant. Doing it for me didn't work.

That was the first of multiple interventions, all of them ultimately failures. The next time he tried to get clean, he took along his baby lizard for emotional support. But once he went into withdrawal, he couldn't control either his emotions or his body. He accidentally stepped on his pet, killing it. He was distraught. The incident sent him into a downward emotional spiral and straight back to his source of comfort. Fentanyl. He still wasn't ready, and nothing I could say or do would change that. Fear for my son became a daily battle.

As Navarone noted after Lisa passed away, he had no idea that he and his sister had been fighting some of the same battles at the same time. He and Lisa were not estranged, but during those years, they were not close, either. Lisa had moved back from England and was now dividing her time between Nashville and LA. She had pulled away from the family in general as her addiction worsened. The personality changes the drugs brought and her need to keep her addiction secret affected all her relationships. What I had first identified as a sort of docility in Lisa gradually became alarming. When I would visit her, she wasn't always dressed, and she seemed out of it mentally. She would still be wearing her pajamas in the middle of the day. One morning when I came to visit, her husband, Michael, was just about to take the twins to school when Lisa appeared. She was half-dressed, with uncombed hair, insisting that she be the one to drive them to school.

She told us, "That's my job. I'm the mother."

Clearly, she was in no condition to drive, and Michael eventually persuaded her to come with them while he drove. All I could think was, *Please don't let the paparazzi be there.* If Lisa were photographed in that state, it would become tabloid gold.

Michael realized I was aware that something was wrong, though Lisa had sworn him to secrecy. He and I finally had a long talk about it. He said that Lisa had been taking pain pills since the twins' birth, but in the beginning, her use had been relatively controlled. But over time, she had started using more and more, and she was now in need of help. When he tried to talk to her about it, though, she resented it and told him to mind his own business. It was creating a wedge between them, and he felt helpless to help her. In her eyes, he had become the enemy. I understood his dilemma all too well. Elvis had reacted the same way whenever I'd gently tried to get him to address his drug usage. And I knew from experience with both Elvis and my son that my talking to her wouldn't do any good. It would simply strain our relationship. An intervention seemed out of the question. As Lisa herself used to say, nobody told her what to do. She was her own woman. Seeking help had to be her decision.

By 2014, the problem had gone well beyond painkillers. As she eventually acknowledged, Lisa was taking both opioids and painkillers while mixing cocaine with large amounts of alcohol. She was well aware that what she was doing was disastrous, but she couldn't stop. She continued trying to hide the extent of her addiction out of shame and fear of losing custody of her children. I didn't learn many of the details until afterward, for I was one of the people she was trying to hide it from. The fact that she knew better only made her feel worse. Her children were the only thing that kept her going.

That year, Lisa entered rehab for the first of many times. She was fighting hard to reclaim her life, but she was losing the battle. In addition to the harmful effects the drugs were having on her physical and mental health, they were also affecting her marriage. Just as Elvis had resented any mention of his drug problems, Lisa resented Michael's efforts to help her. When she told me she didn't want to be married anymore, my heart sank. I cared about Michael, and I knew he loved Lisa. I believed he was good for her.

In June 2016, Lisa filed for divorce, asking for sole custody of Finley and Harper. She knew that the only way she could keep the twins full-time was to claim that Michael was an unfit father, so she filed a variety of accusations against him intended to demonstrate that the girls should not be with him. She was encouraged to do this by someone very possessive of her. They felt threatened by anyone who had a close relationship with Lisa, including me, but they were particularly jealous of Michael. In her suggestible state, with a load of painkillers and opioids in her system, Lisa was vulnerable to the bad advice she was receiving. When she filed her accusations, Michael had to countersue to avoid losing his children. His countersuit cited Lisa's addiction as impeding her ability to care for the twins. In the deposition about her drug use subsequently required by the court, Lisa finally revealed the extent of her usage. I was stunned. I had no idea how much poison she was pouring into her body.

What was happening was heartbreaking. I knew Michael well, and I had always known him to be a loving and devoted husband and father. I also knew that Lisa was very unhappy. She was convinced that Harper and Finley should be with her because she was the mother. She believed that mothers had more rights than fathers since mothers carried and birthed the children. I found her belief ironic because of the way Elvis and I had handled custody of her. We'd shared custody because we believed she needed both parents. Whenever her school calendar and Elvis's performance schedule allowed, I arranged for Lisa to be with her dad. Losing contact with her father would have devastated her. But pointing the analogy out to Lisa in her current state of mind would be useless. She wasn't thinking clearly.

After Lisa's deposition, articles about the divorce proceeding began to appear, and I worried about the rumors that were spreading. Most of all, though, I was worried about Harper and Finley. Their welfare came first.

Because of the custody dispute, the twins legally had to be removed from the home and monitored by designated third parties. They could not see either parent without supervision. None of us wanted the girls to be turned over to Child and Family Services for foster care, so I offered to have the twins live with me while the legal issues were resolved. Both Lisa and Michael agreed to the twins being placed in my care, and Lisa asked me if Benjamin could live with me as well while she concentrated on her health. For a while, we were able to keep the arrangement confidential. But when the press leaked that Harper and Finley had been taken into protective custody, the public assumed they were in foster care. I then released a statement saying that they had been in my care since they were removed from their home, something I would have preferred not to share publicly. What followed was simultaneously one of the best and most difficult years of my life.

Ben settled into my home nicely. He was in his early twenties by then and fascinated with computers. He spent most of his time working on his computer in his room at my home. I was struck by his intense interest and wondered if a career in computers would be a good choice for him. He could create computer games or be a programmer. It would be a way to funnel his creativity into a new medium. I knew he felt some pressure to go into music, and he had even been signed to a record contract. But the albums he was meant to produce hadn't materialized, and I wasn't sure his heart was in music. He was such a lovely young man, easy to have around and thoughtful of me. I was kept in the loop when he was going out with friends. Ben was accustomed to his mom asking lots of questions about his friends and activities whenever he left the house, and I think he liked that I didn't. I had kept an eye on my children, too, but it was different being a grandmother. Ben enjoyed the added freedom. My grandson and I grew close as we spent long periods together for the first time.

Benjamin was good company and made few demands on my time. He was, of course, a legal adult who was free to come and go as he chose. The situation with the twins was dramatically different. Apart from their being only eight years old, my responsibility to them was now legal as well as familial. My role had changed. I was still their Nona, but I was also their temporary guardian. I had to ensure that the directives from the court were followed. I was also responsible for helping to monitor them during visits with their parents. Neither parent was allowed to see the children alone. Because it was a 24-7 commitment, it was impractical for one person to fulfill all the responsibilities involved. Harper and Finley were appointed two monitors: myself and Vikki, who had helped to care for Navarone when he was a child.

I would get the girls up and dressed and take them to school every weekday. I would also pick them up after school and make sure their homework was done. If they were visiting one of their parents, Vikki would take off work early and drive them to see either Lisa or Michael. She had to remain there throughout the visit, which was tiring and awkward for her. Afterward, she would bring them back to my house and go home while the girls took a bath and I put them to bed. On weekends, they would be with me.

From the time Lisa filed her allegations against Michael, the matter was in the hands of the courts. We had no choice but to follow the legal processes. Serious custody disputes entail extensive investigation. There were processes that the girls had to go through. They were interviewed and examined by psychologists, doctors, and social workers. It was confusing and stressful for two eight-year-olds, who didn't understand what was going on. They would sometimes cry on the way home from the appointments and want to know why they had to see all these people. After each session, I did what any grandmother would do. I bought them ice cream. Later, when we got home, we'd have dinner and watch old movies on TV. By the time I put the girls to bed, life seemed happy and normal again.

They stayed with me for almost a year. Unless something happened related to the investigation, we just enjoyed being together. I wanted them to have a wonderful time with me because I didn't want them to think about the tug-of-war between Lisa and Michael. They were being shuttled back and forth between their parents. I wanted my home to be a safe place, neutral ground. I didn't want them to know I was their legal guardian. It was important that I remain just Nona. We had so much fun. We swam and played tennis and ran around the yard playing hide and seek. We cuddled up together and watched old movies and ate bowls of popcorn. That's still Harper's favorite thing to do with me. They played with the dogs. They brought life back into my home in a way I hadn't experienced since Navarone grew up. I knew I would miss them terribly when they were gone.

After a year, Lisa requested a change in the custody arrangements. She missed her girls and wanted a legal way to spend more time with them. So she petitioned the court to make Benjamin and her personal assistant monitors for the girls. Ben would move back home with Finley and Harper. To my surprise, the court agreed, and the twins moved back in with their mother. Vikki continued to pick up the girls from Lisa's house and take them to visit Michael so they could still see their dad. Lisa was upset, feeling Vikki was taking sides against her. She also thought I should be more supportive of her bid for sole custody. The conflict between my daughter and son-in-law was creating fissures within our family like cracks spreading across a sheet of ice. We were slowly but surely being poisoned by drugs, by fear, and by suspicion, and I didn't know how to fix any of it.

The battle over the girls continued until the decree was final in 2021. It seemed endless.

Lisa had gone steadily downhill from the day she first filed for divorce. It was like my daughter was disappearing inside a woman I had never met. She was no longer my Lisa Marie. Her drug usage climbed as high as eighty pills a day. Desperate to keep her girls, she lived in a tornado of drug-fueled emotions with no relief in sight. She no longer had the release of the auditing sessions that Scientology had once provided for her. Though she had left the church, she retained some of its beliefs, including a distrust of psychologists. She was still opposed to therapy, which would have given her a potential outlet for her feelings. It was near the end of this period that she began recording the tapes that would be transcribed and edited for her autobiography. It was a way for her to feel that she had a voice and to release some of the fear, anger, and despair that enveloped her. The pain began to pour out of her onto audiotapes in a mixture of memories and nightmares, of what had happened and what she believed had happened.

In a last-ditch effort to gain sole custody of the twins, she asked me to sign a deposition supporting her allegations that Michael was unfit to have custody of the girls. I told her I couldn't sign it, for I had never seen Michael behave in the harmful ways she was alleging. Signing it would be perjury. In Lisa's mind, I was the last hope to prove her charges. The court's investigations of Michael had failed to reveal any wrongdoing or neglect on his part, so she had exhausted her legal options. Now I was refusing to back her up in court. To her, it was a betrayal. When the divorce proceedings finally concluded, Michael was given regular visitation rights. The girls would live primarily with Lisa, but they would still be with their father part-time. Lisa was unhappy with the outcome. She blamed it partly on my refusal to take a legal stand against Michael. Her anger fueled what I feared most: estrangement from my daughter.

I knew that arguing with her was futile. I would be arguing with her addiction. I also knew with a stab to my heart that she would never completely forgive me. And she never did. I was losing one of the two people I loved the most. I didn't know yet that I would soon lose her permanently. The events poisoning our lives would prove fatal.

CHAPTER 16
Storm and Grace

My heart can't seem to take it
Your storm and your grace

LIFE SEEMS TO ACCELERATE AS YOU GROW OLDER, AND I had reached the time in my life when generations come and go. "Little Riley" was all grown up, an accomplished woman in her own right. My oldest granddaughter has always been a force to be reckoned with. Riley was born independent. In some respects, she is like her mother—a loving, sensitive, talented free spirit with a killer sense of humor. But Riley has always had a focus that my daughter struggled to find. Riley has always seemed to know what she wanted to do and gone after it. She began modeling when she was fourteen and had appeared on several major magazine covers by the time she was fifteen, including the cover of *Vogue* in August 2004. By twenty, Riley was acting in featured roles. By her late twenties, she had attracted not only critical acclaim but multiple award nominations, including her first Golden Globe nomination as Best Actress. She has gone on to direct and produce films and has even started her own production company. As we painfully learned when her mother passed away, Riley is also a talented writer. She embodies both a fearlessness and a tenderness that draw people to her. She is the best daughter and big sister anyone could wish for. Her love and loyalty to both of her parents have been steadfast. I have always been intensely proud not only of what she's achieved but also of who she is.

In 2015, shortly before our family was thrust into the turmoil of Lisa's divorce, Riley married Australian stuntman Ben Smith-Petersen, whom she'd met while filming *Mad Max: Fury Road*. The family quickly dubbed him "Big Ben" to differentiate him from her younger brother, "Ben Ben." The wedding made the February 2015 cover of *Hello!* magazine, with a photo of Riley, Lisa, and me, and the headline "Love Me Tender: Priscilla and Lisa Marie's Joy as Daughter Riley Weds." The headline was a lovely, poignant reminder that her grandfather, Elvis, was still with us in spirit.

The wedding took place at Calistoga Ranch in Napa Valley. It was a picture-perfect day, with the kind of weather only California can provide in February. The large wedding party included friends, siblings, and cousins from both sides of the family, plus Riley's Uncle Navarone, two years her senior. All of the attendants were dressed formally in black, and the look was simple and elegant—right down my alley. Riley looked stunning in a vintage-style white lace dress with long sleeves and a short train. She wore her long hair down in soft curls, with no headpiece. She looked so much like her mother that day. Jerry Schilling officiated. We ate dinner by the lake, and afterward, her father Danny and brother Ben joined the band while we all danced into the night. It was a day of tranquility and joy that came to symbolize the peace of mind we were soon to lose. I looked at my granddaughter, all grown up with a husband of her own, and thought about her grandfather. In another life, Elvis would have been there that day. We might have persuaded him to dance with her. He would certainly have sung to her. Not that day, though. That day, there were only memories.

Three years later, amid the pain and turmoil of Lisa's divorce, my father passed away. Though he was not my biological father, Colonel Joseph Paul Beaulieu was the only father I had ever known. He had married my mother and adopted me in 1948. Paul was a military man through and through. He began his career as a US Marine and entered the air force in World War II. He served as a pilot in World War II, the Korean War, and the Vietnam War. It was while he was stationed in Germany, flying daily missions over the Berlin Wall, that I met Elvis. If my dad had never joined the air force, I would never have met Elvis. More than once, he wished I hadn't.

My dad has taken a lot of flak for letting me date Elvis at fourteen. It wasn't an easy decision for him, and after my first "date," he forbade me to see Elvis again. When I objected, my father consulted Elvis's commanding officer for a character reference and insisted on meeting Elvis personally. He made it clear to Elvis that I was to be treated with respect and that he would be watching carefully to see that I was. I was to be chaperoned at all times. His permission for me to see Elvis was provisional, subject to being revoked if his terms weren't met. It was also the result of prolonged discussions with my mother, to whom I talked more freely. She saw how important the relationship was to me, and she believed me when I told her it was just a friendship. I'm sure she also saw the stars in my eyes, but she believed me when I told her that nothing inappropriate was happening. At the time, neither of my parents thought that the relationship would last more than a few weeks. Elvis would be returning to the United States soon, and that move—they were sure—would be the end of my acquaintance with him.

And the truth is, Elvis and I weren't dating then in the traditional sense of the word. That didn't happen until three years later. The Elvis I met at fourteen was a deeply homesick young man who was grieving the death of his mother. Her death was recent and completely unexpected. He was still traumatized by her passing. I didn't meet the rock star. I met a frightened, lonely young man who was on his own for the first time in his life. His celebrity status just isolated him further in the military. Elvis's deployment to Germany was the first time he had been away from home. Everything in his environment was unfamiliar, even the language. And though he was homesick, he worried continually about what would happen when he went home. Would his fans have forgotten him? Would his music have gone out of style? Rock and roll was still comparatively new, and no one knew if it was a passing fad or a lasting part of American music. Elvis knew his mother wouldn't be there when he got home. Would his career still be there?

I think my primary appeal was that I was a girl from home who was a sympathetic listener. We spent our evenings together talking or listening to music. The vast majority of the time we were alone, Elvis just talked to me, usually about his mother. He still yearned for her. Sometimes, tears would roll down his cheeks. I don't know why, but he instinctively trusted me. I would hold his hand as he talked, and sometimes we would lie down together, and he'd hold me. There were some soft kisses, but he never touched me sexually. He held me in his arms respectfully and tenderly. I think I eased his pain. I believe my parents were right to trust him to treat me like the "little one" he called me. Both my mother and my father allowed the relationship, despite their reservations.

My dad had a very hard time letting me move to Memphis when I was seventeen. Elvis wanted me there, but it wasn't a casual request. He had carefully thought through the arrangement. I would live with his father Vernon and Vernon's wife at their home near Graceland. I would complete the last year of my education at a good Catholic high school. Elvis would treat me with the respect I deserved and guard my reputation. And though he never directly stated it, Elvis implied that his purpose in bringing me there was to ultimately make me his wife. He and my father discussed the arrangement man to man.

My father believed that Elvis was serious, but I don't think he would have allowed the arrangement if I hadn't threatened to run away. By then I was so deeply in love with Elvis that I told my parents I would go to Memphis with or without their permission. I would find a way to get there. I was defiant, and I was sincere. I would have run away, which would have been a greater risk to me than moving there under agreed-upon conditions. My parents reluctantly considered what Elvis was proposing. My dad went to Memphis to meet Vernon and to tour the Catholic school I would be enrolled in. Although it was summer break and he couldn't meet my teachers, he made sure it was a reputable, academically sound school. He discussed the requirements for the move with Elvis, and they agreed on terms. Admittedly, Elvis and I didn't do a very good job of sticking to the conditions my parents had set, for I soon quietly moved to Graceland. But that was my decision, not my parents' fault. I have always been hurt and angered by the blame both my parents endured for a situation that was largely out of their control.

I believe that the main reason my parents moved to California when Dad retired from the air force in 1976 was to get back some of the years they'd lost with me. I bought them a home in Brentwood, near my house in Beverly Hills, and we were able to have an extended family when my sister and one of my brothers joined us. Dad worked as a contractor for several years and then became the neighborhood fix-it guy in his old age. If any of his neighbors had a broken refrigerator or a loose doorknob, they knew to call Paul. He was a well-known and well-liked figure in the neighborhood.

Dad died of kidney failure in 2018. He was ninety-two years old. My parents were Catholic, and my father had chosen to be buried in a Catholic cemetery rather than a military one. His funeral was held at Holy Cross Cemetery in Culver City, California, in February with full military honors. There was a color guard, and my mother was presented with a ceremonial American flag, carefully folded. Our entire family gathered to say goodbye. Paul wasn't always an easy man to have as a father. He had the reserve common to military men, and I was never as close to him emotionally as I was to my mother. But he was an honorable man, an upright man who chose to raise another man's daughter as his own. And for that, I honor him, and I mourned his passing.

Losing your father is a normal, if painful, part of life. Losing your grandson is not. I never had the flicker of a premonition that Benjamin, the little boy with the golden curls I remembered from years before, would precede me in death. Would precede all of us and eventually take his mother with him.

In so many ways, Lisa embodied Elvis's legacy from the day she was born. Part of it was physical. She looked strikingly like her father, and she inherited his physical propensity to addiction as well. She was passionate and moody like her father; she was also charismatic and mercurial. Her musical talent was, I believe, genetic. So was her tendency toward depression and her deep need to find meaning in life. Elvis was a searcher, and though Lisa never duplicated the religious explorations her father made, she pondered the meaning of life from her earliest years. She would thumb through Elvis's religious books, looking at his annotations. And when she committed to Scientology in her twenties, she did it with a zeal that I never duplicated. Though I lived by Scientology principles and practices, I never committed completely to the arduous process of climbing the Bridge to Freedom. Lisa did, and she made it almost to the top.

I believe she also inherited the capacity for intense parental connection like that between Elvis and his mother. Theirs went beyond the typical parent-child bond. Long after her passing, while Elvis and I were married, he would breathe in the lingering scent of his mother's clothing to feel her presence. Gladys could hardly bear to have Elvis out of her sight, in part because of the trauma of losing Elvis's twin. She was terrified of losing Elvis, too. Lisa loved all her children passionately, but it was Ben she had the intense bond with. Like Gladys had been to Elvis, Lisa was connected to Ben's soul.

The trauma of losing Elvis had permanently marked Lisa's life, so when she gave birth to a son who looked strikingly like her father, it was like a gift from heaven. It was as though she got a part of Elvis back again in her son. She watched over Ben just as Gladys had watched over Elvis, keeping him safe. Ben had the same intense blue eyes, and his fair coloring was like Elvis's as a child. The public associates Elvis with black hair, but he was born a blond. He didn't begin dyeing his hair black until his late teens. If you place photos of Elvis and Ben as children side by side, the resemblance is unmistakable. One time when I was at Graceland with Lisa and Ben, we saw a portrait of Elvis. We were in the archives, and there was a picture of Elvis in front of us.

Lisa pointed to the picture and said to Ben, "See there? Look at you. You look like my dad." Then she pointed from the picture to Ben's face and said, "See?"

Ben just mumbled and said, "Yeah."

When she took Ben backstage with her at the Grand Ole Opry, murmurs went through the crowd. People were glancing at Ben and whispering. His resemblance to Elvis became the talk of the evening.

I think this sort of attention was hard for Ben. It couldn't have been easy looking so much like his grandfather. Not that he ever complained about it. As far as I know, he never complained within the family, though his friends said the frequent comparisons to Elvis bothered Ben. It's hard enough for anyone to establish their own identity, but for Ben, it must have been an uphill struggle. So many expectations came with his heritage. People wanted to know if he could sing, if he was musically talented like Elvis. Ben's shyness made the unwanted attention hard to live with. I knew firsthand what it was like to grow up surrounded by admiring fans who searched for a resemblance to Elvis in a child's face. I had spent all of Lisa's childhood and teen years trying to protect her from the implications of being Elvis Presley's daughter. I saw history being repeated with Ben. And emotionally, being frequently perceived in relation to Elvis, rather than as themselves, was confusing for both of them. Who did people see when they looked at Ben and Lisa? Who did people like, Lisa and Ben, or Elvis's daughter and grandson?

Like Lisa, Ben was sweet, sensitive, and introspective. But unlike his mother, he lacked the tough exterior that was part of Lisa's defense mechanism against the world. He had a fragile, soulful quality about him, almost as if he were too good for this world. No wonder Lisa had an overpowering desire to protect him. Just as Gladys had overprotected Elvis out of love and fear, Lisa overprotected Ben. Gladys had walked Elvis to school when he was in high school, afraid he would get beaten up by the neighborhood toughs. He always made her turn back when they got near the school, embarrassed by her protectiveness. Even when Ben was in his twenties, Lisa questioned him every time he went out the door. Where was he going? Who was he going with? When would he be back? Her intense protectiveness made him very uncomfortable. I will admit, though, that my daughter learned that habit partly from me. I used to pepper her with many of the same questions when she left the house as a teenager. Occasionally, I even followed her to make sure she was safe. I still struggle not to check on the safety of my thirty-eight-year-old son. I understand why Lisa did it. Raising a Presley child is a huge responsibility. It came from a place of love.

And of course, she indulged him, as Elvis had indulged her. As she indulged all her children. For Lisa, Elvis's permissiveness was a sign of unconditional love. If she didn't want to brush her teeth, she didn't have to. If her kids didn't want to go to school, she let them stay home. I, of course, was the other extreme with Lisa. I made her go to school whether she wanted to go or not. I kept her to a regular schedule. Bedtime was not negotiable. My firm approach created problems between us because Lisa saw it as a lack of understanding, a lack of love. Lisa and I spoke different love languages when she was growing up. To her, leniency was an expression of love and understanding. She didn't see my careful nurturing of her, my desire to protect her, as an expression of love. To her, my desire to teach her independence was an attempt to distance her from my life. Though she understood cognitively when she grew up that my approach was motivated by love, I'm not certain she ever understood it emotionally. It was only natural that with her own children, her parenting was more like her father's.

One thing was certain: She adored her son. She used to joke with Riley that Ben was her favorite, but Riley took it good-naturedly. She knew she was loved, too. I think the most eloquent expression of Lisa's love for Ben is in her own words. When she recorded her last album, the title song was written for Ben. It was called "Storm and Grace," an allusion to Ben's middle name, Storm. It is my favorite of Lisa's songs. And the most heartbreaking.

> *You are the most beautiful man*
> *That I've ever known...*
> *You blow me away, yeah*
> *Your storm and your grace*
> *My heart can't seem to take it*
> *Your storm and your grace*
> *You have the most beautiful heart*
> *That I've ever known...*

It was a love song to her son. I can hardly bear to listen to it anymore.

In the summer of 2020, during the pandemic shutdown, Lisa became sick with allergies. The cause was identified as a serious mold infestation in her house. She, Ben, and the twins moved into the Beverly Hills Hotel while the problem was being corrected. Ben went back and forth between the hotel and home, where he could see his girlfriend, Diana Pinto. He was at home on July 12 for Diana's birthday. The party was still going on well past midnight.

Accounts of what happened next vary. Some partygoers say Ben and Diana had a loud argument and that Ben disappeared into the bathroom afterward. Others say that he went to get a beer but didn't come back. A few people reported hearing a woman shout "Don't do it!" followed by a gunshot. Some say people went looking for him when he didn't come back after a couple of hours. Whatever the truth, one thing is certain. When his friends picked the lock and went inside the bathroom, they found Ben's body on the floor next to a gun. He had shot himself through the mouth.

None of us saw it coming. For twenty-seven years. Not a glimmer.

It was Riley who got the first call. Lisa's assistant was at the party, and she wanted the family to know before it hit the news. But she didn't want to be the one to break it to Lisa. While the police were called, Riley's phone rang at a little after five in the morning.

The voice on the other end said, "Your brother's shot himself in the head!" Lisa's assistant said it over and over. As the reality of the situation sank in, Riley knew she had to be the one to tell her mother.

My sweet Riley, struggling to function, went directly to the hotel with her husband to wake her mother and break the news. She called her father and then called me. Danny caught the next plane to LA from Portland, where he was living at the time. I called Navarone, and I called Vikki to come take care of my dogs. And then I went to the hotel. We were all like the island of the lost, stunned into silence by pain. I didn't even cry, not yet. All I could think about was Lisa. She would never recover from this. I didn't see how she could outlive it.

Ben's body was taken by the authorities for autopsy the next day. The report verified suicide, and the investigation was quickly brought to a close.

One of the most difficult things about being a celebrity is sharing your grief with the public. We were deluged with requests for comment long before we had processed the news ourselves. Lisa's manager, Roger Widynowski, made the announcement for the family, confirming Ben's passing: "She [Lisa] is completely heartbroken, inconsolable and beyond devastated but trying to stay strong for her 11-year-old twins and her oldest daughter, Riley. She adored that boy. He was the love of her life."

In the depths of my grief, I made my own public statement about Ben's death a few days later:

> These are some of the darkest days of my family's life. The shock of losing Ben has been devastating. Trying to put all the pieces together of all the possible why's has penetrated my soul. Each day I wake up, I pray it will get better. Then, I think of my daughter and the pain she is going through as she was a doting mother. Ben's father, Danny, who is completely lost, as Ben was his only son.
>
> Riley, so loving and so close to him; Harper and Finley, who absolutely adored Ben. Navarone, who struggles deeply with loss and death. Rest in Peace Ben, you were loved.

I coped by focusing on Lisa, Danny, and the girls. I reminded myself that they were the ones bearing the brunt of the loss. For a while, shock kept Lisa on her feet as she and Danny planned Ben's funeral. Riley, however, was barely coping. She stopped speaking almost completely and struggled even to bear her own weight. Her friends would half carry her to the shower to bathe and would wash her hair for her, then try to get her to eat. The twins couldn't stop crying. All of us kept asking ourselves why. Why had he done it? Why hadn't he reached out to one of us? Why hadn't we seen it coming? We were all drowning in whys. There were no family fights, no recriminations, no blaming one another. We were all isolated in our own misery. One of the hardest things for me was that Lisa wouldn't let me comfort her. I knew that she was still angry because I had not supported her allegations against Michael. I continued to remind myself that my own pain had to be secondary to Lisa's grief.

I walked through the days like a zombie. I can barely remember them. As had happened when Elvis died, everything became a blur for me. Even today, when I'm asked about the details of Ben's passing, my mind goes blank. I rely on those close to me to carry the burden of those memories for me.

I do remember seeing Ben. Lisa had him brought home after the authorities released his body. I remember that he was lying on a table, in Lisa's room, I think. I went into the room alone. Given the manner of his death, you would expect to find him disfigured, even unrecognizable. But he wasn't. The back of his head was badly damaged, but his face was virtually untouched. He was still a beautiful boy. I touched his hands and stroked his face. I told him how much he was loved. I told him how much I would miss him. And I wept for all he was and all he might have been.

Lisa spoke to a sympathetic funeral director about the legal requirements for interring a body. She found out that there was no law in California against keeping a body at home as long as certain health requirements were met. By then, she had rented another house in the neighborhood, as none of the family could bear to return to the place where he had died. The new place had a detached room, and they moved him in there and kept the temperature at fifty-five degrees. He was kept in a coffin filled with dry ice. Lisa spent most of her time with him. She couldn't bear to let him go. I remembered over forty years earlier, sitting on the stairs with her at Graceland, looking down on Elvis's body while fans filed by. We would go to visit him afterward, when the house was quiet. I remembered us kissing him goodbye late that last night. Being with Elvis after death had comforted Lisa. So did being with Ben. We all grieve in our own way.

There was a private funeral in Malibu on July 27, two weeks after his death. It was difficult to find a venue because of the pandemic, but Lisa and Danny were able to rent a beautiful location near the ocean. About one hundred family and friends attended, all masked because of the virus. I had been seated across the aisle from Lisa, so I was grateful when Navarone arrived and sat next to me, his arm protectively around my shoulders. Deepak Chopra led the service. Our musician friend Danny, who had traveled from Hawaii for Ben's memorial, played music and said a traditional blessing. Riley's husband, Ben, read a tribute of love that Riley had written for her brother. She was still so traumatized that speaking was difficult. The venue was decorated with cherry blossoms, and Ben lay in an open coffin in a separate room. He looked remarkably serene in his suit and hat. The ravages of his passing did not show on his face.

Ben's body remained at home with Lisa for another two and a half months, until Lisa felt he no longer wanted to be there. He was taken to Graceland for a second, small family ceremony on October 1 and laid to rest in the Meditation Garden near Elvis.

Losing Ben was the beginning of the end for my daughter. She had lost the love of her life. For the second time. She would never get over it. We all knew that with Lisa, we were living on borrowed time.

CHAPTER 17

Peace in the Valley

There'll be no sadness, no sorrow, no trouble I see
There will be peace in the valley for me.

MOST PEOPLE SPENT THE PANDEMIC AT HOME WITH family members, including their pets. For me, that meant my dogs. For others, it meant cats or birds or fish. Not my son. Navarone spent the pandemic with the biggest articulated snakes in Los Angeles County outside of a zoo. Thirteen-foot snakes. His water monitor, Stefan, had passed away by then, and Navarone had turned his attention to breeding snakes. He bred the parents, carefully cut the babies out of the eggs when the time came, and then fed and nurtured the little ones like a doting father. You don't want to know what he fed the parents. All in his backyard in the San Fernando Valley. It wasn't a gimmick for his rock band. He just loved snakes. He'd loved them since he'd captured his first little garden snake as a boy. My son, the snake whisperer.

The isolation of the pandemic was hard on everyone, especially our family in the wake of Benjamin's passing. For Navarone, it was a time of introspection. He was dealing with the shock of Ben's suicide, as we all were. He was taking fentanyl around the clock, at least every hour. He was hiding his drug habit from his girlfriend, who was living in Europe, though he could no longer hide it from me. He knew his body was breaking down. Two weeks after Ben's interment at Graceland, Navarone decided to go off fentanyl. Not wanting to add to my grief and anxiety, he decided to detox on his own. It was a bad idea. A very bad idea.

Navarone called me one afternoon that October from a gym near his house. He'd decided to go to the steam room there to sweat the drugs out of his system. He thought that doing so might make him feel better. It had the opposite effect.

I heard his voice on the phone, saying, "Mom, I need help. I'm a week into withdrawal. I thought I could do it by myself, but it's getting bad. Can I come over?"

I told him, "Of course, you can. Where are you? Do you need soup?"

I mobilized the troops. First, we had to get Navarone to my house. Then somebody would need to go over to his place every day to check on the snakes and feed them. Somebody would have to pick up clean clothes for him. We would get his old bedroom ready, and yes, we would need soup and other liquids.

Vikki would make the soup. Navarone loved her soups, especially the creamy chicken one.

While we got things ready at home, Vikki drove as fast as she could to the gym to pick up Navarone. I couldn't go myself because if I were seen, there would be photos and rumors on the internet. He couldn't stand by himself, but Vikki managed to get him to his feet and half carry him to the car. When they reached home, the two of us got him out of the car and up the stairs to his room. My son is nearly a foot taller than I am, so it was no easy task. We got him undressed and into bed, where he would remain for the next three weeks. Twenty-two days, to be exact. He counted every one of them. He was in and out of consciousness all the time, but he later said that he knew exactly where he was. Being in his childhood room, in familiar surroundings, helped him feel safer.

I had never seen anyone as violently ill as my son was. It was frightening. His body was struggling to rid itself of the poison in his system. He retched over and over. His body and sheets were soaked with vomit, diarrhea, and sweat. One of us would strip the bed and throw the linens in the washer while I helped him crawl to the bathroom. He couldn't get there on his own. I would fill the bathtub with warm water and suds for him to soak in. It soothed his muscles and his mind. Afterward, we'd get him in clean clothes and put him back to bed. We did this endlessly, over and over, for weeks. In between, we tried to get fluids into him. He could swallow liquids, but he struggled to keep them down.

And then there was the pain. His entire body was racked with terrible pain, in his head and stomach, and in his arms and legs. I would put cool compresses on his head and stomach to soothe him. Watching his suffering felt almost unbearable. I stroked his head and arms. When all else failed, I would lie down next to him and hold him gently in my arms. I couldn't stop his pain, but I could make sure he knew he wasn't alone.

He couldn't sleep. For three weeks, he was awake around the clock, desperate for sleep, for a respite. Knowing I couldn't care for him alone, I sought help. As we had done when he was a little boy, Vikki, Marta, and I sat with him in turns so that each of us could get some rest and eat. I took the night shift. He dreaded the nights. Fear overwhelmed him in the dark. He was afraid he was going to die; he was even more afraid that he wouldn't die, and he'd feel like this forever. The first light of dawn became a symbol for him of another endless day. I struggled with my own fear as I comforted my son. There was a heart-stopping moment when I thought he was gone. Then he started breathing again, and I breathed with him.

The hallucinations were almost as bad as the pain. Navarone had never been a religious man, but now his mind was flooded with images of heaven and of hell. Sometimes he thought he was Jesus, carrying his cross along a river, desperately thirsty and staring at the water he couldn't drink. Just as Navarone was struggling to drink the water we offered him. Sometimes he thought he was being assaulted by devils around and within him. One night, he retched so hard that he felt the devil inside his body ejecting. Afterward, he felt better, less afraid.

No one who has experienced what my son and I did that month would knowingly consume fentanyl. Nightmare doesn't begin to describe the agony of the experience.

Finally, on the twenty-third day, Navarone fell asleep shortly before dawn. He woke a few hours later with his mind clearer, asking to eat. The poison was finally gone. He recovered steadily after that, for his young body was basically healthy, thank God. When he began asking to borrow my car keys, we knew he was going to be all right. My daughter had lost her son four months earlier. My son had been spared.

When he felt better, he traveled to Brazil to visit his father's family. Brazil has strict drug laws, and it is almost impossible to get heroin or fentanyl there. The country was a haven for Navarone, a drug-free zone where he could spend time with the other half of his family. His father was no longer in his life, but his aunts and uncles and cousins were. He had recently changed his last name to Garcia, like the rest of his Brazilian family. He loved it there. When his visa was up, he returned home. I would like to say that at this point, like in the fairy tales, Navarone lived happily ever after. Unfortunately, real life doesn't work that way.

It was not much of a homecoming.

Our family was still awash in grief and sorrow. Benjamin's loss remained raw, and Lisa had withdrawn into a very dark place. Michael was afraid she would relapse under the strain of Ben's passing. He worried about the effect the trauma was having on the twins. He also wondered how keeping Ben's body at home had affected them. Lisa, meanwhile, was holding on to the girls for dear life. Her daughters were her only reason for living. Brazil must have seemed like the promised land to Navarone when he walked back into the turmoil at home.

In the midst of all this, his former drug dealer—who had been missing in action for several years—walked back into Navarone's life. Navarone was still terrified of fentanyl, but his drug dealer offered him something very appealing. Pure heroin. Although Navarone had always loved the way heroin made him feel, pure heroin had become impossible to get in the United States. The dealers always laced it with fentanyl (which can create a similar high in far lower amounts) to drastically increase their profits. Now his old dealer had a source of unadulterated heroin, guaranteed to be pure. Navarone couldn't resist. He bought some, and the drug gave him the pleasurable high he remembered so well. He began taking it regularly and might have continued to use it indefinitely if his dealer hadn't disappeared without a trace. Once again, withdrawal set in, and once again, Navarone called me. I couldn't believe he was using again—and that, again, we were about to go through withdrawal. But I couldn't say no, either.

Thank God, though heroin withdrawal is bad, it is not as bad as fentanyl withdrawal. My son says that withdrawing from fentanyl was a 10. Withdrawing from heroin was a 6.5. Whatever the numbers, the second withdrawal was bad enough. Again, we marshaled the troops. This time, we did it in a new house, because a few months after Ben's passing, I had sold the home my children grew up in. And again, my son pulled through. But this time, there was a difference. Navarone finally—finally—took a long, hard look at himself and realized that drugs were taking his life. He would never have a life until he chose to live it sober. For those who loved him. For me. And most of all, for himself. So far, he has kept that commitment. I am grateful for every day I have with him.

My mother, Anna Iversen Wagner Beaulieu, passed away a year after Ben did. Navarone says my mother was the sweetest woman you'd ever meet. It was impossible not to love her. He is right. She was my guide, my anchor, and my role model from the day I was born. I am proud that my middle name, Ann, is in her honor. As the oldest of six children, I had a special relationship with my mom. It has been three years since she left us, and I still miss her every day.

She didn't have an easy life. She lost her first husband, Jim—her first and lasting love—when I was only six months old. Because he died in an airplane crash, there had been no warning. I still remember the pain and wistfulness in her eyes when she told me about my biological father, the handsome young pilot who was known for his smile. I don't think she ever completely recovered from the shock of his loss. I always felt that my mother and I had a special bond because I was her only remaining link to Jim.

I remember telling Elvis about my father. I confided, "My real father died in an airplane crash."

He was enthralled. "Really?" As far as he knew, my stepfather was my dad. He was concerned. "How is your mother with that? I mean, was your real father the love of her life?"

"Yes."

"Well, how does your dad feel about that?"

I told him, "My mother would never share that. Ever. In fact, she made me swear that I would never tell him I knew about my real father. She didn't want to hurt him. You can't let him know that you know."

The father I grew up with was my stepfather, Paul. He was a good man, but he wasn't always an easy one. Marriage to a career military officer is never easy. Every few years, my mother had to pack up six children and help us make the difficult adjustment to a new home in a strange place. Mom dedicated herself to soothing our sorrow and anxiety about leaving our friends behind while she was adjusting to leaving hers. The story of our lives is written in my siblings' birthplaces. The youngest of us, my twin brothers, Tim and Tom, were born in Germany the year I met Elvis. They were fifteen years younger than I was. My mother was dealing with a teen daughter in love with the world's biggest celebrity while she was nursing newborn twins. I don't know how she did it.

Paul was a typical husband of the 1950s, just a little more rigid. We all knew that he was the head of the household and that his word was law. My mother's choices were subject to his approval. If he didn't like one of her new outfits, she took it back to the store. Sometimes, my father could be demanding, an attitude that would bother my mother. She would grow quiet, and my dad would be doing all the talking. But she had a way of always making things fine. We children didn't need to worry.

My mom was the perfect homemaker of the era. She was an accomplished cook who catered to her husband's appetite. She kept a clean, well-regulated home. She never "let herself go," as the phrase went at the time. My mother was beautiful, always well dressed, well coifed, and well made up. She had lovely manners, and she taught us to emulate them. She was a wonderful, loving mother who never played favorites. We all knew that we were loved. And she always put our needs and our father's ahead of her own. Quietly, graciously, she put us first. All seven of us. She was remarkable.

I know that I tested her limits during my teen years. She was my only confidante during my first months with Elvis, and it couldn't have been easy for her to listen to what I had to say. I marvel at her ability to listen and empathize when she must have been struggling with her own emotions. She was a protective mother who let me go when her strongest instincts were to hold me close. Years later, when I was deciding to leave Elvis, it was my mother I talked to. Divorce went against her faith and her belief system, but she never made me feel wrong for my decision. She put my well-being first. When we were able to live near one another again, over twenty years after I'd left home, we were both thrilled.

When I was growing up, it never occurred to me that my mother wasn't entirely satisfied with her role in life. She certainly never showed it. But once all of us children were grown and gone, and my dad was no longer dealing with the demands of a military career, things began to change.

If it had been up to my dad, my mother would have stayed home, available to wait on him, for the rest of their lives. He was still the king of the table. He wanted a home-cooked breakfast, lunch, and dinner every day. I mean, who wouldn't? My dad's routine in retirement was to get up, have breakfast, read the paper, and watch TV all day. He wanted his wife available to him the entire time he did that. I can still hear him.

"Annie? Annie, where are you? Come watch TV with me."

"Can you get me some coffee? Where are you? Where'd you go? Where's my coffee?"

My dad had no concept of personal time where my mother was concerned. Her existence, he assumed, revolved around him. He was dismayed when he discovered that my mom had developed boundaries. She had raised six children. She wasn't willing to spend the rest of her life raising a seventh. She still cooked him a homemade dinner every night, for they never went out. Dad was always too, well, cheap. So my mother cooked every night, but she no longer cooked three times a day. Worse yet, she wanted her own room, a private space where she could lock the door. After years of sharing a house with seven people, this desire was small wonder. My father did not welcome the changes. He didn't know how to deal with a wife who had a mind of her own. Who said no to him. He would complain. When he got like that, we'd call him Grumpy. Not to his face, of course. But my mom knew it, and it made her smile.

My mother was a doer. If something needed to be done, she was the first to volunteer. She hated sitting around with nothing to do. She seemed to have boundless energy, even into old age, and she was a good businesswoman. I get both those qualities from her. She had become a real estate agent shortly before my parents moved to California and remained a successful one in LA. And on the days she had no clients scheduled, she still liked to get out of the house.

Mom would call me and say, "What are you doing today?"

If I had nothing going on, I'd say, "Nothing."

"Do you want to go to lunch?"

"Yeah, let's go to lunch."

She'd lower her voice. "I've got to get out of here. I can't take it."

"Okay, Mom. I'll pick you up."

She'd be dressed and waiting by the time I got there. She'd probably been dressed before my father even got up.

Every Sunday night, we would have family dinners. All but one of my siblings lived in LA by then, and they'd come with their spouses and children and, eventually, grandchildren. Lisa Marie, Michael, Danny, Navarone, Riley, Ben, Harper, Finley, my nieces and nephews from the Beaulieu side of the family. The table would be full of kids, noise, and laughter. Sometimes I brought food (which I ordered, of course, not willing to inflict my cooking on anyone). Most of the time, my mother cooked for us all. My mom made the best spaghetti in the world. Then we'd settle back and watch TV. It was a wonderful time, a tradition we all cherished. Riley and Navarone still talk about it. That's why, since my mother's passing, we have our family dinners on Sundays when we can. We miss those times together, and we miss her.

My dad's death hit my mother hard. We were all in the hospital room with him, expecting him to rally, but he didn't. We knew he was seriously ill, but the doctors thought he would recover, so his sudden passing was a shock. Even though their marriage was imperfect, my parents had been together for most of my mother's life. She had already lost my brother Tom (one of the twins) a few years earlier, and Benjamin the year before. The losses added up. Her health began to deteriorate. We all embraced her and tried to keep life as normal as possible for her. She was afraid to live alone. She had never lived by herself in her entire life. So I told her she could live with me, and a few weeks after Dad's passing, she moved into my home.

I had help taking care of her. A couple of years before my father died, I had gotten a caregiver for my parents. Her name was Claudia, and she was from Mexico. She cared for my parents at their home five days a week, and when Mom moved in with me, Claudia continued to help me care for her. She was a wonderful, wonderful woman, a true gift. My mother adored her. Mom called her "my friend," and she wanted her friend with her all the time.

In the year after Benjamin died, Mom declined rapidly. She grew progressively weaker and no longer wanted to dress or to leave the house. Knowing she was slipping away, I arranged for hospice. My sister and brothers visited as often as they could, and I spent most of my time with her. It helped me deal with Ben's loss. I couldn't do anything to help him, but I could help my mother. Claudia read stories to her, read the Bible to her, talked to her, listened to her stories, and watched TV with her. My mother had me play Elvis's gospel music all day long. Her favorite song was "How Great Thou Art." The music comforted her. I told Mom over and over how much I loved her, that she was the best mother in the world. I wanted her to take that with her as her life closed, to validate her. She knew she didn't have long, and she was terrified of dying. I would wait until she was asleep to slip away from her bed for a few minutes. If I was gone for even a moment, she would panic.

"You're not leaving me, are you?"

"No, I'm coming right back, Mom."

"Are you sure?"

"Yes. I'm just going to get some water." I would sit with her, stroking her hand, murmuring soothing words.

I will never forget the moment she passed. It was nighttime, and I had put her to bed. She seemed to be asleep, but when I went back to check on her, she was wide awake.

Instead of panicking as usual while I was gone, though, she said, "Hi," welcoming me back.

I replied, "Hi."

"Who are they?" she asked. She was pointing at the door. There was nobody there.

I said, "Who?"

"Them. Those three people."

I didn't want to make her wrong, so I said, "Oh, those are your friends, Mom. They're your friends."

"Oh…" And she smiled, a radiant smile that transformed her. The fear and tension faded from her face as serenity enfolded her. Then she looked at the ceiling and closed her eyes. I could feel her spirit leave her body. It was like the whisper of a gentle breeze caressing my face. Her friends were taking her away. Chills washed through me. Then she was gone, and everything was calm. It was the most beautiful thing I had ever experienced.

"Oh my God," I whispered.

I have thought about that moment many times. So many times. I have never feared death in the same way since that night.

On August 2, 2021, I announced her passing:

I am heartbroken. My beautiful mother died today. She was the light of our lives. She never wanted any attention on herself. Her children were her everything. May you Rest in Peace mom. You will always be with us.

Riley posted her own announcement:

We lost our beautiful Nana this morning. She was an incredible woman and mother. Rest in Peace nana.

We interred her at Holy Cross Cemetery with my father. My brothers and sister attended, along with Navarone and Riley. All my mother's friends were gone by then. Her epitaph was simple: "Wife, Mother & Nana." My mother had a long life. She was ninety-five years old when she passed, sixty-eight years older than Ben when we lost him. It still wasn't long enough for me.

CHAPTER 18

Don't Be Cruel

Don't want no other love
Baby, it's just you I'm dreaming of.

I DON'T KNOW HOW MANY MOVIES AND DOCUMENTARIES have been made about Elvis. The number changes yearly, sometimes monthly. I haven't seen them all, and I don't want to. Imagine what it is like to watch movies about cherished family members made by someone who never met them. You notice every little factual error, resent misjudgments about their character, wonder why they didn't include the things you consider most important. Why they did include things that you think are inconsequential. Now imagine that you lost this family member at a young age. The mist of nostalgia, of unresolved grief, hovers over the entire film. I approach any new film about Elvis with apprehension. So did Lisa Marie. So when Baz Luhrmann sent me the script for his new movie, *Elvis*, after he started shooting in 2019, I was cautious. I knew that Baz is gifted and that he is also an out-of-the-box thinker. What might he do with a film about Elvis, whose entire life was out of the box?

When I read the script, I liked it immediately. So many films about Elvis focus on tabloid aspects of his life. The women. The drug dependence. The health problems. His sudden, undignified death in his bathroom at Graceland. All were factually accurate to varying degrees, but none of them captured the man behind the tasteless headlines. Baz did. He focused on Elvis's extraordinary gifts as a musician, his struggles to navigate a world he wasn't raised for, his social consciousness and sense of history. The script considered his roots in the forces that shaped him—family, poverty, religion, Black culture. The darker parts of his life were alluded to but not focused on. Baz presented the conflicted idealist I had known. He told my own love story with sensitivity. When he offered me the opportunity to meet the lead, Austin Butler, I was happy to accept.

Lisa and I were naturally concerned about how Austin would portray Elvis. We had seen so many stereotyped portrayals that mimicked his mannerisms but failed to show his depth and complexity. I had seen Austin as Tex Watson in *Once Upon a Time in Hollywood*, and I thought he was excellent. I was optimistic about his taking on the challenge of playing Elvis. When Lisa called me to ask what I thought about his casting, I did my best to reassure her. I told her that I thought he would probably do a good job.

Meeting Austin was a joy. He was nervous, anxious to please. I can only imagine what it would be like to meet the wife of a legendary man you are about to depict on film.

"I want to make this good for you," he told me. "I want to make you proud of me. I hope I do a good job for you and Lisa. This is the biggest role I've ever done, and of course, it's Elvis Presley. I'm a nervous wreck."

I said to him, "You know, you've got big shoes to fill."

I could practically see him sweating, and he said, "Please. Don't even."

I could have asked to watch the filming, but I didn't want to intimidate him. Austin was very brave to take on the challenge. He took nothing for granted, studying for two years to play that part. With shooting postponed because of the Covid-19 pandemic, he used the time to prepare. He took voice lessons to learn how to talk like Elvis, deepening his voice a little and adding that little Southern touch. He took dance lessons to master Elvis's moves and body language. He watched all the footage of Elvis he could find—films, documentaries, concerts, performances, and interviews. Austin practically absorbed Elvis through his pores. He worked incredibly hard, avoiding the impression that he was an Elvis impersonator. It was never *Look at me. I'm doing Elvis.* It was clear from the beginning that he knew what he was doing, and I didn't feel the need to offer advice. Instead, I offered encouragement.

I waited for its release to see the film, choosing not to attend the premiere, because I didn't want to validate it until I'd seen it. My presence would have drawn attention from the press and been a statement in itself. Instead, I saw it privately on the studio lot, alone in the screening room. Afterward, I left without comment. Lisa had wanted me to go first and tell her whether she should go. She was hopeful that the film would portray her father accurately. So many films in the past had not, so seeing Baz's interpretation for the first time was an emotional thing for her. Her hopes were high, and she didn't want to be let down.

When I called her afterward, she said, "Mom, what do you think?"

I just said, "I think you should see it. I think Austin did a nice job."

I didn't tell her my real feelings about the movie. I wanted to rave "Oh my God, Lisa, it's amazing! You're going to love it!"

But I didn't, because I know my daughter. If she didn't like it as much as I did, she'd come back and say "I can't believe you told me that. What were you thinking?" I didn't want to get her hopes up and have her be disappointed. So I left it up to her to form her own opinion.

I arranged another showing in the screening room for the two of us. While we watched it, we were both so fixated on the film that we didn't say a word to each other for the entire two hours and thirty-nine minutes it ran. When the movie ended and the credits rolled, we both let out our breath and went, "Phew!" I didn't realize I'd been holding my breath until that moment.

Lisa was over the moon. We went out and stood by the car afterward, and she kept saying, "Oh my God, Mom, he's amazing. Oh my God."

He *was* amazing. His voice sounded so much like Elvis's that it was uncanny. Of all the actors I'd seen play Elvis, I'd never seen anyone who could compare with Austin. Neither had Lisa. He is a true actor. He stepped into the part and embodied the man I knew.

Perhaps the best example of his extraordinary portrayal comes at the end of the movie. Baz chose to end the film with Elvis's iconic first performance of "Unchained Melody" two months before Elvis's death. To do the scene, Austin wore heavy prosthetics that transformed him into the bloated, unhealthy man that Elvis had become at the end of his life. But the remarkable thing wasn't the physical transformation. Austin was able to portray the deep emotion and to duplicate every nuance of that storied performance. His voice blended seamlessly with Elvis's. Baz's last, brilliant directorial sleight of hand was to segue to footage of the real Elvis for the last lines of the song. Even for me, it took a moment to realize what had happened. One moment, I was watching Austin; the next, I was watching Elvis. The transition made me catch my breath.

Months later, at Graceland, I told Austin, "You're going to get a lot of people loving you. You did such a great job on this that some people will want you to remain Elvis. You've identified yourself with him so closely. Don't lose yourself in it, Austin. I want you to stick to who *you* are."

Austin has done a good job of avoiding that trap, reclaiming his own identity. He's not only a good actor but also a good man. Lisa and Austin developed a close relationship. She saw her father in him, and it created a powerful bond. Lisa and I both embraced him as a family friend. We were honored to have him in our lives.

The most controversial character in the film, of course, is Colonel Tom Parker, played by Tom Hanks. People who have seen the film ask me how I felt about the Colonel. I liked him. So did Jerry Schilling, George Klein, Alan Fortas, and some of Elvis's other closest friends. The Colonel wasn't quite the villain he seems to be in the movie. He was a complicated man, and contrary to public perception, he loved Elvis like a son.

In a sense, there were two Colonel Parkers. One was the manager who would do anything to make a dollar, the man who sold Elvis for a living. He was self-serving in that role, putting profit above everything else. The snow man, as the movie calls him. I saw this man in action. He was a coldhearted negotiator whom you didn't want to cross. But there was another Colonel Parker, the one who lived a great love story in his relationship with his wife. The Colonel was one of the most tender and devoted husbands I've ever seen, and he would do anything for his wife, Marie Francis "Miss Marie" Parker. This included walking away from business to take care of her himself when she was ill. That Colonel Parker was not in the movie.

The Colonel has taken a lot of criticism for booking Elvis so heavily during the last couple of years he toured. Undoubtedly, Elvis's health was failing then, and it was increasingly difficult for him to get through a performance. But Elvis also had a big payroll to meet every month, as his father often reminded him. Many people depended on Elvis for a living. And though he loved relaxing at Graceland, he would miss performing after a while. He needed his fans, just as they needed him. Elvis came alive onstage. He wanted those tours.

Even the scenes where the Colonel has Elvis's head plunged in ice water to get him onstage weren't as coldhearted as they appear in the film. There were days when Elvis's health and drug intake were debilitating. When he did go onstage, he struggled to get through his act. On rare occasions, he had to cancel shows. Because his shows were always sold out, canceling them meant leaving a thousand or more people in their seats disappointed when an announcement was made over the PA system. And every time he stumbled onstage or canceled, speculation ran wild. The tabloids blared sensational headlines speculating about what was wrong with Elvis Presley. Getting him onstage by whatever means necessary wasn't solely a financial decision. It was also a way of avoiding a public relations nightmare.

I understand, though, that Colonel Parker's depiction in the film and his role as narrator make for an interesting cinematic point of view. Baz told Elvis's story with great artistry. He contextualized Elvis's life within the social issues of the time, something that is rarely done in depictions of Elvis. He showed the influences on Elvis, both musical and cultural, when he was growing up. The impact of Black culture and interracial friendships on his life and music was made clear. The "If I Can Dream" scenes were powerful, the song's lyrics echoing Martin Luther King Jr.'s "I Have a Dream" speech as Elvis paid tribute to him in the weeks following King's assassination:

> *If I can dream of a better land,*
> *Where all my brothers walk hand in hand,*
> *Tell me why, oh why, oh why can't my dream come true?*

> *And while I can think, while I can talk,*
> *While I can stand, while I can walk,*
> *While I can dream, please let my dream come true…*

The entire film was deeply moving. Beautifully done. Truly, beautifully done.

I had seen myself in films and documentaries about Elvis, but it had never occurred to me that someone would want to make a film about me. I was surprised when Sofia Coppola called to say she wanted to make a movie based on my book, ***Elvis and Me***, telling the story of my life with Elvis from my perspective. It was clear from the beginning that she was concerned with doing things sensitively and getting the story right. She told me what she envisioned, and after our first conversation, she sent me a copy of the script. Other talks followed, and I felt safe entrusting my story to Sofia. She made me executive producer of the film.

Sofia was embarking on my life story with challenges that would have been insurmountable to most directors. The project was so underfunded that she had to shoot the movie digitally, in thirty days, with only twenty extras for the whole film. Even if she hadn't made the artistic choice to keep the camera focused on me, it would have been necessary anyway. There wasn't the time or enough cast to people the fictional Graceland with the full Memphis Mafia. The cast didn't fill the screen the way they had filled my life. The emphasis was on me and the loneliness I struggled with when Elvis was away from home. I think Sofia did an amazing job with the resources available to her.

My only concern about the film was Lisa. The movie would look at Elvis from a different perspective, and I wasn't sure Lisa would be comfortable with that.

She wasn't, to say the least. She was appalled by Sofia's script. I could understand her feelings. I put myself in her position and realized I'd have mixed emotions, too. This was her father, and now a woman who'd never known him was making a film about him. Any daughter would have a hard time with it. Complicating matters was the reality that Lisa didn't know the whole story about her dad. She was a little girl when she lost him. She never knew him when she was an adult. Before the film was even made, Lisa objected to it. She felt that it would be damaging to her father, especially on the heels of his heroic portrayal in the *Elvis* film.

Lisa emailed Sofia to voice her strong objections before the film began shooting. She said the script portrayed her father as "vengeful and contemptuous." Lisa believed that Elvis was being characterized as a predator and manipulator. She also thought that Sofia was manipulating me and that the film would portray my perspective on Elvis inaccurately. My daughter was concerned that when the film was released, she would be forced to speak out publicly against Sofia, against the film, and, in doing so, against me.

Sofia responded to Lisa: "I hope that when you see the film, you will feel differently, and understand that I'm taking great care in honoring your mother, while also presenting your father with sensitivity and complexity."

I tried to give Lisa context for some of the scenes in the film. I acknowledged that by contemporary standards, her dad came across as controlling, but it wasn't seen that way at the time. He was a man's man, which back in the day meant that he was the boss. He was very open about that, and he expected his opinions to be respected. He didn't like domineering women. I had been raised not to push my opinions on a man, so I was not surprised when he got upset if I disagreed with him. I would never put up with it now, but at the time, it seemed normal.

What Sofia presented was largely accurate. There are many scenes in the movie showing Elvis picking out my clothes and expressing his opinions on them. It was true. He did. Sometimes I'd be disappointed if he didn't like something I had picked out, but for the most part, I didn't resent it. I was dressing for him, not for anyone else. The film was portraying me in 1963, when I was still an eager-to-please young woman. For women who grew up during the feminist revolution of the 1970s and 1980s, as Lisa did, having your husband choose all your clothes was completely unacceptable. I tried to explain that to her.

Some of the scenes where Elvis lost his temper bothered her as well. Lisa knew that her father had an explosive temper and sometimes threw things when he got angry or frustrated. So did his mother, Gladys. So did Lisa. Occasionally, they were like children throwing their toys in a tantrum. I don't believe that Elvis ever intentionally tried to harm me. He would explode in a rage and, oblivious to his surroundings, throw whatever was at hand. When Elvis threw the chair in real life, the incident was a little different from how it looked in the film. The records that had sparked Elvis's anger in the first place were stacked on the chair. When I told him I didn't like the song, he picked up the chair and threw it. One of the records flew off and hit me. Elvis was horrified that I'd been hurt and immediately took me in his arms and began apologizing. What Elvis had done was childish and dangerous; I'm not condoning it. But it wasn't the same as hitting me intentionally. I did, however, want Lisa to think about how she would have felt if she'd been the one standing where I was.

The pillow-fighting scene is another example. I had started a pillow fight with Elvis. At first, we were laughing and having fun, but as it continued, we both started getting carried away. That evening, we'd taken too many uppers, the pills Elvis took to stay awake. I was taking them in an effort to keep Elvis company until dawn, then go to school after very little sleep. I got caught up in the moment and hit Elvis hard with my pillow. I caught him off guard. Elvis was shocked and furious. He hit me back with the same pillow and bruised my eye. He felt terrible, but I wasn't going to let him off the hook. When we went to the movies that evening, I wore an eyepatch to draw attention to my bruised eye. That was the closest we ever came to blows. At the end of the scene in the film, I tell Elvis that maybe we were taking too many pills. That line is barely audible in the movie, but there is no doubt that at that time in our lives, the pills were complicating our relationship.

When your life is portrayed in a film, some things inevitably look different from what you experienced. The camera's lens isn't like your own. It was startling for me to watch some of the scenes from my own life from the outside, not the inside. I couldn't always reconcile the two. *Priscilla* is very much a generational film. Lisa's generation sees a different story than what many of my generation do. That was clear from the critics' response. And that's a good thing. Women's rights have come a long way, and I am no longer the teenager in the film. For Lisa, though, it was impossible to be objective.

She told me, "But Mom, it's about my dad."

I said, "I know, but honestly, the story is not that bad, Lisa. It really isn't. It just feels that way because it's your dad. He was human, like everybody else."

It was difficult for her to accept that. When she had seen her father angry, the anger was always aimed at someone else. She never had that anger directed at her. She didn't know how it felt to be on the receiving end of it, because Elvis protected her. I don't know how she would have felt if she had actually seen the movie. Lisa passed away just six weeks after Sofia finished shooting the film. I hope she would have been proud of me. I never got to find out.

Is my view of the film objective? Probably not. Nobody is objective about their own life. And it is different when you love somebody. I loved Elvis deeply, and sixty years later, I see him through a tender haze. When I lost him, he became the man of my dreams in a different sense. I cherish both the man he was and the man he wanted to be.

Sofia did a remarkable job of capturing my emotional journey. She approached the film with exceptional skill, a strong desire to do justice to my life story, and great sensitivity to the memories I carry with me. In most respects, the movie was spot-on, and I am grateful to her. I entrusted my story to the right person. I believe that audiences understood the heart of the story, despite the unavoidable generation gap. I am honored that Sofia chose me for a project close to her heart.

While the film *Priscilla* was in postproduction in 2023, I was busy creating a strikingly different kind of Elvis project. It was an animated Netflix series titled *Agent Elvis*. Ever since he was a young boy, Elvis had been fascinated by comic books. Though he lived in poverty throughout his childhood, he was rich in imagination. In his mind, he was the hero of every comic book story. Back when superheroes were in books rather than on theater screens or streaming platforms, Elvis wanted to be a cross between James Bond and Superman. He wanted to be an impossibly heroic and talented secret agent with karate moves that would baffle a Kung Fu master. So I decided to make him one. I wanted to give him that, however belatedly.

The premise is not as far-fetched as it sounds. During his famous visit to the White House in 1970, Elvis had talked to President Nixon about it. He'd arrived at the Oval Office carrying a handwritten letter asking to be made a "federal agent at large," to serve his country in any capacity the president chose. After talking with President Nixon for a while, Elvis asked for a badge designating him an agent for the Bureau of Narcotics and Dangerous Drugs. (The irony was lost on everybody, especially Elvis.) He thought the badge would give him the powers of a federal agent. Jerry Schilling was with him that day and says that the "king" and the president genuinely hit it off. Elvis even gave the famously chilly Nixon a hug. He left the office thrilled with his new badge, but sadly, the insignia did not turn out to make him a secret agent. Can you imagine him trying to go incognito? Elvis Presley would be the worst-kept secret in any crowd. He wouldn't exactly blend in.

When I made my pitch for the animated series, the studio loved the idea of Elvis being a secret agent. We lined up a great cast, with Matthew McConaughey voicing Elvis and Don Cheadle as the commander. I had a small running part playing myself, the woman the secret agent came home to. There were some wonderful guest spots, including Baz Luhrmann as, fittingly, the director. It even featured Scatter, Elvis's real-life drug-addicted, sexually harassing chimpanzee. It was set in the period when Elvis met Nixon and when Lisa Marie was a babe in my arms. There were contemporary characters in every episode, with actors portraying everyone from Charles Manson to Howard Hughes. We made ten episodes for the first season. Each episode was filled with inside jokes for Elvis fans. For instance, Agent Elvis blows up the villain's tape recorder when it auto-plays Robert Goulet recordings over and over.

Some episodes were comic book versions of real-life events. For example, one episode showed Elvis in Vegas, trying to keep one step ahead of a would-be assassin. In real life, Elvis had received a warning note telling him to be careful because somebody was trying to kill him. From then on, Elvis was accompanied everywhere by his armed bodyguards. The guys—the Memphis Mafia—were hypervigilant, locking and guarding all entrances to the theater when Elvis was performing. It was a frightening time for all of us. Another episode featured the Manson family. After the Tate-LaBianca murders, everyone in Hollywood was nervous. Nobody knew who would be targeted next, and Elvis was afraid Manson would come after him. No one knew Manson's identity yet, but we all knew his handiwork. During that period, Elvis wanted Lisa

Marie and me in Vegas when he was there. Manson's killing sprees were in the Los Angeles area, and Elvis didn't want to leave us alone there.

The show lasted only one season; it wasn't renewed. I'm not sure why. The reviews were mixed. Some critics loved it; others didn't. The series might have been aimed at the wrong generation. Most comic book fans are too young to know stories from the 1960s, even if they know who Elvis was. It could also have been the mature-audience rating. There was foul language, sexual references, and cartoon-style blood and gore. Most current superhero movies are rated PG or R. We might have been better off with a softer rating. Whatever the reason, I was sorry to see it end.

By then, I was in my fifth year of touring with my own live show. I had been approached by a friend who asked if I would like to do a program where I could share my life with a live audience. I could show home movies and pictures and talk with a moderator about my life with Elvis and the years afterward—the kind of things people asked me about whenever I did an interview or a special appearance. When I finished the formal presentation, I could answer questions from the audience.

I told my friend that I would enjoy such a program. It would be billed "An Evening with Priscilla Presley." I had reached the age where I wanted to reflect on my life and share it with others, the loyal fans who had supported me for decades. It would be a chance to clear things up, too, to separate the reality from myth. I want the truth to be out there, to respond directly to what people wonder about Elvis and me, about what they've heard.

In these appearances, I let the audience ask anything they want. I've never had to draw a line, and I've always answered whatever question they pose. The questions are often quite personal. They want to know why Elvis and I divorced. How close was I with Elvis after the marriage ended? Most of the questions are respectful and positive. Some of them are funny. Everyone wants to know if Elvis was a good kisser. That was the first question I was asked.

I answered, "Was he a good kisser? What do you think? Look at that mouth! Of course! Yes, he was a very good kisser."

Sometimes, the questions are bizarre. I've been asked if Elvis wore underwear. I answer that it depended on what else he was wearing. Sometimes yes, sometimes no. It gets a big laugh. They can't believe I answer that. So far, no one has asked me if I wear underwear, but I'd answer that one, too. Can you imagine the elegant Ms. Priscilla Beaulieu Presley pulling the elastic up to show them? Now there's an image changer!

Sometimes, people want to talk to me one-on-one afterward. Accommodating their hopes is a little difficult. By the time the show ends, I have often had an eighteen-hour day. The travel, the appearance itself, and the Q&A portion of the show can leave me depleted. Anything afterward takes even more energy. Once, I stayed for three hours after the show, talking with fans well past midnight. It was exhausting, but I couldn't say no.

My assistant kept saying, "You've got to get going. It's really late."

But when I looked at the people still waiting patiently in line, I said, "No, it's okay."

I know that some of them had been waiting far longer than three hours. They had been waiting for forty years, ever since Elvis passed away. I'm the closest they can still get to him now that Lisa is gone. I know I'm the fortunate one. Imagine what Elvis would give to be there with me, to be with them, no matter how late the hour.

CHAPTER 19

Lights Out

*Someone turned the lights out in Memphis.
That's where my family is buried and gone.
Last time I was there, I noticed a space left
Next to them there.*

I was recently told in an interview that the Presley family, like the Kennedy family, is dogged by tragedy. I understand that sentiment, for we have had our share of heartbreak over the years. I look at it more like my granddaughter Riley does, though. In an interview after her mother's death, she said that the losses we've suffered are no different from the losses experienced by other families. No one is immune to death or pain. The difference is that when you're famous, the eyes of the world are on you. The headlines ricochet across the internet within minutes of the event. You lose the ability to mourn in private, for photographers compete to sneak pictures of you at your own child's funeral.

In another respect, too, the Presley family has endured a particularly painful kind of loss. Lisa Marie and Navarone were supposed to lay me to rest together. That can no longer happen. For generations, we Presleys have had to bury our children. Gladys had to bury Elvis's brother, Vernon had to bury Elvis, Grandma had to bury Vernon, Lisa Marie had to bury Benjamin, and I had to bury Lisa Marie. The pain of burying your child is beyond description. I had no way of knowing when I celebrated the New Year at midnight that within two weeks, I would lose my daughter and almost lose my son. It is still unthinkable.

During the first week of January 2023, my friend and photographer Christopher and I went with Navarone to visit an animal refuge in the San Fernando Valley. It was supposed to be a carefree outing on a pleasant California winter day. My friend who runs the place had taken in two camels to foster until she could find a permanent home for them. Both camels had been performers in a circus and had been abused. As they stood together munching their feed that afternoon, they looked harmless. They were certainly a novelty. You can pet a horse at most animal rescues, but camels are a rarity. Because Navarone has always been fascinated by unusual creatures, he asked if he could go into the pen with them. Nobody thought his going in would be a problem; both animals looked calm and relaxed. Navarone walked into the enclosure with Christopher while I stayed on the other side of the chain-link fence to watch. Like me, my son knows how to handle himself around animals, so I wasn't worried.

At first, everything went well. The camels didn't seem concerned by his presence. When Navarone asked the handler if he could feed them, the handler handed him two bags of popcorn. The first camel grabbed one bag of popcorn out of Navarone's hand and began to eat it. To avoid a repeat, Navarone opened the second bag and offered a handful of popcorn to the other camel. But instead of taking the food, the camel took Navarone's hand in its mouth. When Navarone tried to pull away, the animal gripped him harder. Then, to my horror, it twisted Navarone's arm and threw him to the ground, lying down on top of him.

Navarone was screaming as the camel began to crush him. "Mom, I'm going to die! I'm going to die!"

Then he could no longer breathe or make a sound. An adult camel weighs an average of a thousand pounds, and this animal was crushing Navarone. As he struggled, the camel opened its mouth and bit down, taking Navarone's head in its teeth. Blood was pouring down Navarone's neck.

I knew he couldn't survive much longer. He was already losing consciousness.

I screamed for help and crawled over the chain-link fence into the enclosure. Christopher and the handler were trying to move the camel. Christopher was beating it with a stick, but the camel refused to move or let go of Navarone's head. I was watching my son die before my eyes.

And he would have, without the interference of the refuge dog. The big German shepherd was barking frantically, and when the camel wouldn't move, the dog attacked. It flew at the camel's face and sank its teeth into flesh. The camel reluctantly let go of Navarone's head and lumbered to its feet. Navarone's legs were numb, but he managed to pull himself away. His head was streaming blood, he was groggy and disoriented, and he couldn't stand up. But he was alive. When I got to him, I helped him up, crying with relief.

We called 911, but Christopher and I ended up taking him to the hospital ourselves since we could get there faster. The doctor determined that Navarone was bruised but that no bones had been broken. The biggest problem was the cut on his scalp where the camel had bitten him. It took thirty-four staples to repair the gash. The doctor told Navarone he was incredibly lucky; the camel's tooth had almost pierced his brain. All that mattered to me was that my son was going to be all right. I had no premonition that a week later, I would be in another hospital room, this time with my daughter.

Lisa's last duet with her father was the title track for a new gospel compilation titled **Where No One Stands Alone**. When she played the video for me, I thought it was so beautiful, it brought tears to my eyes. The way she sang it, her demeanor, everything was touching. It was amazing to hear her sing gospel with Elvis.

As everyone close to him knew, he was at his most authentic when he sang gospel. He sang it around the house and to warm up for his concerts as well as singing it onstage. It gave him a sense of peace that nothing else did. I remember one time, years ago, Elvis and I heard voices singing "How Great Thou Art" as we passed a Church of Christ in Memphis. The Church of Christ doesn't use musical instruments in worship, so what we heard were powerful voices in harmony as they sang the hymn without accompaniment. Elvis and I stood outside the open window of the church and listened to the singing until the voices fell silent, and the service carried on. The congregation never knew we were there.

Gospel music evoked her father for Lisa, and she loved it as he had. I think that's why she chose a lyric from "Where No One Stands Alone" as the title for her memoir. It was a difficult time in her life, and she needed to believe that she would not be alone "from here to the great unknown." And she wasn't.

A few days after the camel attack, Lisa Marie flew to Memphis for the January 8 celebration of Elvis's eighty-eighth birthday at Graceland. It had been a few years since she'd attended, but this year, there was a special exhibit honoring Baz's film *Elvis*. Costumes, props, and artifacts were on display. The tremendous success of the film brought out record crowds for the event and coaxed Lisa out of her comfort zone for a rare public appearance since Benjamin's death. She talked about her pride in the film and her gratitude for all the fans who continued to honor her father so many years after his passing. Afterward, she cut the "Aloha cake," decorated in honor of the fiftieth anniversary of Elvis's landmark Hawaii special. She was thin but otherwise seemed to be doing well.

Before she left for Graceland, Lisa had called to see if I wanted to go to the Golden Globe Awards with her. We were both invited, and she wanted us to go together. The ceremony was being held at the Beverly Hilton on January 10, the day after she was returning from Memphis. *Elvis* had three nominations that year: Baz for Best Director of a Motion Picture, *Elvis* for Best

Motion Picture–Drama, and Austin for Best Actor in a Motion Picture–Drama. Lisa and I were excited about the film's nominations. Among other things, the film had been good for our relationship. She had been resentful toward me since the custody dispute. I understood that her anger made perfect sense to her and that there was nothing I could do about it. But the *Elvis* movie—particularly Austin—had given us common ground again. It reminded us of what we shared, and it united us in our love for her father.

I was a little worried about her as well. When we had talked over the last couple of months, she would sometimes mention that she had pain in her stomach. She said she didn't know why. What she wasn't telling me, perhaps because she didn't recognize its relevance, was that she'd had a gastric bypass a couple of years before. I wasn't sure when. At the time of the bypass, she had just told me she was having "a little cosmetic surgery." Because she did have these procedures now and then, I hadn't thought much about it this time. But Lisa wasn't one to complain to me about physical ailments, so it rang a warning bell when she mentioned recurrent pain. I told her she needed to see a doctor, and she promised she would. Of course, she didn't, and I eventually learned she was also ignoring Riley's suggestions that she see a physician. Her failure to follow through was frustrating and worrisome, but Lisa wasn't a child anymore. When she was six, I could simply put her in the car and take her to the doctor. It doesn't work that way when your child is fifty-four. It hadn't worked with her father, either.

Lisa had also invited Jerry Schilling to join us for the Globes, and the three of us were meeting at the event. The moment I saw her that evening, I knew something was wrong. Her loose black dress had long sleeves and a halter collar that closed in front of her throat, but the dress didn't camouflage her thinness. She was wearing thick five-inch heels that she'd worn before with no difficulty, but this night, she couldn't navigate in them. She asked Jerry if he'd hold her up as we walked the red carpet, so that she wouldn't fall. He kept a firm grip under her elbow and around her waist as we made the slow trip past the cameras. I remembered how Jerry would watch Lisa at Graceland when she was learning to walk. Fifty years later, he was there again to make sure she didn't fall, the kind surrogate uncle still watching out for his friend's daughter.

Something was off with Lisa's behavior that night, too. She seemed a little out of it, and her speech was slightly slurred as if she'd been drinking. At the time, I thought she might be under the influence, but in retrospect, I'm not so sure. Both Jerry and I monitored her carefully, trying to keep her upright and off camera as much as possible. Doing so was difficult because she was excited for Austin and eager to talk about him to anyone with a microphone.

Finally, we were seated. The Golden Globe Awards are a dinner event, unlike the Academy Awards, but we ate almost nothing. Lisa leaned over and told me her stomach was starting to hurt again. I had no appetite because I was both excited for Austin and worried about Lisa. I seldom eat at formal events, anyway. After what felt like an eternity, the award for Best Actor in a Motion Picture–Drama was presented. Hearing Austin's name announced was exhilarating for Lisa and me. I am so grateful we were given that moment of joy together. Austin was overwhelmed by humility, by gratitude, and by emotion. So were we as we listened to the end of his acceptance speech.

Speaking to Lisa and me, he said, "Thank you, guys. Thank you for opening your hearts, your memories, your home to me. Lisa Marie, Priscilla, I love you forever. Lastly, Elvis Presley himself. You are an icon and a rebel, and I love you so much." Both Lisa and I fought back tears and held our hands to our hearts as he spoke. It was a memorable moment. The last great moment of Lisa's life.

Shortly after Austin's speech, Lisa leaned into me and whispered, "Mom, I need to go. My stomach hurts." I let Jerry know, and we guided her out of the ballroom and called for our cars. But despite her pain, Lisa wasn't quite ready to let go of the magical evening.

She told me, "Let's stop at Chateau Marmont for a drink on the way home."

I said okay, and we agreed to meet there. Jerry handed her carefully into the waiting car. We had taken separate cars. I had come from Beverly Hills, and she had come from Calabasas, twenty miles away through heavy traffic. By the time we met at the hotel restaurant, though, Lisa had changed her mind.

She was very pale and said, "Mom, my stomach really hurts. I need to go home."

"Of course, sweetheart. We'll get the car."

When the car was brought up, I supported her over to where the valet was holding the car door open. I gave her a hug and said, "Let me know when you get home."

I didn't know it was the last hug. When she called to say she was safely home, I would have stayed on the line if I'd known it was the last time I'd hear her voice. But I didn't know. So I asked her how she was feeling and told her for the last time that I loved her. Then I hung up the phone.

Two days later, on the morning of January 12, my phone rang early in the day. It was Danny. He was staying with Lisa at her house in the valley. I knew immediately that something was wrong.

Danny said, "Nona, Lisa's unwell. You need to come."

Swallowing my panic, I asked Danny what had happened. He had gotten up early that morning and come downstairs to find Lisa on the floor. She was unresponsive. He couldn't feel a pulse. He called 911 and did CPR, then sat on the floor, holding her in his arms, until the paramedics arrived. When the EMTs got there, they confirmed that she had no heartbeat. After shocking her with a defibrillator and injecting her heart with epinephrine, they were able to get a heartbeat. They transported her to West Hills Hospital.

Danny knew the protocol if there was an emergency. Although the hospital knew Lisa's real identity, he checked her in under a false name and asked for an information blackout. No one was to be admitted to that area of the hospital without his permission, and no cameras were allowed. While the medical staff put Lisa in a room in ICU, Danny called Riley and me. Riley was out of town, working, but she told her dad she'd be on the next plane. Then he called Michael to bring the twins.

I went into emergency mode. Soldier mode, as my stepfather would have seen it. I didn't have the luxury of falling apart. I called my cousin Ivy at work and told her what was going on.

Vikki said she'd pick Ivy up and bring her back while I called Navarone. When Ivy got to my house, we left for the hospital in Woodland Hills, breaking a few speed limits on the way. There were already two paparazzi hiding on the hill when we arrived at the back entrance, waiting for me. So much for the information blackout. I texted Danny, who came to walk me inside to Lisa. Ivy went to park the car and then waited outside for Navarone. Close family and friends were arriving by then, but there was no private place to put them. The hospital staff scrambled to find a room for them to wait in and then escorted them inside. Danny and I identified everyone, and they were given passes. Michael had arrived with the twins, and Jerry was there. He had been in the next room with Elvis when Lisa Marie was born. He was there again as she lay dying.

I knew from the first moment I walked into Lisa's hospital room that she was already gone. She was hooked to a machine that was breathing for her, and she had a heartbeat. There was little brain activity. Her spirit, always so vital, wasn't there. Riley later told us that while she was still on her flight, she had felt her mother's spirit pass. But none of us was ready to give up yet. A nurse came to tell me that Navarone had arrived. I asked her to bring him into the room. Then we began to wait. Finally, Navarone voiced the question we were all thinking. How long until we knew if she was going to start breathing again? The doctor said it could be two minutes. Or it could be two days. After two hours, Navarone couldn't take the anxiety any longer. He left to go into the other room. The others were allowed in one or two at a time. Danny and I remained, holding Lisa's hands, stroking her face, telling her we loved her.

At some point, I remember that a nurse took me into the other room, where Ivy stepped forward to meet me. The nurse told Ivy to see to it that I ate and drank something. My cousin took my arm, but then we heard an emergency alarm from Lisa's room. It was a code blue; Lisa's heart had stopped. As I started back to my daughter, the nurse detained Ivy and spoke to her in a whisper.

Nodding toward me, she told Ivy, "Come with us. I need you to stand right behind her. She's going to fall, and you will need to catch her."

The next thing I remember is the doctor talking to me. He asked me what I wanted him to do. They had restarted Lisa's heart, but there was no guarantee it would keep beating.

I asked the doctor, "What kind of life will she have if we keep her on that machine?"

He looked at me with compassion and shook his head. "No quality of life at all."

I thought about my girl, my wild, rebellious, passionate girl, lying in a vegetative state for the rest of her life.

I said what I had to. "Take her off the machine, Doctor." My voice was barely above a whisper.

The nurse began to unhook the apparatus that kept Lisa's chest rising and falling. I looked at Danny and said, "We have to tell them, Danny. So they can say goodbye."

But as I began to move toward the door, I heard Danny's anguished cry. "No, Nona! Don't go! We can't leave her all alone!"

It was unbearable. I began to sob. I don't remember falling. I know that Ivy caught me. After that, everything went dark. I can't remember. I don't want to remember.

When they took me out through the back entrance of the hospital later, more paparazzi were on the hill, their telephoto lenses aimed at my face. When Danny left a little while afterward, a helicopter followed him. They had already noted his license plate. The helicopter followed him to my house, where it hovered overhead, hoping for shots of the family arriving.

Everyone gathered at my home. Riley and her husband arrived. We were scattered throughout the rooms in small groups, crying quietly, seeking comfort. A little later, my Beaulieu family arrived, Michelle and my brothers. Somebody arranged for food. Probably Vikki. I don't remember.

Late that night, after everyone had left, I made the announcement that is required when your child is famous:

> It is with a heavy heart that I must share the devastating news that my beautiful daughter Lisa Marie has left us. She was the most passionate, strong and loving woman I have ever known.

And I asked for privacy.

By the next morning, fans were bringing flowers to Graceland. Tributes poured in from around the world.

My former son-in-law, Nicolas Cage, wrote, "Lisa had the greatest laugh of anyone I ever met. She lit up every room, and I am heartbroken."

Tom Hanks, who played Colonel Parker in Baz's film, shared, "We are heartbroken over the death of Lisa Marie Presley. Absolutely heartbroken."

Baz Luhrmann offered his condolences to my granddaughters and me and told Lisa, "We will miss your warmth, your smile, your love."

Austin said his heart was "completely shattered."

John Travolta told Lisa, "Baby girl, I'm so sorry."

Yoko Ono told me that her heart ached for me.

There were many more, too many to share.

The doctors eventually determined that Lisa had died of a small-bowel obstruction, a result of her bariatric surgery. The dangerous complication ultimately stopped her heart. But Riley and I knew that Lisa's heart had really stopped beating the day Benjamin died. I like to believe that her son and her father were there to see her over. I need to believe that my girl is not alone.

CHAPTER 20
Midnight

Trying to be strong...
Oh, but it's midnight, and I miss you.

Like an old manor house in England, Graceland has its own private cemetery. Some would say it has its own ghosts. It wasn't planned that way. The Meditation Garden started out as a place of peace and reflection where Elvis and I could look at the stars at night. But when he passed, it became apparent that the family crypt at the nearby cemetery wasn't secure. So within days, he was moved to the Meditation Garden and placed in a beautiful marble sarcophagus. Gladys was moved next to him. When Vernon and Grandma passed, it was only natural that they would be buried there, too. I have mixed feelings about the garden's transformation. It is where my family would want to be, close to their beloved home and to each other. It is where I have chosen to be laid to rest. But the decision to bury the family there brought something melancholy to Graceland. The house took on a poignant air of mortality, our shared mortality, when it ceased to be just our home. The graveyard bothered Lisa, whose song referred to the psychological toll of having a cemetery "in the damn backyard" with a space left for her.

Lisa's public funeral was to be held on January 22. Graceland was handling the logistics, because a large crowd was expected. At home, I concentrated on keeping the family—and myself—together. Part of the legacy of growing up in a military family is learning young to control your emotions in emergencies. When you start to fall apart, you remind yourself to pull yourself together. The British call it keeping a stiff upper lip. Years of being in the public eye had taught me the same lesson. When Elvis left Germany, I was fourteen and never expected to see him again. All I wanted to do was cry. But he wanted me to put on a cheerful face for him when we said our public goodbye. So I fought back the tears and smiled and waved at him as the cameras clicked away. I didn't want to share my grief with the rest of the world, anyway. I am naturally a private person, and I find it painful to expose my intimate feelings publicly. I also have a strong sense of responsibility, and as the matriarch of the family, it was up to me to provide support and leadership in the wake of Lisa's passing. I had three granddaughters who had lost their mother. Their needs came first.

Our extended family and some of our close friends flew to Memphis on January 20, on separate flights. Nobody could accommodate all of us at once. A private service was planned for January 21, the night before the public funeral. In addition to the family, close friends would be attending. Security for the private service was tight. There was a guest list, and everyone outside the immediate family was checked in by Graceland security. There was also a bag check; no recording devices were allowed inside. Guests had to sign a confidentiality agreement that they would not take any pictures, record anything, or publicly disclose any details of the evening. It was a viewing, and our fear was that someone would take and leak a photo of Lisa Marie in her casket. Once guests passed security, they were given a badge. Security was so tight that my brother's wife almost wasn't admitted. Her husband's name was on the list, but hers had inadvertently been left off. Other family members had to advocate for her before she was allowed inside.

The service was held at the Chapel in the Woods, usually referred to simply as the Graceland Chapel, which had been built in 2018 in the woods adjoining the Graceland property. The venue is beautiful: The small chapel nestled among the trees accommodates about a hundred people. It is a simple structure that evokes the churches of the early twentieth century. There are two rows of wooden pews, and beams crisscross the white ceiling. There is no pulpit or choir loft, just a space for a congregation to gather. Windows run from floor to ceiling, bringing the forest into the church, like a mural that changes with the seasons. The front of the sanctuary consists entirely of glass panels, with nature as the backdrop. Lisa's casket was placed in front of the windows. The trees outside were bleak and frosted with winter, with a crescent moon in the sky. The light was gentle on Lisa's face.

The temperature was nearly freezing by the time we gathered that evening. People huddled in groups, talking quietly. I remember that our family friend Sarah Ferguson was there, but overall, the evening is a blank. I sat on the right side of the sanctuary, with Navarone next to me, his arm around me. I dimly recall people coming up to me and offering their condolences. Everyone was kind. I thanked them for coming, but I was barely registering my surroundings. I was enclosed in a cocoon of grief. My cousin Ivy was there, sitting behind and to the right of me. I didn't realize it then, but she was keeping watch over me. She never let me out of her sight that evening, ensuring that I ate and drank something, and ready to run interference if the social demands became overwhelming. Ivy recognized something that I didn't. I felt contained and in control, as I had been much of the time at the hospital when Lisa passed. As I had been right before I collapsed. My cousin saw how pale I was, saw the pain behind my eyes, and she knew what it could mean. She was my loving shadow all evening, poised to catch me if I fell again.

After everyone had a chance to talk to one another and say goodbye to Lisa, they were shepherded outside the chapel into a small clearing, so the family could say goodbye privately. I lingered until the end. I had brought a memento with me, a small object that Lisa had loved as a toddler. I'd kept it ever since, safely tucked away, a precious reminder of the little blonde girl my daughter once was. Before they closed the lid to her coffin,

I gently tucked it under her hand so she could carry it with her the way she used to. Then I kissed her goodbye for the last time, as I had kissed her father almost fifty years earlier, only a hundred yards away. The coffin lid was secured, and I stepped outside to where everyone was waiting.

The family had agreed on the manner of Lisa's final journey. Her coffin was carried out and placed carefully on one of her beloved golf carts for transport. With the pallbearers walking on each side of the cart, we followed her out of the woods and down the main driveway of Graceland, coming to a stop near the Meditation Garden. It was there that everyone said their farewells to Lisa and returned to the hotel to sleep before the public memorial the next morning. Only Riley and I stayed behind, keeping Lisa company, watching the workmen ready her sarcophagus. It was identical to Benjamin's. We had even been able to procure some of the same marble to construct it. Ben had been moved over a few inches to make room for his mother to lie beside him. Late in the night, Lisa's coffin was placed next to his. My sweet Riley was with me as we said our final goodbye.

The next morning, five thousand people gathered along the driveway by the front lawn of Graceland, waiting for the service to begin. People huddled together for warmth against the bleak gray sky. Some of them had been there all night. As they had for Elvis's passing, they came from all over America, some from overseas. Another hundred thousand viewers tuned in for the livestream broadcast once the service began. It was barely above freezing, and everyone was bundled up in parkas and heavy coats. Most people stood; some in the front were sitting on their backpacks or camp chairs because the ground was frozen. The grass was stiff and tipped with gray ice. Everyone held memorial programs with Lisa's photo on the front as they looked expectantly toward the front door of the mansion. Most were solemn; some wept quietly as they waited.

Inside, the family was gathered in the front entryway, waiting to make the interminable walk to the white tent that had been pitched in front of the house. A temporary stage had been erected there, with a small grand piano at one end and steps at the other. Most of the invited guests were already present and seated, under strict security like the night before. We would be taking our seats in the front row: Michael and the twins next to Riley and her husband, Ben; then me and Navarone; and next to him, Jerry and Danny. As we waited in the Graceland foyer to face the public, the family was ranged behind me. It was my responsibility to take the lead. I took a deep breath and nodded to have the door opened.

The cold air was like a slap in the face as we moved onto the porch. Riley and the twins were beside me, and the flashbulbs started going off. It was quiet except for the sound of Elvis's voice filling the air. He was singing one of his favorite songs, his voice sounding achingly sweet: "I come to the garden alone, while the dew is still on the roses." It was beautiful, but the dew that morning was frozen, and the roses were cut flowers lying on Lisa's grave.

We made our way to the tent, stopping occasionally to talk or confer. It wasn't a formal procession, just a family walking together to a destination they dreaded reaching. Navarone stayed next to me the whole way, his hand supporting my elbow, his arm encircling my shoulders. He was holding me up the same way Jerry had kept Lisa on her feet just two weeks earlier. We finally got settled in the front row, and the service began.

Joel Weinshanker, managing partner of Graceland, took the microphone first, telling the audience that Lisa had not wanted her memorial service "to be sad."

He was followed by Dwayne Hunt, pastor of the Abundant Grace Fellowship in Memphis, who gave a moving invocation, asking God to give our family peace in our pain and light in our darkness. Pastor Hunt returned for the benediction to pray for comfort for our family as we said "Goodbye, goodbye for now," to Lisa Marie. His prayers that day were poetic and powerful.

My friend A. C. Wharton, mayor of Memphis, spoke next about Lisa's unique connection to Memphis: "Before Jay-Z and Beyoncé had Blue Ivy, our own royal couple, Elvis and Priscilla, had a beautiful bundle of joy named Lisa Marie in 1968," a "star of hope" after the assassination of Martin Luther King Jr. a short while before she was born. The mayor said she would live on in the heart of a city that "loved her tenderly, loved her sweetly, and loved her truly."

Then Billy Corgan played his guitar and sang "To Sheila" with the refrain, "A summer storm graces all of me." It was a poignant reminder of Lisa's song "Storm and Grace," her tribute to the son she had now joined in death.

Sarah Ferguson spoke next. Despite being a duchess, she is one of the most unassuming, authentic people I know. She referred to Lisa as her sissy, her sister in friendship. Strands of red hair blew across her face as she quoted her mother-in-law, Queen Elizabeth II, who had told her, "Nothing can take away the agony of these moments, for grief is the price we pay for love." She looked right at me as she said, "We look to Priscilla, a mother, who has lost Lisa Marie; Lisa Marie, who lost a son... Losing children, there are no words for it." And she told the girls and me that if we ever needed her, we could just put out a hand, and she would be there.

Afterward, Lisa's friend Alanis Morissette sang a moving rendition of her own song "Rest."

Jerry led off for the family, talking about "me and a girl named Memphis," speaking directly to me for most of his time onstage. He was funny and tender as only someone who loved Lisa deeply could be. He told us that he had called Lisa "Memphis" from the day Elvis introduced her to him as a newborn. Then he got a laugh by saying, "And she always called me 'Jerry Schilling,'" imitating Lisa with a quick, funny voice. He talked about the day Lisa had called him and asked for a job when she moved into her own place. She insisted on being called his assistant, not his secretary. Every couple of weeks, he said, she would complain, "Somebody wants to talk to you about Lisa Marie." The people asking had no idea they were talking to her. Jerry got another laugh when he said that Lisa was the only person he'd ever known who could intimidate Jerry Lee Lewis. I could well believe it. Lisa could stare anybody down. The last thing she had said to Jerry, as he helped her into her car at the Golden Globe Awards, was "Jerry Schilling, I love you."

I was the next person to speak. I held myself upright and slowly climbed the stairs. It was lonely walking across that stage. When I reached the microphone, I told the audience, "I am going to read something written by my granddaughter. That says it all."

I struggled to raise my voice above a whisper as I read the words written by my fifteen-year-old Harper:

> The old soul. I have no idea how to put my mother into words. Truth is, there are too many.... Mama was my icon, my role model and my super hero.... She was born into our world, born strong but was delicate, filled with life.... She always knew she wouldn't be here long.... She lost her second child...a broken heart was the doing of her death. My heart is missing her love. She knew that I loved her. The old soul is always with me.

Then I looked up and said, "Our hearts are broken, Lisa. We all love you." Those were all the words I could manage. I walked back across the stage and down the steps, back to my family waiting in the front row.

Afterward, Riley's husband, Ben, mounted the stage to read a letter on Riley's behalf, as he had at Benjamin's funeral. He looked as though he had the weight of the world on his shoulders as he looked down at the words his wife had written. They were titled "A Letter to My Mama."

Riley told her mother that she remembered everything, from Lisa bathing her as a baby to listening to Aretha Franklin in her car seat:

> I remember how it felt to be loved by the most loving mother I've ever known. I remember how safe it felt to be in your arms....
> I remember that feeling as a child and I remember it two weeks

ago on your couch. Thank you for showing me that love is the only thing that matters in this life. I hope I can love my daughter the way you loved me, the way you loved my brother and my sisters.

I was proud of Ben. He choked back his tears and read each word his wife needed to tell her mother that day. And he reminded us all of the future when he read Riley's words about their daughter, my first great-grandchild, named Tupelo Storm, in honor of her great-grandfather and uncle.

Afterward, Axl Rose played the piano and sang his ballad "November Rain": "Nothing lasts forever... And it's hard to hold a candle in the cold November rain." After Pastor Hunt's blessing and benediction, the rest of the ceremony was simply music, as was fitting for Elvis's daughter.

The Blackwood Brothers started it off. I remembered them well from my years with Elvis. He had worked with them professionally, but he also counted them as friends. The group had been founded by James Blackwood, who had passed away since Elvis left us. Elvis would sometimes call James on the spur of the moment to ask if the singer could round up the "boys" and come over to Graceland for an evening of gospel singing. James's younger son, Billy, now the lead baritone for the group, was the spokesman when they took the stage that cold morning to sing Elvis's favorite hymn, "How Great Thou Art." The familiar notes settled over me with a soothing familiarity, and I remembered standing outside the church window with Elvis that long-ago day as he and I listened to the same song.

Afterward, Billy told us a story. He said that one night when he was a teenager, his father answered the phone, and Billy heard him say, "Oh hi, Elvis."

Billy perked up. It was always exciting when Elvis called. When he hung up, his dad looked at Billy and said, "Elvis wants me to come over and meet someone. Do you want to come with me?" Of course, he did. It was Elvis.

Billy and his dad drove to Graceland and were invited inside. They were told that Elvis would be down in a minute. A few minutes later, Elvis appeared at the top of the stairs and walked down toward them, carefully holding a small bundle.

When he reached the bottom of the stairs, he said, "Mr. Blackwood, this is my little girl, Lisa Marie. Lisa, this is Mr. Blackwood, one of my heroes." Billy still remembered that moment.

Billy's dad and uncles had sung at Gladys's funeral when Elvis lost his mother. They had sung in the living room at Graceland for Lisa Marie and me on the day we laid Elvis to rest. As Billy looked at me, he choked up and said, "And now we're singing for Lisa Marie. I guess things have come full circle."

Still looking at my granddaughters and me, he said that I'd remember the next song because Elvis always asked the audience to maintain a sort of holy silence when the Stamps Quartet sang it in his concerts. He prayed that it would now comfort us.

As they begin to sing "There's a sweet, sweet spirit in this place," I remembered. I remembered the song and the spirit and the way Elvis closed his eyes when it was sung. As the melody came to a close, Billy looked at me with tears in his eyes and pressed his hand to his heart as he left the stage. Billy was right.

A sweet spirit had filled the tent, and in that moment, there was comfort.

Jason Clark and the Tennessee Mass Choir brought the service to a close with a beautiful hymn of praise beginning "The lord of God is mighty, the lord of God is magnificent."

As I stood to file out behind my granddaughters, with Navarone holding my arm, the sounds of Lisa and Elvis singing "Where No One Stands Alone" followed us as we walked to the Meditation Garden and to Lisa's grave one last time. I knew that behind us, thousands of mourners would soon be following in our footsteps.

How do you explain the loss of your child to others? How do you explain it to yourself? Every morning, I wake up and realize that a big part of me is gone forever. Lisa lived inside me for nine months. I gave birth to her. I held her, and I nursed her. For so many years, she was my first thought in the morning and my last thought at night. We shared a deep and abiding love for the man who transformed both of our lives. We shared the wrenching pain of his departure. It never really went away.

I remember so many things. I remember cradling her tiny body in my arms for the first time. I remember gazing with wonder at her beautiful little face. I could not fathom that such a lovely, fragile creature had come out of my own body. I remember lying next to Elvis with our newborn daughter between us. We touched her tiny hands and feet, counted her fingers, stroked her silky dark hair. I remember the little girl, her face lighting up when she smiled, and her brow furrowing into a pout when she didn't get her way. I remember her springing out of bed on Easter morning to see what the Easter Bunny had brought, rummaging excitedly through the eggs and Hershey bars, then hugging the Barbie doll. I remember how beautiful she looked in her Easter dress with the fluffy skirt. I remember her "helping" decorate the Christmas tree while Daddy threw gobs of tinsel on the branches that Mommy would sort out later. I remember her having a tantrum one minute, then crawling into my arms a few minutes later, saying, "I'm sorry, Mommy." So much like her father. And I remember the bedtimes when I would read her a story or play her a song, then say the Lord's Prayer with her before kissing her and saying, "Sleep well, my love." I remember her sleeping face on the pillow, angelic after a day of making mischief.

And I remember the woman she grew up to be. I remember my twentysomething daughter digging through the Easter basket I gave her, then hiding the eggs for two-year-old Riley to find over and over again. I remember her stroking baby Navarone's blond curls. I remember how excited she still got over Christmas presents. I remember going to her concerts and feeling so proud of her, I thought I might burst. I remember her calling me for no particular reason, just to say hi. I remember her radiance on the day she married Danny in that small office in the Scientology Celebrity Centre. I remember the late-night calls when she was struggling in her marriage. I remember walking along the sand in Hawaii in the moonlight, holding her hand as she shared her confusion over Michael Jackson. I remember listening to her vent her frustration that two people who loved each other as much as she and Nick did couldn't go a day without fighting. I remember the tenderness beneath the public persona of "Lisa Marie F***ing Presley." And I remember walking the side streets of Beverly Hills with her, hand in hand and talking, as we had done when she was a child.

Lisa liked to write letters. She wrote me letters for much of her life. I keep them in a scrapbook on my coffee table and read them on the bad days. On the days her absence is a physical ache, on the days I wish I'd listened to her more or been the perfect mother I tried so hard to be. I read them, and I hear her voice reassure me again:

> *Mommy,*
> *This is supposed to be a card of thanks, happiness, care, loyalty, and love most of all for being my mom. There's been lies and there's been upsets, which neither of them you deserve, and what you do deserve is the best and that only. No kid in the world has or will have a mom like you. Someone who cares and someone who will understand as much as you do. And I know that now I have so many dreams I'd like to live. But we will both help each other live them. And from here on out, I'm gonna take care of you! And protect you! Because you're just not gonna get hurt anymore by anyone, <u>especially me</u>. I love you, Mommy. You are the <u>most</u> important person in my life, and forever will you be that.*
>
> *L*

My little wild child, I love you forever.

Epilogue

RAVEN

Go on, dry your eyes,...
Beautiful lady
...I'll hear your stories
That fill your sad eyes
When you had raven hair.

IT IS A DIFFICULT THING TO TELL THE STORY OF YOUR LIFE. You struggle with what to put in and what to leave out, for telling your own story means telling other people's stories, too. You don't want to hurt the people you love. You wonder what readers will think of you. Will they understand? Will they judge you? Believe you? Will they even find your story interesting?

All these things were on my mind when I went to the Venice International Film Festival with Sofia Coppola in September

2023 for the premiere of her film *Priscilla*. It was eight months after Lisa's passing. She never got to see the movie that had stirred such strong emotions in her. I wondered what she would have thought if she'd been with me the night of the premiere. Sofia sat next to me on one side. Cailee Spaeny, who plays me in the film, was on the other. She looked almost as nervous as I felt. I like Cailee. I gave her the best advice I could about playing me in the movie. I told her to be sensitive to Elvis. And Cailee was. She later said she was very nervous sitting next to me while the movie premiered. I can understand that. But she had nothing to fear; she was wonderful in the film.

Cailee wasn't the only one unnerved by the premiere. Even in the dark, I felt as if all eyes were on me as my story unfolded on-screen. I found myself holding my breath by the time the credits rolled. What did they think? That question was answered the moment the lights came up. The audience members rose to their feet and, turning to Sofia and me and the cast, gave us a standing ovation that lasted almost eight minutes and that followed me until I left the theater.

I couldn't hold back the tears. I kept thinking, *Oh my God, thank God. Thank God.* And I wished my mother were there to experience it with me. The moment was embracing and affirming and, most of all, humbling. It remains a pinnacle in a life that is filled with great moments.

The film covers fourteen years of my life. This book covers eight decades. Writing it has been a learning experience on many levels. I have seen how memories change with the passage of time. What is raw and immediate while you are young may soften with context and experience. We remember the things that are important to us at the time, but our priorities change. That is true of my memories of Elvis. I have always loved and admired him, but the more than four decades of living without him have taught me how rare and extraordinary he was as a human being. How rare and extraordinary our love for each other was. I have never felt anything remotely like it since.

Reliving the trauma in my life has also been challenging. I've learned that my mind simply refuses to remember certain things. It blocks them out to protect me. In reconstructing the experience of losing my loved ones, I have had to rely on the memories of those closest to me—people who were there at the time. I have even consulted the footage that was shot of those events, sometimes by paparazzi who filmed me without my consent. I remember many individual moments, and I remember the feelings, but there are gaps. My interview with Piers Morgan in the wake of Lisa's passing is an example. Piers was empathetic and kind, and I allowed myself to connect emotionally with my grief. But in the process, I confused the chronology of the events following Elvis's passing. My mind went into overload, and I didn't realize it until much later.

Conjuring up eight decades of memories is challenging for anyone, even more so for someone who has lived a life as eventful as mine. People my age often have bucket lists. I don't, because I have already experienced everything I've dreamed of. I have traveled the world, met hundreds of thousands of people, and attended some of the most glamorous events on the planet. I had my fairy-tale wedding to the most famous celebrity in the world. I had the children I wanted, both a daughter and a son. I have created, produced, or performed in a long list of films, documentaries, albums, and books. I have had the profound satisfaction of improving the lives of both people and animals through my charity work. Few people can say they have had every experience they aspired to. I know how extremely fortunate, extraordinarily blessed, I am.

I am also fortunate to have inherited my mother's good genes. She remained energetic and active into her nineties and was rarely ill. I have the same sort of stamina she did. My staff has nicknamed me the Energizer Bunny. My friends are envious because at eighty, I can still read the small print without glasses. I can also still manage a decent karate kick. I walk the dogs every day. I continue to work, traveling around the country nearly every week to do my show or attend conventions and other events. I have carried on my charity work on behalf of animals and people who are terminally ill. I continue to create new projects. Just last year, I cocreated and produced with Jerry Schilling a documentary titled *Return of the King: The Fall and Rise of Elvis Presley*, for Netflix. The reviews have been rewarding. And though I continue to attend galas for my charities and go out with friends for special occasions, I'm most content at home with my loved ones and a dog or two flaked out next to me. I travel when I need to, but like Dorothy in *The Wizard of Oz*, for me, there's no place like home.

Though I have suffered deep losses, I choose to focus on what remains. It gets me through the bad days. I lost my mother, but I carry on her spirit and her traditions. I lost my daughter, but I still have a son who loves me deeply. I lost my grandson, but I have three remarkable, loving granddaughters who give my life meaning. I have my sister and brothers and cousin.

We have weathered the struggles that all families have and remained intact. And we have weathered the drama created by the press that could have divided us. On holidays and birthdays and at times when we're all in town, we sit down at the table together to eat, to laugh, to talk, and to share memories. I also have an extended family in my household staff, who have been with me for almost forty years. We share a deep mutual trust and affection, and they see to it that I am well taken care of. I have a houseful of rescue dogs curled in beds on the floor or on the couch with me. They love me with the unconditional devotion that only a faithful animal has. And I have my friends, some of whom go back to my teenage years at Graceland. We are bound by an affection that comes from a lifetime of shared experiences. When I fear I might fall, I know someone will always be there to catch me.

I know a great deal about leaving the ones you love. I left the love of my life because I could no longer endure our *way* of life. I had to find my own life before I could figure out how Elvis fit into it. I left as gently as I could, but there was no way to do it without pain. When my mother left me in death, she also did it gently, but the pain remained. Benjamin's departure was not gentle; it was so wrenching that it almost destroyed our family and led directly to the biggest loss of all—my daughter's life. You cannot leave without leaving someone else behind to grieve. I live with grief, and I have learned that it never goes away. I will never outlive it, but I move through it one day at a time. I carry every one of the people I have lost with me. I feel their presence, and I believe that my journey will eventually bring us back to one another. I walk forward even when my mind turns toward the past. I am not trapped by those behind me. I am supported by them on the path.

Above all, I believe that love endures. I continue to be asked why I never married again. The answer is simple: I never wanted to. Even though we divorced, Elvis and I remained together spiritually until he died. He is still with me. One of my most precious memories of him occurred in the years following our separation. Though he formed other relationships after we parted, he still came by to visit sometimes when he was in town. One memorable evening, we embraced closely as we always did before he left.

This time, though, he looked me in the eye as we let go and said, "I will always love you, Sattnin'." It was important to him that I knew that.

And as he went out my door and down the path into the night, he began to sing, his voice soft in the evening air:

> *So I'll go, but I know, I'll think of you every step of the way.*
> *For I will always love you, I will always love you...*

What would I tell my fourteen-year-old self if I could go back in time?

Get ready. Hold on tight, sweetheart. It's going to be a wild ride. It will be the trip of your life.

Acknowledgments

WITHOUT MY COMMUNITY OF SUPPORT, THIS BOOK WOULD never have been written. My sincerest thanks go to the following:

My agent, Alan Nevins, of Renaissance Literary and Talent, whose advocacy, creativity, and support made this book possible.

My editors, Ben Schafer, Lauren Marino, and Seán Moreau, and the team at Hachette Book Group, for believing in my vision for the book and bringing it to fruition.

My friend and photographer, Christopher Ameruoso, whose artistry created the back cover photo and many of the other photos for this book.

Vikki Hakkinen, for organizing my days, for her uncanny recall of dates and places, and for sharing nearly forty years of memories for this narrative.

Marta Garcia, for sharing her memories of Navarone and for archiving hundreds of photos, magically locating the ones I needed.

Francisco Ayala, who is always there to help, even when it means feeding the snakes while Navarone is gone.

The Dream Foundation and Last Chance for Animals, for their ongoing advocacy and compassion for all God's creatures.

The fans, who have supported me through joy and heartbreak and ensured that Elvis's legacy lives on.

My son and protector, Navarone Garcia, who brings joy to my days.

My granddaughters, Riley Keough, Harper Lockwood, and Finley Lockwood, who give me hope and a window to the future.

My cousin Barbara "Ivy" Iversen, who remembers the things I cannot bear and is there to catch me if I fall.

My sister, Michelle Beaulieu, who has been with me throughout my journey.

And my collaborator, Mary Jane Ross, who put words to the music of my heart.

About the Authors

Priscilla Beaulieu Presley is a businesswoman, author, designer, producer, and actress best known for her roles in the television drama *Dallas* and the *Naked Gun* movies. As the cofounder and former chairperson of Elvis Presley Enterprises, she is credited with turning Elvis Presley's mansion, Graceland, into the second most visited historic home in the United States. As a key architect of the Elvis Presley legacy, she has curated and produced albums, books, films, and concerts honoring the late music legend. She lives in Los Angeles near her son and grandchildren, where she continues her lifelong commitment to animal advocacy.

Mary Jane Ross is an award-winning college professor and writer, honored with the NAACP Image Award for Best Biography or Autobiography with Ray Charles Robinson. Her collaborations span diverse subjects, such as Judy Garland, Frank Sinatra, Piper Laurie, Mafia hitman Roy DeMeo, and Congresswoman Nancy Mace. *Softly, As I Leave You*, with Priscilla Presley marks her ninth memoir. Her compositions also include poetry and an online grammar textbook for second-language students. She lives in her native Southern California.